Dedication

"Let us fix our eyes on Jesus, the author and perfecter of our faith...."

—*Heb. 12:2*

*To the author and redeemer of life, my Father and Friend,
who has walked with me every step of this journey.*

*To the called, who have heard His voice and put aside the things
of this world to follow Him who is faithful.*

Contents

Part 1: Responding to the Call   **1**

Chapter 1:   Where Are You Headed?   3
      God's Four Key Purposes for Work   *4*
      Availability vs. Ability   *8*
      Help Wanted: Applications Accepted Via Prayer   *13*

Chapter 2:   Created to Be Called   17
      Career Questions About Calling   *17*
      Called to Be, Do, and Persevere   *19*
      Biblical Principles of a Calling   *21*
      How to Hear from Heaven   *22*
      Chapter Wrap-Up   *27*

Chapter 3:   Reconciling Your Master F.I.T. with God's Master Plan   33
      Visioning and Planning   *34*
      Identifying Your Master F.I.T.   *35*
      Career Assessments to Discover Your Master F.I.T.   *49*
      Chapter Wrap-Up   *51*

Chapter 4:   Making the Right Career Decision   55
      Brainstorming Options   *57*
      Investigate with Legwork   *65*
      Consider the Steps to Get There   *70*
      Weigh the Pros and Cons   *70*
      Commit to a Decision   *74*
      Create Your Focus Statement   *75*
      Chapter Wrap-Up   *77*

Part 2: Planning Your Campaign and Creating Your Career Marketing Documents   **81**

Chapter 5:   Getting Your Job Search Plan Together   83
      12 Tips for the Road to Self-Employment   *84*
      Break Your Job Search Plan into Small Steps   *87*
      Five Phases of a Job Transition   *88*
      Plan A—Create a SMART Goal   *90*
      Plan B—Give Yourself Options   *101*
      Job Search Resources and Budget   *102*
      Your Support Team   *102*
      Avoid the Traps, Temptations, and "Yes, Buts"
        That Keep You from Your Calling   *104*
      Chapter Wrap-Up   *108*

The Christian's Career
Journey

Finding the Job
God Designed for You

Susan Britton Whitcomb

The Christian's Career Journey

© 2008 by Susan Britton Whitcomb

Published by JIST Works, an imprint of JIST Publishing

7321 Shadeland Station, Suite 200

Indianapolis, IN 46256-3923

Phone: 800-648-JIST   Fax: 877-454-7839   E-mail: info@jist.com

Visit our Web site at **www.jist.com** for information on JIST, free job search tips, tables of contents and sample pages, and ordering instructions for our many products!

Quantity discounts are available for JIST books. Have future editions of JIST books automatically delivered to you on publication through our convenient standing order program. Please call our Sales Department at 800-648-5478 for a free catalog and more information.

All scripture quotations, unless otherwise indicated, are taken from the Holy Bible, New International Version®. Copyright © 1973, 1978, 1984 by International Bible Society. Used by permission of Zondervan Publishing House. All rights reserved.

The "NIV" and "New International Version" trademarks are registered in the United States Patent and Trademark Office by International Bible Society. Use of either trademark requires the permission of International Bible Society.

Trade Product Manager: Lori Cates Hand

Cover Designer: Trudy Coler

Cover Photo: Robert Glusic/Photographer's Choice/Getty Images

Interior Design and Layout: Toi Davis

Proofreaders: Paula Lowell, Jeanne Clark

Indexer: Cheryl Lenser

Printed in the United States of America

12 11 10 09 08   9 8 7 6 5 4 3 2 1

Library of Congress Cataloging-in-Publication Data

Whitcomb, Susan Britton, 1957-

The Christian's career journey : finding the job God designed for you / Susan Britton Whitcomb.

    p. cm.

Includes index.

ISBN-13: 978-1-59357-518-2 (alk. paper)

1. Vocation--Christianity. 2. Job hunting--Religious aspects--Christianity. I. Title.

BV4740.W45 2008

248.8'8--dc22

2007044990

We have been careful to provide accurate information in this book, but it is possible that errors and omissions have been introduced. Please consider this in making any career plans or other important decisions. Trust your own judgment and align it with Biblical truths above all else and in all things.

Trademarks: All brand names and product names used in this book are trade names, service marks, trademarks, or registered trademarks of their respective owners.

ISBN 978-1-59357-518-2

Chapter 6:   Capturing Your Value with "Smart" Success Stories   111
          Conveying Value to Employers   *112*
          Inventorying Your Success Stories   *115*
          Using the SMART Format to Answer Behavioral
              Interview Questions   *119*
          Writing Your Success Stories   *123*
          Chapter Wrap-Up   *128*

Chapter 7:   Communicating Your Value Via a Career Brand   131
          How Can a Career Brand Help?   *132*
          The Elements of Your Brand   *133*
          The Essence of Branding   *133*
          Verbal Branding: Creating Your Sound Bites   *134*
          Visual Branding: Look and Act the Part!   *142*
          Chapter Wrap-Up   *147*

Chapter 8:   The Blueprint for a Masterful Resume   151
          The One Hard-and-Fast Rule for Resume Writing   *152*
          Two Tried-and-True Winning Formats:
              Chronological and Functional   *153*
          What to Include on Your Resume—and What Not
              to Include   *160*
          Putting It All Together   *162*
          Chapter Wrap-Up   *170*

Chapter 9:   Accomplishments: The Linchpin of a Great Resume   173
          What Employers Really Want in a Resume   *175*
          Words to Woo Employers   *177*
          Strategies for Presenting Accomplishments   *178*
          Where to Find Material for Your Accomplishments   *183*
          Impact-Mining: Probing Questions to Unearth
              Hidden Treasures   *184*
          Sifting Through the Accomplishments You've Gathered   *184*
          Finalizing Your Resume with Formatting, Editing,
              and Proofing   *185*
          Chapter Wrap-Up   *187*

Chapter 10: E-resumes, Cover Letters, and Other Career Marketing
          Documents   191
          Creating ASCII Plain-Text Resumes   *192*
          Creating an E-portfolio   *195*
          Getting on the Blog Bandwagon   *196*
          Cover Letters and Other Correspondence   *198*
          Chapter Wrap-Up   *206*

Part 3: Executing Your Job Search   **209**

Chapter 11:   Tackling Your Job Search with New Economy Strategies   211

*Six Misconceptions and Mistakes Christians Can
    Avoid in Their Job Search*   *212*
Tap the Hidden Job Market with a Targeted Search   *215*
The Difference Between Openings and Opportunities   *215*
Seven Steps to a Targeted Search   *217*
Chapter Wrap-Up   *238*

Chapter 12:   Covering Your Bases with Traditional Search Strategies   243

*Why People Continue to Use Traditional Search
    Strategies*   *243*
The Seven Venues of a Traditional Search   *244*
Keeping the Momentum Going   *255*
Chapter Wrap-Up   *255*

Chapter 13:   The Four Cs of Interviewing: Connect, Clarify,
    Collaborate, and Close   259

*Phase 1: Connect with the Interviewer—How
    to Create the Right Chemistry*   *261*
Phase 2: Clarify What Needs to Be Done   *264*
Phase 3: Collaborate on How to Do the Job   *268*
*Phase 4: Close with Professionalism—How to
    Wrap Up and Win*   *269*
How to Determine Whether This Is the Right Position   *270*
Measure Your Performance in a Post-Interview Analysis *273*
Chapter Wrap-Up   *274*

Chapter 14:   Salary Negotiations: Truths and Tips for Christians
    in the Marketplace   279

*Seven Situations That Cause Christians to Stumble
    over Salary*   *280*
Five Truths to Take to the Salary Negotiation Table   *281*
Preparing for the Salary Dance   *282*
How to Deflect Salary Questions Until the Offer   *285*
When an Offer Is Made   *287*
How to Initiate a Counter-Offer   *289*
*Negotiating Additional Elements of Your
    Compensation Package*   *293*
Get the Offer in Writing and Think It Over   *293*
Chapter Wrap-Up   *293*

Chapter 15:   Your New Job Description: 10 Career Commandments   297

Appendix: Christian Career and Leadership Coaches   301

Index   303

Acknowledgments

First and foremost, I give thanks to the Lord who has given me the indescribable honor and delight of being employed in His service—what an unpredictable and wild ride it has often been, and yet I wouldn't trade a minute of it. It is Christ who equips me to deliver the message that every human being is uniquely gifted and infinitely important, whether street sweeper or CEO. I am truly grateful for the work He has assigned to me!

Heartfelt thanks go to Lynn Guillory, Executive Director of Career Transition Ministries, who had the initial vision for this book. In addition to his demanding work as a human resources executive, Lynn has faithfully ministered to job seekers on a weekly basis for more than a dozen years. He has also volunteered his time to help churches nationwide launch similar job seeker ministries. Lynn wanted a resource for churches that would help people navigate career/job transition from a Biblical perspective. I am honored that he thought of me as "the one to write it."

Behind *The Christian's Career Journey* is a terrific team at JIST Publishing. Special thanks go to Lori Cates Hand, Trade Product Manager, for the commitment she brought to this project. Lori offered the wisdom to take the best of *Job Search Magic* (my fourth book, part of the *Magic* Series also published by JIST) and ground it in Biblical principles for those who want to honor Christ in their careers. Applause to Cheri Clark, my eagle-eyed editor, who added clarity and accuracy to many a page. In addition, a big thank you to Trudy Coler, Toi Davis, Paula Lowell, and Cheryl Lenser for behind-the-scenes work with expert production, design, desktop publishing, proofreading, and indexing.

Sincere appreciation goes to those who contributed insider tips, insights, and industry knowledge to the original book *(Job Search Magic)*, portions of which are included in *The Christian's Career Journey*:

> Dana Adams, Microsoft Corporation
>
> Lou Adler, Adler Concepts
>
> Reginna K. Burns, AT&T
>
> Freddie Cheek, Cheek & Associates
>
> Gerry Crispin, CareerXroads
>
> Mary Ann Dietschler, Abundant Life for U
>
> Kirsten Dixson, Reach Branding Club
>
> Christine Edick
>
> Dean Eller, Central California Blood Center
>
> Meg Ellis, Type Resources

Debra Feldman, JobWhiz.com

Julianne Franke, The Right Connections

Sheila Garofalo, SFC Consulting

Dr. Charles Handler, Rocket-Hire.com

Beverly Harvey, Beverly Harvey Resume & Career Services

Barry Hemly, Corning, Inc.

Mike Johnson, Corning, Inc.

Valerie Kennerson, Corning, Inc.

Kate Kingsley, KLKingsley Executive Search

Louise Kursmark, Your Best Impression

Murray Mann, Global Career Strategies

Mark Mehler, CareerXroads

Don Orlando, The McLean Group

Dr. Dale Paulson, Career Ethic/Allegiance Research Group

Jean Hampton Pruitt

Pamela Ryder, Wyeth Pharmaceuticals

Kevin Skarritt, Acorn Creative

Dr. John Sullivan, San Francisco State University

Eileen Swift, Swift Graphic Design

Peter Weddle, Weddles.com

Gwen Weld, Isilon Systems (formerly of Microsoft Corporation)

Judy Wile, New England Human Resources Association

Deborah Wile Dib, Executive Power Coach

Michael A. Wirth, Talent+, Inc.

In addition, thanks go to my colleagues who shared insights about career management from a Biblical perspective:

Kim Batson, Career Management Coaching.com

Kathy Bitschenauer, New Pathways

Nancy Branton, People Potential Group, Inc.

Robyn Feldberg, Abundant Success Career Services

Terri Ferrara, Summit View Career Coaching

Al Lopus, Best Christian Workplaces Institute

Ron Rutherford, Intercristo

Judy Santos, Christian Coaches Network and JudySantos.com

Shandel Slaten, True Life Coaching

Heartfelt thanks go to my "Aaron and Hur" (Exod. 17:11-13)—Jean Gatewood and Myrna McDonald—for "holding up my arms" and helping me win the battle of getting this book out of my heart and onto paper. Judy Santos of the Christian Coaches Network brilliantly supported me in moving my chapter drafts from conceptual to concrete, and Scott Tompkins of YWAM/University of the Nations offered his years of editorial expertise to help decide on a title that is both apropos and alliterative. Sincere thanks to both. And to the many prayer partners who covered me during the writing process, thank you, thank you, thank you. Your fervent petitions have, indeed, accomplished much.

To my husband, Charlie, thank you for challenging me to read the Bible with my head as well as my heart (and teaching me the difference between exegesis and isogesis!), as well as helping me stay grounded as I lunge at life. And to daughter Emmeline, thank you for giving me a priceless reason *not* to succumb to the temptation of being a workaholic!

Writing this book has been an awesome privilege. To be immersed in God's promises has encouraged me of His purposes, love, and compassion for each of us. I have attempted to apply scripture to the subject of career transition with wisdom and love. There will likely be places where I may have missed the mark on wisdom (if so, feel free to e-mail me with your insights). After reading this book, I hope you will decide that I have not missed the mark when it comes to love. God has given me a heart of compassion for you who desire to honor Him in your work. I know there are days when you feel weary, face opposition, and fight battles that are "not against flesh and blood." (Eph. 6:12) My prayer is that this book helps you realize that in every trial you are more than conquerors. Nothing can separate you from the love of God that is in Christ Jesus our Lord! (Rom. 8:35-39)

Contact the Author

Thank you for selecting *The Christian's Career Journey*. The author welcomes your comments about this book. E-mail to let the author know what you found helpful, what you would like more information on, or what could be done to make this book stronger. Also, feel free to share how this book helped you find significance and incorporate faith into your work life. Please be sure to mention this book's title in your correspondence.

Susan Britton Whitcomb, ACC, CCMC, MRW
Fresno, CA
E-mail: susan@christiancareerjourney.com
Web site: www.ChristianCareerJourney.com

About This Book

This resource is for those who are committed to (or even curious about) following Christ in their career, whether they work in the marketplace or in the ministry. For the committed, God has amazing delights in store for you. Hold fast to the promise of Galatians 6:9: "Let us not become weary in doing good, for at the proper time we will reap a harvest if we do not give up." For the curious, God loves you and has patiently waited for and watched over you for years and years (just as He did for me). If you are a seeker, I invite you to seek with your heart and not just your head. God's promise in Jeremiah 29:13 is that you will "…find me when you seek me with *all* your heart."

Whether you're committed or curious, God created you to play a significant role in this world. He gifted you with a combination of talents and experiences like no other human being, which makes you irreplaceable. Using those gifts to the fullest will bring indescribable joy to you, blessings to those you work with, and infinite glory to Him.

There is power in numbers. To benefit from this book, pair up with an accountability buddy or prayer partner. You'll gain even more value by assembling a small group of Christians (or joining an existing group) who are committed to making progress in their career journey. (For free assistance in learning how to start a group in your church, visit Career Transition Ministry Network at www.CTMNetwork.org.) If you'd like to hire a career coach to support you in your transition, scan the appendix of *The Christian's Career Journey,* where you'll find a list of Christian career coaches who have graduated from Career Coach Academy and Leadership Coach Academy, my coach training organizations.

On your journey, you're likely to find scenic byways along with some boring stretches, places to climb and places to coast, straightaways and delays, points where you'll need to rev up and periods to rest and refuel. There will be valleys with shadows, as well as vistas that give you a glimpse of the Big Picture, where God's awesomeness shakes your soul and you're reminded that nothing is impossible with God.

You'll learn that finding the job God designed for you starts on the inside with your mind and heart. Yield your will and your dreams to Him and He *will* give you the desires of your heart. You'll also discover that the career of your dreams won't materialize without unrelenting action and street-smart strategies. This book addresses both the internal and the external sides of the equation for career success.

The Christian's Career Journey is divided into three parts. Part 1 establishes the all-important foundation for career success. Chapter 1 reveals God's four key purposes for work and reminds us that the Lord is more interested in availability than ability. Chapter 2 answers questions about your calling and offers a formula to help you hear from heaven. Chapter 3 introduces the Master F.I.T.™ tool and offers seven steps to hone in on your career calling. In chapter 4, you'll learn insider tips on how to brainstorm and investigate career options, as well as how to come to a decision that brings peace and fuels the fires of passion and enthusiasm.

In part 2 of *The Christian's Career Journey,* you'll equip yourself with the essentials for a successful job search. In chapter 5, you'll learn the five phases of a job transition and how to craft SMART career goals. You'll also learn how to avoid the traps, temptations, and "yes, buts" that can keep you from your calling.

In chapter 6, you'll catalog a series of SMART Stories™; these success stories will help you provide employers with hard evidence of how you can deliver a return on investment (ROI) to the organization by solving problems or serving needs. Chapter 7 then takes you through the steps to create a memorable career brand—that unique combination of skills or competencies that employers are willing to pay a premium for!

Chapter 8 walks you through easy steps to outline and plug in keywords to your resume, and chapter 9 will help you unearth accomplishments, the linchpin of a winning resume. Chapter 10 covers e-resumes, cover letters, and other pieces of the puzzle.

Part 3 contains a wealth of job search strategies for both targeted/active searches and traditional/passive searches. Chapter 11 shares six misconceptions and mistakes that Christians can avoid in job search. You'll also learn why it's important to uncover opportunities in addition to openings and how to manage the seven-step process for conducting a "new economy" search. You'll also see scripts that will help open doors to important networking contacts—the people who can help tip the job search scales in your favor. Chapter 12 will help you leverage the seven venues in a traditional/passive search, including online searches, resume posting, resume distribution, recruiters and agencies, classified ads, direct inquiry, and career events.

Chapter 13 prepares you for interviews with a foolproof method for connecting with interviewers, clarifying what they need, collaborating on how you

(continued)

would meet those needs, and closing the interview with professionalism and confidence. Chapter 14 reveals the seven situations that cause Christians to stumble over salary and gives you five truths to take to the salary negotiation table so that you can enter negotiations as a confident optimist. With a clear picture of your "reality," "comfort," and "dream number" salary ranges, you'll find the secret to negotiating with power and integrity!

Finally, chapter 15 offers "10 Career Commandments" to adopt as your new job description. These commandments are portable and permanent—they apply to those in the mail room and those in the boardroom, to graduating seniors and 70-somethings nearing retirement. Live by them and you will earn the trust of all and experience good success, just as Joshua did in claiming Canaan, the long-awaited Promised Land.

Finally, an important feature of this book is the tips found at the end of most chapters. The "10 Quick Tips" will give you a quick overview if you're in a hurry, and the coaching tips will help you take charge and move your career forward with commitment, intention, and momentum. You'll also find a "Pocket Prayer" at the close of each chapter to help you talk with God about various aspects of your career transition. Downloadable copies of these prayers are also available at my Web site so that you can carry them with you in your briefcase, PDA, or wallet.

The companion site to this book, www.ChristianCareerJourney.com, contains downloadable forms and additional resources that augment the book. Be sure to visit the site.

If you're ready to experience the encouragement of God, be led by divine direction, and marvel at the miracles He wants to do in your work-world, read on!

PART 1

RESPONDING TO THE CALL

CHAPTER 1

WHERE ARE YOU HEADED?

You are on a journey—a purposeful and poignant pilgrimage through life. Your journey was conceived in the heart of God in a realm beyond this earthly one. He loved you before time began, fashioned you in your mother's womb, gifted you with unique talents, and continues to plant dreams and desires in your soul that will fulfill His timeless purposes and your divine destiny.

God, your ultimate job coach, has plans for your career that are beyond what you could conceive or accomplish on your own—plans from a bigger perspective with limitless possibility...plans with divine purpose and eternal payoff. He guarantees provision for the pilgrimage and joy for the journey. With your every step through work and life, God is drawing you into the way of grace. Ultimately, your travels will lead you back into the arms of His holy Son, Christ the Savior, who has been faithfully at your side every step of the way.

God is intensely interested in your career because He is intensely interested in the marketplace. In his book *The 9 to 5 Window* (Regal Books, 2005), Os Hillman, a prominent leader in the marketplace ministry movement, points out that "Jesus' ministry focused on the marketplace, where people spent most of their time. Of His 132 public appearances in the New Testament, all but 10 of them were in the marketplace, and 45 of His 52 parables had a workplace context." Hillman emphasizes that every Christian is in full-time Christian work, whether driving nails or preaching the gospel.

Add to those statistics the fact that most adults log between 100,000 and 125,000 hours in the marketplace during their careers, and you get a glimpse of why God is keen on careers.

As you prepare for the next leg of your career journey, this initial chapter will allow you to

- Learn about God's four key purposes for work.
- Get a glimpse of how ordinary people have put God at the center of their work (and see if you personally relate to one of these situations).
- Understand that God is more interested in availability than He is ability or talent.
- Discover that every career is a kingdom career, whether in the marketplace or in the church.
- Understand that believers do "double duty" in their work.
- Remember that obedience has a cost but the payoff is eternal.

In the chapters that follow we'll look extensively at the mechanics of career change and job search. But to start off on the right foot, let's first review God's purposes for work.

God's Four Key Purposes for Work

In God's eyes, work appears to have four key purposes:

- A setting to write your life's story
- An incubator in which to grow your faith
- A training ground to increase your capacity and influence
- A stage on which to reflect God's image

Let's look briefly at each purpose.

Purpose #1: A Setting to Write Your Life's Story

God desires that you live a life of significance...a life of character, contribution, and consequence...a life of blessing. Because God is in the business of doing beyond all that we ask or think, He is able to take your career beyond the dreams that you have for it. Your work life is part of history—*His* story—and it's a story of His faithfulness to you. He knows the beginning, the middle, and the end. Characters (co-workers, colleagues, customers), challenges, and victories will be woven throughout your story. The Lord sees the big picture and has big plans for you. The blank pages to unfold have works of grace and mercy already penned by God. He has prepared good works for you to walk in and will be with you every step of the way. He is enabling you to make wise choices and finish the course so that you will one day hear, "Well done, good and faithful servant."

Travel Tip: On your career journey, be prepared for high points and low points. The Israelites' journey from Egypt to the Promised Land was full of extremes: the parting of the Red Sea and the waters of Meribah (Exod. 14:13-31; Num. 20:9-13); the glory of God revealed on Mt. Sinai and the debauchery of Aaron and his golden calf (Exod. 33:18-23; 32:1-35); the appointment of the Levites to minister in the temple and the bickering over who should be in charge (Num. 18:1-7; 16:1-4); the sneak peek at the wonders of the Promised Land and the 40 years of waiting as a consequence of the explorers' detestable unbelief (Num. 13:23-30; 14:23-24). And yet, woven throughout the pages of this amazing story is God's tender love and amazing provision for the needs of His children. His love and provision await you on your journey, as well.

Purpose #2: An Incubator in Which to Grow Your Faith

Your career is an incubator that will nourish your spiritual growth. In this "controlled" environment, *God wants to grow your faith.* He will do that by showing you His goodness and faithfulness. He will also do that by allowing trials to come into your life. Jesus allowed the biggest trial of Mary and Martha's life—the death of their brother Lazarus—so that they would experience more fully the extent of His power, love, and compassion toward them (see John 11 for the full story of Lazarus's resurrection). God wants you to experience that same degree of power, love, and compassion.

Though challenging times are inescapable, God will show you how to break down insurmountable tasks into small steps and whom to partner with to help navigate the road ahead (picking up this book is a good start!). He will supply you with strength, strategy, and solutions for success, especially when things look confusing or overwhelming. He promises to prosper you (Jer. 29:11), weave all things together for good (Rom. 8:28), and take you to "higher ground"—a place of shelter, protection, and blessing (Ps. 61:2-4).

Difficulties plant the seeds of spiritual growth. I'm sure we can all attest to the fact that work is, indeed, very difficult at times. Projects get delayed, computers crash, e-mail never ends, people renege on promises, misunderstandings happen, raises don't materialize, companies downsize, and more. And, if we think holding down a job is difficult, finding a job can feel like an overwhelming challenge.

After 20-plus years of standing with people as they navigate career change and job search, I've come to the conclusion that looking for a job is one of the toughest jobs in the world. It is fraught with uncertainty, bringing up concerns such as these: "How long before I land a job?" "Will my savings hold out until I find a new position?" "Will I have to take a cut in salary to find a position I really like?" "Employers want me to have more experience before they'll hire me, but how can I get that experience if they won't give me a job?" "What new set of difficulties will I encounter when I get hired?" For others, painful questions may surface, such as "Why would God allow my boss to backstab me like that?" or "How could my company fire me without cause when I've been such a loyal employee all these years?"

Making matters more difficult is the fact that in job search there's no on-site supervisor to offer you kudos or encouragement, nor do you get paid for all your hard work (at least, not until you land a new job).

Job search is definitely the soil in which faith is tilled. Now, more than ever, you'll benefit from working with a career coach who can stand with you, pray for you, offer encouragement, challenge you, and share career transition resources as well as biblically sound strategies (to find a Christian career coach, see appendix A or visit www.ChristianCoaches.com).

A Job or a Career?

Throughout this book, the terms *job* and *career* are used synonymously. Some people much prefer *career,* as it implies ownership of work that brings both fulfillment and financial reward—*career* conveys something you "want to do." *Job,* on the other hand, may imply an unwilling servitude—something you "have to do." The reality is that the world uses the term *job* frequently and so, throughout this book, I use the terms interchangeably. If *job* doesn't conjure up positive images for you, I encourage you to think of it in light of this acronym:

J—Journey
O—Of
B—Becoming

Your JOB is, indeed, a journey—a journey of becoming more like Christ.

Purpose #3: A Training Ground to Increase Your Capacity and Influence

God delights in you as His unique creation. He purposefully planted gifts within you, and He has plans to continue to grow those gifts, as well as your skills and experiences. God will often put you into a position that is a training ground to build your capacity and influence. He is the ultimate recycler and will not let anything go to waste.

Judy Santos is a prime example of this. Little did she realize that accepting a customer service position with Xerox while the company was in its infancy would equip her later to establish several entrepreneurial ventures of her own. She notes that the Xerox position wasn't a perfect fit with her strengths or her Myers-Briggs type (more on this in chapter 3), but it brought first-class on-the-job training in marketing and customer service. She remembers a branch manager there, Gord Davidson, who had a significant impact on her career. Judy shares, "Gord would ask me what I thought was going well and what wasn't. There is one conversation I shall never forget. He said simply, 'If you want to make points with me, anticipate me. If you want to make points with your customers, anticipate them.' That advice has served me well over the years." Today, Judy's increased capacity has led to increased influence. She is the executive director of Christian Coaches International, which she founded in 1998 as a companion to her work as a professional coach.

Zechariah 4:10 reminds us to not despise the day of small things—never think that seemingly insignificant skills aren't important in God's kingdom. To increase your capacity and influence, it might be that you need to increase your technical skills (computer programming, web design software, and so on), emotional strength (coping skills, perseverance, and so on), "soft" skills (leadership skills, communication skills, and so on), or "hard" skills (project planning, negotiations, and so on). God may have hand-picked people, like Judy's mentor, at your next position who can teach you important lessons, even if they don't yet know the Lord in a personal way. Most often, the training ground will build your capacity to be faithful, obedient, and trustworthy. Don't resist a "recycling" position!

GO AND GROW

The parables of Jesus illustrate the importance of being faithful in small matters. In Matthew 25:23, the parable of the talents, the servant who had increased his talent was told by the master, "Well done, good and faithful servant! You have been faithful with a few things; I will put you in charge of many things. Come and share your master's happiness." And in Luke 19:17, the parable of the 10 minas (a mina was about three months' wages), the faithful servant is told, "Because you have been trustworthy in a very small matter, take charge of ten cities."

It's important to note that the master was pleased with both the servant who increased in a small way and the servant who increased in a large way. He was not more impressed with the one who brought in the greatest increase. From this parable, we learn that God simply wants you to **go and grow—to take the gifts He's given you and put your best effort toward creating something more for Him.**

In general, the greater your capacity for handling responsibility and important tasks, the greater your influence. The greater your influence, the more opportunity you have to fulfill His fourth key purpose for work.

Purpose #4: A Stage on Which to Reflect God's Image

Every position has a job description that guides you in what you're supposed to do for your employer. God also has a "spiritual" job description for you: He wants you to be His ambassador to the people whose paths you cross. Sometimes you will be a silent witness, reflecting Him by your conduct, ethics, and excellence. Sometimes you will be a "semisilent" ambassador, dropping a timely word about God's truths, sharing a prayer with someone in need, or doing an act of selfless service. And sometimes God will call you to be a spokesman for His truth and an agent of His miracles, taking a spiritual leadership role that will transform the lives of those in your workplace. As you abide in Christ, He will equip and guide you to be a powerful reflection of His love and accomplish His purposes!

> **Travel Tip:** 1 Peter 2:12 reminds us: "Be careful to live properly among your unbelieving neighbors. Then even if they accuse you of doing wrong, they will see your honorable behavior, and they will give honor to God when he judges the world" (New Living Translation). In the work world, "living properly" means acting with impeccable ethics, demonstrating selfless love, and pursuing excellence in your craft or profession.

Availability vs. Ability

It's been said that God is more interested in our availability than our ability. Let me introduce you to some "extraordinary" ordinary people who have said "yes" to being used by God in the marketplace.

God Uses Ordinary People to Build His Kingdom

Chaz became an auto mechanic because he always enjoyed taking things apart and putting them back together. It was not a spiritually based decision, but a very pragmatic one. Although he went to college to be a teacher, he found he could make more money on weekends working on cars than he could all week teaching kids.

Can an auto mechanic be a tool in the hands of God as he goes to work every day? You bet. Chaz reflects the Lord in both his honesty and his extraordinary talent (which I can personally attest to). He also listens for opportunities to bring God into the conversation and remembers one customer in particular who had a son bouncing in and out of drug rehab. Chaz reported, "I invited the man to church—he is now attending regularly and involved in a Celebrate Recovery program!"

God Faithfully Redirects Us and Helps Us Discover Our Strengths and Gifting

Joan spent 28 years in federal government, including 15 years in managerial and executive positions. As time went on, she became more and more restless, moving from job to job every couple of years. Finally, she realized that the problem was not the position, but that God wanted something more and different. At the same time, she became more and more involved with equipping ministries at church and also felt drawn to attend seminary, which was life-changing. God gradually clarified for her that He had other places for her to go. Through others, she discovered (or actually rediscovered) her gifts for encouragement, teaching, and counseling. Two weeks after completing a Christian coach training class, she was given an opportunity to retire early from her federal job, by trading jobs with someone who was about to be downsized out of a job. Joan explains, "I can't tell you how rare this set of circumstances is—it literally almost never happens. It was abundantly clear that God was saying, 'Okay, you're ready—let's go!'" She adds, "While I don't expect this transition to be without struggles, I have everything I need to move as God directs and, most of all, I have *joy*."

God Shows Us That His Purposes Trump Our Passions

A few years ago, Terri completed a career coach training program that I lead through Career Coach Academy. Although I'd never met her face to face (Terri lives in Traverse City, Michigan, and I am in Fresno, California, but training was conducted via telephone bridge line), she impressed me greatly with her coaching talent, effusive warmth, and love for the Lord. After she graduated from the program, I asked her if she would be interested in working part-time for my organization in a program management capacity. At first, she responded that she was appreciative of the offer but would like to instead pursue her passion for coaching. Terri is a true gem and would have been a wonderful addition to our team, so I was disappointed (and confessed to the Lord so!). About a week later, she called and told me she had been praying about it and felt she should ask if the opportunity was still available. I was thrilled.

Does God draw us away from our passions? Sometimes, but always with good reason. In working for Career Coach Academy, Terri has been able to work flexible hours while still pursuing her passion, coaching. Although the program management work isn't her first love, she relates, "I am so thankful for the Lord leading me to this opportunity because it's made me a much better career coach. I am able to take advantage of other training that Career Coach Academy offers, and I've had lots of enlightening conversations with others in the career field that I wouldn't have had without my position as Program Manager. Perhaps the best part has been working with committed believers. So, doing what I believe God was leading me to do, even though it wasn't my original goal, has been the best for me, and I am so thankful how God has led!"

OBEDIENCE BLESSES

One of the most popular career trends today centers on passion: Pursuing one's passion is seen as a sort of North Star for career direction. Of course, God does plant passions in our heart that can be helpful in career decision-making, but we must be careful not to assume that every hour of our workday will be filled with fulfilling them. God works miracles in the mundane, sometimes unbeknownst to us, when we abide and obey.

William Barclay, in his commentary on *The Parables of Jesus* (Westminster John Knox Press, 1999), describes just such a case with Johann Sebastian Bach:

> For years he was teacher and organist in St. Thomas' School, Leipzig. For £125 a year he had to train the boys' choir, play at services, weddings and funerals, and—most amazing of all—produce new compositions every Sunday. They were never published; they were simply written, sung and then piled into a cupboard to grow old and dusty and forgotten. Priceless music—"Sheep may safely graze," "Jesu, joy of man's desiring," all kinds of things—was written, used and piled away. In the day's work in Leipzig he produced 265 church cantatas; 263 chorales; 14 larger works; 24 secular cantatas; 6 concertos; 4 overtures; 18 piano and violin concertos; 356 organ works and 162 pieces for the piano.

Bach did not pursue his passion at the exclusivity of all else. Had he not been obediently engaged in his everyday duties, he would not have produced the voluminous works that have blessed millions over the past centuries. Barclay draws this eloquent conclusion:

"It is not in longing for some other task than our own, but in doing our own faithfully and well that we find happiness and God."

God Uses "Boring" Jobs to Prepare Us for Bigger Responsibilities in the Future

While a college student, Lyndsey worked as a personal assistant to a busy mother who had a home-based business. Her job description included everything under the sun, from updating the company database and assembling training binders for the business to helping put on birthday parties for the children, washing the car, and polishing silver on the home front. An English Literature major with aspirations to write or teach at the university level, Lyndsey felt that this part-time position wasn't her permanent dream job, but she focused on the good things about the job such as the flexibility and her boss. In the meantime, the job helped buy books and pay some bills. Because she had such an incredibly positive attitude and always went the extra mile, she was recommended highly by her boss when she left and moved on to other jobs.

Was there purpose in that position? Certainly. Lyndsey relates that although she didn't necessarily learn important technical skills (seriously, how many jobs these days require knowing how to polish silver!), she learned the discipline of doing things that weren't necessarily fun and working with a commitment to excellence. Some of the "little" things she learned were how to follow through and think beyond basic instructions so that there weren't any loose ends for the boss to have to clean up, and how to keep lines of communication open so that her boss knew the status of a project and didn't worry that details were forgotten or swept under the rug. That attention to detail helped earn Lyndsey a coveted marketing internship with an international engineering firm after college, which opened up a variety of career doors for her.

God Allows Jobs to "Blow Up" for Sometimes Unknown Reasons, Even When We're Obedient

Sylvia is a successful mortgage broker who went through a very challenging time in her career recently. After working for one mortgage firm for approximately 10 years, she felt sure that the Lord had led her to move to a new company (company "A"); yet, after just a short time, the honeymoon quickly ended. Management wasn't following through on its promises and support staff seemed to be undermining her efforts, making it nearly impossible to service new loan business. This, of course, impacted her income as well.

Sylvia is a very mature believer, but there were times when she was in tears over the situation, uncertain about whether to change employers or stick it out. With prayer support, counsel from godly friends, and personal prayer and fasting, Sylvia followed the advice of 1 Peter 4:19. She committed herself and continued "to do good," but it wasn't easy. Eventually, Sylvia sensed God releasing her from the position as He clearly opened the door to move to another company.

Did Sylvia make a mistake in going to company "A"? Absolutely not. Looking back, Sylvia senses that she was obedient in following the Lord's guidance and knows that seeds were planted with several unbelievers there. Additionally, her teammate, also a believer, was greatly encouraged in her faith-walk as a result of the trial. Obedience can be a steep and painful climb in your professional pilgrimage. The ultimate reason for Sylvia's short sojourn at company "A" may never be revealed this side of heaven.

In the meantime, in her new position Sylvia is faithful and prays without ceasing for her customers, co-workers, and industry colleagues. She often thinks about going into full-time ministry, but her husband just chuckles when she mentions this. He reminds her that she *is* in full-time ministry—it just happens to be in a business setting.

God Redeems Work, Even When We're in the "Wrong" Job Just to Pay the Bills

Charlie is a gifted teacher, but he doesn't love his teaching job. Every day, he makes a two-hour round-trip commute to a rural agricultural area to teach alternative-education high-school students. Some days it feels more like babysitting than teaching. Most of his students are tough characters, often showing up to class with ankle bracelets (a "keepsake" from their overnight stays at Juvenile Hall). Fights, drug-sniffing dogs, and getting cussed out are routine; but Charlie has a family to support, so the good paycheck, excellent health benefits, and summers off with his family outweigh "escaping" the job to pursue his lifelong dream of being a forest ranger.

Years earlier, he had done everything he could think of to get on with the forest service. Despite perfect scores on preemployment exams, his lack of veteran or minority status prevented him from being hired. With doors closed to the forest service, he reluctantly opted to return to school to get a teaching credential. He was hired immediately—even before his credential was completed—just in time to earn health insurance to cover his wife's pregnancy expenses for their first child.

Has Charlie missed out on God's best for his career? Not necessarily. The years with these challenging students have stretched him and definitely grown him in the area of patience and self-discipline. And there are occasions when he can share the things of God with his students and their parents. Only time will tell what kind of eternal impact he is having. In the meantime, to bring the intellectual stimulation that is missing from his day job, he has pursued teaching night classes for a local university, which has brought him significant personal rewards and recognition. One of the humanities classes he teaches is world religions, and you can be sure he challenges his students with thought-provoking questions. His favorable student evaluations caused the administration to take notice of his skill, which led to added responsibilities in training other adjunct professors for the university.

God Uses Our Job to Get Our Attention and Correct Our Spiritual Course

Dan has a 20-year career in sales management with Fortune 500 companies. More than a year ago he underwent a six-month job search to pursue his dream of working on a national sales team that sold to Wal-Mart. People told him it was impossible to land such a job without direct Wal-Mart experience, which Dan did not have. Nonetheless, he admirably pursued this difficult road and eventually was hired by a well-known company for a team that sold to Sam's Club. He took the position thinking that it would later allow for a lateral move to the Wal-Mart account team. The position brought some significant and unexpected challenges— increased competition and factors outside of his control had led to declining sales. At the time, Dan was not a believer, but the difficulties caused him to start seeking God and return to church for the first time in a long time.

Not long after that, a surprise call from a recruiter brought an invitation to interview with another company for a Wal-Mart account team. Dan went on the interview and was eventually offered the position. It happened that the new company was going through change, with Wall Street rumors of a possible sale or merger. This caused Dan to wonder whether the new position was the best career move. He called a colleague to discuss this. During the course of the conversation, she asked Dan whether this potential merger was a calculated risk or a red flag. Dan figured it was a calculated risk. The colleague then talked about the unseen spiritual side of the story—that God desired good for him but that the enemy desired destruction. She explained to him how sin separates us from God and asked if there had been a point in his history where he had put his trust in Christ as Savior. He said no. She asked him if he wanted to do that now. He said yes. Dan is now experiencing new life in Christ as a true child of God.

Does God use job uncertainty or job search to correct our spiritual course and draw us to Him? You bet. Whether it's to meet Him the first time or experience Him in a deeper way, God's first desire is for relationship. He uses circumstances to get our attention. Romans 2:4 tells us that the kindness of God leads us to repentance. God lovingly gave Dan a new position, which got his attention.

From each of these varied stories, we can see that there's meaningful work to be done in this world. Chaz, Joan, Terri, Lyndsey, Sylvia, Charlie, Dan, and countless others have found it. You can, too.

Help Wanted: Applications Accepted Via Prayer

God is looking for people to be a part of His purposes. That doesn't mean you have to go to work for a church or become a missionary. Yes, you can certainly serve God by being employed with a church, parachurch organization, or missionary organization, but it's time we redefined careers in business, education, and government as essential places to serve God in "full-time ministry." *Every* career is a kingdom career!

There are millions of job openings in God's "company." His business is in growth mode and He's recruiting right now. His job postings might simply read:

> *Help wanted to facilitate life-changing behavioral transformation. Ideal candidate will be service-oriented, prepared to be on call 24/7, and willing to sometimes be vulnerable. No experience needed. On-the-job training and mentoring included. Opportunity to work with winning team. Global opportunities. Great life insurance plan. Send resume with prayer letter to God@work.com.*

God wants to walk with you on your career journey and has given the Holy Spirit as your "mentor" and on-the-job trainer. In your work life, He longs to bless you—to give you divine favor and prosper you. In addition, He wants you to experience the unfathomable depths of His love—to know Him and make Him known, to walk in the resurrection power given to His believers, to function fully in the physical world as well as the faith realm, and to do the good works—work with eternal significance—that He has prepared in advance for you to do (Eph. 2:10).

So what are the "good works" that God has handpicked for you? Complete the Chapter Wrap-Up Worksheet that follows. Then turn to chapter 2 to begin the next leg of your career journey.

CHAPTER WRAP-UP WORKSHEET

God's Purposes for Work

As you review the four purposes God has for your career (a setting to write your life's story, an incubator to grow your faith, a training ground to increase your capacity and influence, and a stage to reflect God's image), what new insights has God given you about His desires for your work?

_____

_____

_____

Availability vs. Ability

As you read the stories near the beginning of this chapter about God working in ordinary people's lives, which ones do you relate to the most?

____ God uses ordinary people to build His kingdom
____ God faithfully redirects us and helps us discover our strengths and gifting
____ God shows us that His purposes trump our passions
____ God uses "boring" jobs to prepare us for bigger responsibilities in the future
____ God allows jobs to "blow up" for sometimes unknown reasons, even when we're obedient
____ God redeems work, even when we're in the "wrong" job just to pay the bills
____ God uses our jobs to get our attention and correct our spiritual course
____ God uses the job search to show us His faithfulness

What might be keeping you from committing your career completely to God?

____ I am afraid God will ask me to take a vow of poverty if I commit my career to Him.
____ I am fearful of being accused of being a religious zealot or embarrassing myself if I represent God fully in the workplace.
____ I am concerned God will ask me to do things that I don't want to do.
____ Other

What does God say about fear in Hebrews 13:5-6 and about trying to win the approval of men in Galatians 1:10?

_____

_____

_____

What will it take to trust God with your career? Read Psalm 84:11-12, Psalm 125:1, Proverbs 3:5-6, and Matt. 6:31-32. What do these verses say about the benefits of trusting God?

_____

_____

_____

In 1914, Ernest Shackleton, the famous Antarctic explorer whose ship the _Endurance_ was trapped in ice for more than a year before slowly sinking, had the challenge of leading his 27-man crew to rescue on foot through 200 miles of treacherous ice floes. He limited each man to two pounds maximum of personal items. To demonstrate his commitment to doing the same, he discarded in front of his crew the "things of this world"— gold sovereigns, a gold watch, and silver brushes and dressing cases. He then ceremoniously took a treasured Bible, given to him by Queen Alexandra, and tore out only a few pages of his favorite verses to accompany him on the journey (a crewman later retrieved the whole Bible for their dangerous trek). Of course, your conditions promise to be much easier and you have access to the entire Bible during every step of your journey. Nonetheless, Shackleton's actions lead to a helpful question: As you head out on your journey toward a meaningful kingdom career, what special verse(s) do you want to hold onto as your constant companion for the days ahead?

_____

_____

_____

If you haven't already memorized these verses, I urge you to start today!

At the conclusion of each chapter, you'll find a Pocket Prayer that will help you talk with God about the various facets of your career journey. For downloadable copies that you can print and carry with you in a pocket, purse, or briefcase, visit www.ChristianCareerJourney.com/pray.html. I encourage you to pray the Pocket Prayers aloud and, when possible, ask another believer to join with you in prayer. Jesus reminds us in Matthew 18:20, "For where two or three come together in my name, there am I with them." (To learn more about the importance of assembling a support team for your career transition, see the worksheet at the end of chapter 2.)

Pocket Prayer

Father in heaven, You are the author of the good works that await me in my career. Thank you for forming me, gifting me with unique abilities, and perfectly preparing me over the past years to take on this upcoming chapter in my career journey. I do not know what the future holds, but I know who holds the future. I commit my career to You from this day forward and lay my hopes and dreams, as well as all my cares and concerns, at Your feet. Lead me to opportunities that will allow me to use the gifts You have entrusted to me. May they bless and bring benefit to others. Help me cooperate with You in creating a kingdom career—one that acknowledges Your Son as Lord and furthers Your work here on earth, and eternally. I am Yours. Use me. In Jesus' name, Amen.

CHAPTER 2

CREATED TO BE CALLED

"Christianity has preserved the fundamental idea that our lives count for something because God has a direction in mind for them…. If the God who made us has fig- ured out something we are supposed to do… —something that fits how we were made, so that doing it will enable us to glorify God, serve others, and be most richly ourselves —then life stops seeming so empty; my story has meaning as part of a larger story ultimately shaped by God."

— William C. Placher

You are God's workmanship—a hand-crafted vessel that He desires to fill and use. As a believer, the Savior dwells within you—you are to be the hands, feet, voice, and heart of Christ to those you work for and with. God has a strategic position for you in the workplace—a place where you can reflect His pres- ence, purposes, and power…a place where you will be significant for Him.

Career Questions About Calling

Despite the truths that you are important to God and He wants to use you, I find that most Christians still have puzzling questions about their career journey. For instance:

- If God has a plan for me, does that mean there is only one "right" job out there for me—and if so, won't that be a bit like finding a needle in a haystack? And how will I know when I've found it?

- If God really loves me and wants to use me, won't He make it easy for me to know what to do next?

- If God has given me specific gifts, does that mean I am supposed to work only in positions that use my gifting?
- Is it okay to work for a "questionable" employer, such as a publisher of supermarket tabloids?
- What if I make a mistake and miss God's will for my work life?
- Do I have to sacrifice income or other things if I follow God's leading in my career?
- If I'm following my calling and walking in obedience, does that mean I'll be happy with every aspect of my job?
- Will God be pleased with me if I simply show up at work and do a good job, or do I also have to witness?

If you were to assemble a room full of Bible scholars, you'd likely find no definitive answers to these questions. Debate would depend on denominational traditions and biblical interpretation. However, there are some questions that can be answered with an unequivocal "Yes!":

- Is God "on my side" and does He want to bless me in my career? Yes!
- Has God gone ahead of me and prepared "good works" that He wants me to do? Yes!
- Has He gifted me with certain talents and abilities that He wants me to use? Yes!
- Will God correct me if I get off course? Yes!
- Can God use me regardless of where I work? Yes!
- Will God supply me with the strength and resources I need to make this next career move? Yes!
- Will God never leave or forsake me on this journey? Yes!

As you continue to find answers for your career, this chapter will do the following:

- Outline three different aspects of calling: the call to be, do, and persevere
- Explain the career "DNA" of your calling
- Review biblical examples of callings
- Offer a formula for hearing from heaven to aid you in making wise career decisions

Called to Be, Do, and Persevere

"...in truth we are not called once only, but many times; all through our life Christ is calling us. ...whether we obey His voice or not, He graciously calls us still. If we fall...He calls us to repent; if we are striving to fulfill our calling, He calls us on from grace to grace...."

—*John Henry Newman*

Newman, an influential English theologian in the early 1800s, suggests that we are not called once, but throughout our lives. If so, then perhaps we might describe God's callings in these categories:

- The initial, priority call: This is a call **to be His follower.**
- The secondary, career call: This is a call **to do His work.**
- And, the ongoing, faithful call: This is a call **to persevere** and **become like Christ.**

Let's look at each one briefly.

Your Priority Call: To Be His Follower

The initial, priority call, is a call to be a follower of Christ. God's invitation is, "Come, *be* with Me." It is a call to treasure His presence, to marvel at His majesty, and to bathe in His love and forgiveness.

William C. Placher, in his book *Callings: Twenty Centuries of Christian Wisdom on Vocation* (Wm. B. Eerdmans Publishing Co., 2005), adds insight to the priority call:

> *More generally, when the Bible talks about "call" or "vocation," it charac-teristically means a call to faith or to do a special task in God's service. ...In the New Testament the word klēsis ("calling," from the Greek verb kaleō, "to call," used eleven times, mostly in letters by Paul or authors influenced by him) consistently refers to God's call to a life of faith...the "call" was to come, be a Christian.*

As an example, Paul, when writing to the Christians in Rome, uses the term twice in Romans 1:6-7a: "And you also are among those who are *called* to belong to Jesus Christ. To all in Rome who are loved by God and *called* to be saints...."(For other illustrations of how this word is used, see Rom. 8:28, 1 Cor. 1:26, and 2 Thess. 1:11.)

Even if you've walked with the Lord for many years, He continues to call you to a fresh experience of His nature. He calls with love that is more tender than the moth-er of a nestling newborn, and more forgiving than the father of a prodigal son. He calls you "beloved." He is the most benevolent boss you could ever imagine. His banner over you is love (Song of Sol. 2:4)—a proclamation of His devotion to you.

If it's been a while since you've quietly basked in His presence, take time today. He bids you simply, "Come, be with Me. I want to show you more of who I am."

As we learn more about who God is, we learn more of who we were meant to be, too. Knowing Christ gives you the freedom to become all that He intended you to be and to do all that He intended you to do.

Your Secondary Call: To Do His Work

The secondary call is a call to do. Christ calls us, saying, "Come, *do* something significant with your life. I made you and am filling you, and I want your voice to be heard and your presence to be known." Significance may be lived out in multiple forms as a spouse, parent, volunteer, and/or career professional, whether in the marketplace, in a church organization, or on the mission field.

This is the call to perform work that will fulfill His commandments, such as "love your neighbor as yourself" (Mark 12:31); "make disciples…teaching them to obey everything I have commanded you" (Matt. 28:19-20); and "work with your hands…so that your daily life may win the respect of outsiders" (1 Thess. 4:11-12).

We are to do things *with* and *for* Him: *with* Him because we can do nothing apart from Him (John 15:5, Rom. 11:35-36) and *for* Him because we are to live a life of love that pleases Him and bears fruit in every good work (Rom. 12:1, Col. 1:10).

God is calling: "Come, abide in Me and bear much fruit."

It is worth noting here that, despite God's desire that we do good and bear fruit, our salvation and security in Christ are not based on works. Ephesians 2:8-9 reminds us: "For it is by grace you have been saved, through faith—and this not from yourselves, it is the gift of God—not by works, so that no one can boast."

Your Ongoing Call: To Persevere and Become Like Christ

Finally, the ongoing call throughout our lives is a call to persevere. He urges us to run the race with endurance and to persevere when we're weary, to rekindle our commitment when our hearts are lukewarm, and to repent when we've missed the mark. He continually encourages, corrects, and restores.

The language of Christ in this call might be, "Come, follow Me. I know you've stumbled. I know you're weary. I know you've had thoughts of giving up, but I am still here, calling you, waiting for you, equipping you, and praying for you. I am committed to a lifetime of loving you and helping you run this course with endurance." (See Matt. 11:28, 1 John 1:8, Isa. 40:28-31, 2 Pet. 1:3, Rom. 8:26, Heb. 7:25, Phil. 1:6.)

If you're discouraged in your career, hear His voice today of encouragement. Eugene Peterson puts it in modern-day language in *The Message,* his paraphrase of the Bible: "Are you tired? Worn out? Burned out on religion? Come to me. Get away with me and you'll recover your life. I'll show you how to take a real rest. Walk with me and work with me—watch how I do it. Learn the unforced rhythms of grace. I won't lay anything heavy or ill-fitting on you. Keep company with me and you'll learn to live freely and lightly" (Matt. 11:28-30, *The Message*).

Biblical Principles of a Calling

God offers us some interesting insights into a calling as we look at the examples He's given us in scripture.

Characteristics of a Calling

In studying examples of calling in the Bible, we can make several observations about the characteristics of a call:

- God often surprises His people, calling them in the midst of the mundane and expecting an immediate response.
- The person called is usually an unlikely candidate by the world's standards— God anoints availability, not ability!
- God's call has both immediate and eternal outcomes.
- The purpose of God's call is to free people from slavery (whether physical or emotional) and deliver them to a good place. Caveat: As with Joseph of the Old Testament, your deliverance may feel long in coming, but God intends things for good and not for harm (Gen. 50:20).
- There are personal implications for the person called and big-picture ramifications for God's grand design.

Examples of a Calling

These characteristics of a calling are apparent in the following examples:

- **Abram (Abraham) in Genesis 12:1-4:** Abram (Abraham) was asked to leave his household (perhaps a foreshadowing of Jesus' instruction in Matt. 19:29) to be brought to the good land of Canaan. Not only Abram was blessed by following His calling, but an entire nation (and eventually the whole world).
- **Moses in Exodus 3:1-10:** While doing the mundane work of shepherding sheep, Moses was called to rescue his people and bring them to a good place.
- **Saul (Paul) in Acts 9:1-6, 19b-20:** Paul's call had major implications for his life. He was knocked off his career course and transformed from persecutor to promoter of "the Way." His call also had major ramifications for Christendom, because his letters compose a large part of the New Testament.

DIG DEEPER

For other examples of calling, look for the characteristics of a calling as you read the call of these people:

- Samuel in 1 Samuel 3:1-10 and 1 Samuel 16:1-13

- Isaiah in Isaiah 6:1-8

- Jeremiah in Jeremiah 1:4-10

- Mary in Luke 1:26-56

- Simon Peter and Andrew in Matthew 4:18-22

- Philip in Acts 8:26-38

- Barnabas and Saul in Acts 13:2-5

How to Hear from Heaven

Absent a burning bush or a blinding light from heaven, you'll need some help in hearing from God. As you begin to seek His will for your career, it will be important to have a clear channel to hear Him, with no interference or white noise!

What does it take to hear from heaven—to perceive God's wisdom for your work? In a survey developed for this book, dozens of Christians shared their stories of how they went about making a career change. When asked how God made it clear that they were to pursue different work, they responded as follows (respondents were asked to check all that applied):

- **Circumstances:** Circumstances occurred that seemed to have God's finger-prints on them (70%).
- **Prayer:** It became clear as I prayed (60%).
- **Peace:** God gave me great peace about the move (57%).
- **Godly Counsel:** It became clear through the godly counsel of others (54%).
- **God's Word:** It became clear as I read God's word (25%).
- **Faith:** I didn't have clear direction, but I moved ahead in faith anyway (22%).

The results show that circumstances, prayer, and peace are some of the highest markers for confirming a decision.

Will you hear an audible voice from God? Not likely. It's more likely that you'll have an impression of something you should do while praying (or after praying) and, if it's a major step, there will be confirmation by other trustworthy people and circumstances. After you follow through in that step, there will be revelation for the next step. Rarely does God give us all the steps at once. Your course of action should always align with God's word. Sometimes a good check is to ask yourself, "Would I be embarrassed if I had to explain to Jesus why I'm doing what I'm doing?"

A Formula to H.E.A.R. God

"...he goes on ahead of them, and his sheep follow him because they know his voice.... My sheep listen to my voice; I know them, and they follow me."

—*John 10:4b, 27*

How do you hear God's voice? One of the most notable stories about hearing from God is Moses' encounter at the burning bush in Exodus 3. I'll recap the story here, breaking it down into an acrostic for HEAR:

- **H—Hunger:** Step 1 in hearing from God is *wanting* to hear from Him! Perhaps the greatest gift God can give us is hunger—hunger to need Him and know Him. Whether a tiny hunger pang or complete famishment, hunger reminds us that nourishment is needed to fill us and fuel us. Hunger gets our attention. God caught Moses' attention with a burning bush. The sight caused Moses to come closer to the bush, which God had consumed (but not destroyed) with His presence (Ex. 3:2). This is God's goal in hunger—to draw us closer to Him.

  What has God used lately to catch your attention and draw you closer to Him? Perhaps it is a need, a difficulty, or a longing. Your need may be to bring home a bigger paycheck, or your difficulty might be a toxic work environment, or perhaps you have a longing for a change from inconsequential work to meaningful work.

  God also uses other people to make us hungry for Him. Perhaps God has put a believer in your pathway recently who lives life with faith and joy and you want to experience that blessing, too. Whatever gets our attention can create hunger for God.

- **E—Exalt:** Step 2 in hearing God is to exalt Him—admire and praise Him for who He is and commit to setting yourself apart for His use. Exalting is another way of saying, "God, You are who You say You are. I am humbled in Your presence."

  Returning to the story of the burning bush, when God got Moses' attention to come closer, we see a surprising turn of events. In Exodus 3:5, God tells Moses, "Do not come any closer." Why would God call Moses and then warn him to stay away? God then instructs Moses to take off his sandals. In other words, remove the dirt from his commonplace life and be consecrated to the things of God. God expects the same of us. He wants us near Him but also requires that we be clean and consecrated. Moses' response in removing his shoes acknowledged that God was holy and he wasn't.

It's interesting to note that in the next verse, Moses hides his face and is afraid to look at God. This can be a typical reaction when we first experience God. His invisible nature and holiness may cause us to be frightened or put off. You may feel that way at this point in your walk with the Lord. But as Moses learned more about God, he *wanted* to look at God and to have His presence with him (Ex. 33:15-20).

- **A—Accept:** Step 3 in hearing God is to accept what He tells you. In Moses' case, God told him that He had seen the misery of the Israelites while they were enslaved in Egypt and that He was going to send them a deliverer to bring them out of bondage. What is God telling us today? The same thing He told Moses thousands of years ago: Mankind—me, you, everyone—is a slave to sin and cannot free himself apart from a deliverer. Moses was a foreshadowing of the Messiah, the ultimate Savior. Beyond deliverance, there is also a "Promised Land" that God wants to take each of us to—a land of spiritual abundance and victory.

  Think about the things you would like to be free of ... the hurts, habits, hang-ups, and hungers that plague every one of us. Perhaps it's a bad attitude about a co-worker that you can't seem to shake, or a tendency to use company resources for personal use when you know it isn't quite right, or a case of insecurity that won't seem to heal, or a longing to do more with your career but the opportunities won't seem to open up.

  Likewise, think about the Promised Land you'd like to walk in—abundance in relationships, self-discipline, meaning, and provision. God is here to heal and help you. Believe Him. Accept that His promises are true!

- **R—Respond:** Step 4 in hearing God is to respond with action. I don't recommend responding as Moses initially did! He had a host of arguments for God: I am not qualified (Ex. 3:11) ... What authority do I have to do this? (v. 13) ... What if they don't believe me? (Ex. 4:1) ... I don't have the right skills (Ex. 4:10) ... I don't want to do it, send someone else (Ex. 4:13). Note that even when the Lord's anger burned against Moses for all his reluctance, God graciously provided by sending Aaron to help, even *before* Moses agreed to cooperate with God (Ex. 4:14-16).

  God doesn't always call the equipped, but He equips the called.

  God has set the wheels in motion to graciously help you, too, even before you agree to respond to Him. He has helpers awaiting you on your career journey. Your job is to move forward...act...respond!

If you're thinking, "That's all well and good, but how exactly am I supposed to respond?" recall from the end of chapter 1 that we are to function fully in the spiritual realm and fully in the physical realm. It appears from scripture that we are to start with the spiritual:

- *One* thing I ask of the Lord, this is what I seek, that I may dwell in the house of the Lord all the days of my life (Ps. 27:4, emphasis added).
- Mary has chosen what is *better,* and *it will not be taken away from her* (Luke 10:42, emphasis added).

A word of caution: The four-step formula associated with the HEAR acrostic is not a magic potion that will coerce God into telling you what you want to hear. The steps are guidelines for carrying on a conversation with God. In learning how to respond to Him (step 4), consider a scripture passage that has caught your attention recently. Ask God to reveal to you what this verse means (or, if you're new to Bible study, ask for insights from a mature Christian) and how to apply the verse to your life today. God will make it clear, perhaps not in an instant, but very soon, because He *wants* a relationship with you.

Pocket Prayer

Dear Lord, I praise You because You are the same yesterday, today, and forever—never changing, always faithful. Thank you that You still speak to your children today, through Your Word and through Your Spirit. Give me the gift of hunger for You, for You promise that those who hunger and thirst for You will be satisfied and You promise to satisfy with good things. Speak to me today through Your Word. If there is sin that is getting in the way of my hearing You clearly, bring it to mind. Forgive me and correct my course. Thank you that You give wisdom generously to those who ask. Make clear to me the next steps to take, and help me respond by pursuing a career course that will please You. In Jesus' name, Amen.

Three Conditions That Make It Difficult to Hear God

Of course, God is never silent because He has given His Word, the Bible. However, in general, there are three conditions that might prevent you from hearing God clearly:

- **Incorrect Beliefs:** There may be times that you don't hear clearly from God because you have misinterpreted or misapplied scripture. This is why it's important to surround yourself with people who can offer Godly counsel.
- **Unconfessed Sin:** Proverbs 15:29 tells us that God is far from the wicked but does hear the righteous. Ask God to bring to mind any unconfessed sin and then celebrate this verse from 1 John 1:8-9: "If we claim to be without sin, we deceive ourselves and the truth is not in us. If we confess our sins, he is faithful and just and will forgive us our sins and purify us from all unrighteousness."
- **Unexercised Faith:** If it seems that God is silent, it may be that He is simply stretching your faith and wanting you to be faithful in the things that you already know to do.

Clues That You May Be Ignoring God

Sometimes the easiest way to know if you're hearing God is to listen to the chatter inside your head. You might be off course from God's will if you're thinking about doing something and these phrases come to mind:

- "It won't matter if I do this."
- "What's the use?"
- "I'm sure God wouldn't mind just this once."
- "I hope I don't get caught."
- "Hmmm, I wonder if this is God's will" (and then you don't take the time to pray and wait for direction). "Oh well, I don't want to wait to find out, so here goes!"

This last item brings up an important point. There will be times when you'll need to make a decision quickly. That's when it's especially important to be "prayed up." Having had sufficient prayer time at the start of your day will make it easier to make decisions throughout the day.

Here are some other clues that you might be ignoring God:

- There is no peace of mind.
- You're consumed with thinking about what it is you want to do, and plotting how to make it happen.
- When you're trying to say something that God doesn't want you to say, there's no room to break into the conversation. (This is often His way of protecting you from sticking your foot in your mouth!)
- You seem to be blocked from taking action, no matter where you turn.
- You take action and painful consequences result from it.
- Your intentions are self-focused rather than God-focused, with thoughts of: "This will definitely impress them" or "I hope I'll get noticed when I do this."
- Your motives fall short of absolute agape love, with thoughts toward others of: "I hope this teaches her a lesson" or "He needs to see that I'm right in this."

As a point of encouragement, if you ever feel that you have to "be good" in your own strength, you are striving to attain God. Instead, simply abide in God.

Pocket Prayer

If you find yourself striving instead of abiding, you may find it helpful to stop and say this simple prayer aloud: "Lord Jesus, You tell me in John 15 to 'abide in me, and I will abide in you.' So I intentionally do that right now. Thank you for abiding in me and equipping me to do what needs to be done. Amen."

Career Choices: Door No. 1 or Door No. 2?

Os Hillman, in his daily devotional *TGIF—Today God Is First* (available free at www.marketplaceleaders.org), shares how one leader of a marketplace organization poses a critical question to workplace believers:

> *"What if there were two doors to choose from; behind one door was the complete will of God for your life and behind the other door was how life could be according to your own preference. Which door would you choose?" The struggle for most lies in the desire to follow God completely and the fear of what might be behind the door of full surrender. Most of us desire to follow God, but few of us will do it at any cost. We do not really believe that God loves us to the degree that we are willing to give Him complete permission to do as He wills in us.*

If you're like me, there may have been many moments when you said, "I don't want 'full surrender.' I'll just keep doing things my way, thank you very much!" Sadly, there are times I have defiantly chosen the way of the world instead of His way of wonder, wisdom, and love.

Imagine a parent who sees his child doing something that invites destruction—a toddler wandering out into the street, a child playing too close to an open flame, a teenager speeding recklessly, an adult daughter dating a man who beats her. The parent's heart breaks over the danger and destruction; he wants not to take away the child's fun, but to protect, provide, and pour out his blessing. And so it is with our Abba Father who wants the best for us. God is committed to a lifetime of loving us and drawing us to the door of destiny that He has intended.

Chapter Wrap-Up

God created you and has called you—called you to be His own, called you to do His work, and called you to persevere and become more and more like Christ. Over the course of your career, God may call you to do different things. The packaging may change (for example, a new role or new industry), but the essence of the work remains the same. With the call, He will grow your relationship with Him and reflect Himself to others as you serve as His hands, feet, voice, and heart.

10 QUICK TIPS FOR CALLING

1. **Listen for a lifetime.** Listening for God's call is a lifelong process. God calls you not once, but continually, because He loves you and is committed to finishing the good work He started in you.

2. **Belong to God.** God first calls you to belong to Him—to be His follower. It is a call to treasure His presence, to marvel at His majesty, and to bathe in His love and forgiveness.

(continued)

3. **Live a life of significance.** God also calls you to do His work. It is a call to do something significant with your life. It is a call to have a life-changing effect on your corner of the world.

4. **Follow forever.** The perpetual call of God is to persevere in becoming like Christ. He wants you to run the race with endurance, to repent when you've missed the mark, and to press on when you're tired or weary. He continually encourages, corrects, and restores.

5. **Recognize the characteristics of a calling.** God often surprises His people with "career callings" to specific assignments for specific purposes. He is more interested in your availability than your ability, and He can anoint you for whatever task He calls you to. There will be personal implications for you and big-picture ramifications for God's grand design.

6. **Understand the essence of a calling.** Throughout the Old and New Testaments, the underlying purpose of God's call on people's lives was to bring others into a place of abundance. The lives of Moses and Paul are prime examples.

7. **Use the H.E.A.R. formula to hear God's call.** "H" stands for <u>H</u>unger. God loves it when you are hungry for Him—hungry to hear and obey His voice. He often uses circumstances to catch your attention and draw you closer, whether it be a need, a longing, or a blessing. "E" stands for <u>E</u>xalt. Admire and praise Him for who He is. Be grateful for all He's given you. "A" stands for <u>A</u>ccept. Accept what He tells you—there's a treasure trove of promises in His Word that He wants you to accept. "R" stands for <u>R</u>espond. Respond with action. Your job is to move forward…act…respond!

8. **Learn the three conditions that make it difficult to hear God: Incorrect beliefs**—Surround yourself with Godly counsel to avoid misinterpreting or misapplying scripture. **Unconfessed sin**—Proverbs 15:29 reminds us that God is far from the wicked, but 1 John 1:9 tells us that God forgives us the minute we confess. **Unexercised faith**—if it seems that God is silent, it may be that He is stretching your faith and wanting you to be faithful in the things that you already know to do.

9. **Watch for clues that you're ignoring God!** Some clues that you might be ignoring God include the following: You have no peace of mind. You are consumed with thinking about what you want to do, plotting how to do it, and convincing yourself and others that it's the right thing to do. You seem to be blocked from taking action, no matter where you turn. Your intentions are self-focused rather than God-focused. Your motives fall short of agape love.

10. **Choose "Door No. 1" for your career.** There are two options for your work and life: The first is the complete will of God; the second is life lived according to the song made famous by Frank Sinatra, "I Did It My Way." God's complete and perfect will is like the will of a loving parent who doesn't want to take away your fun, but wants to protect, provide, and pour out his blessing. Choose to follow His call!

CHAPTER WRAP-UP WORKSHEET

Your Calling

The Old Testament story of God calling Cyrus to rescue Israel from its captivity in Babylon is found in Isaiah 45:1-5. Read the passage from Isaiah and check all that apply regarding Cyrus's calling:

- ❏ God anoints him for his calling.
- ❏ God holds his right hand.
- ❏ God goes ahead of him to subdue the Babylonian nation (the bad guys).
- ❏ God gives him treasures of wisdom.
- ❏ God does this so that he will know that God is the Lord.
- ❏ God strengthens him for the task, even though he had not yet acknowledged the Lord.

As this passage illustrates, when God calls you, He also anoints you, holds your hand, goes ahead of you, gives you wisdom, deepens your understanding of who He is, and strengthens you, even before you acknowledge Him. Let that sink into your heart for a minute!

Ephesians 1:4 tells us, "For he chose us in him before the creation of the world to be holy and blameless in his sight." From this verse, when would you say God called you?

- ❏ At the time of my birth
- ❏ After I became a Christian
- ❏ Before the creation of the world

The works we do for God will be acted out in the physical/material world, but they will also have an effect in the spiritual realm. Regardless of what you do in the physical/material realm with your career, what are some of the outcomes you would like to effect in the spiritual realm? (For further Bible study, see John 4:34, 6:28-29, and 17:4; 1 Cor. 3:10b-14 and 15:18; Col. 1:10; and Heb. 6:10-11.)

_____

_____

_____

Regarding the call to persevere, what does God say about perseverance in the following verses?

Romans 5:3-4: _____

_____

James 1:3-4: _____

_____

2 Peter 1:6: _____

_____

Want to dig deeper? Enjoy these scriptures, each of which contains the word "calling" in the original Greek: Romans 11:29, 1 Corinthians 1:26 and 7:20, Ephesians 1:18 and 4:1-4. Philippians 3:14, 2 Thessalonians 1:11, 2 Timothy 1:9, Hebrews 3:1, and 2 Peter 1:10.

(continued)

CHAPTER WRAP-UP WORKSHEET *(CONTINUED)*

Hearing from Heaven

Recall the statistics on the different factors God used to help other Christians get clarity on their career change (see "How to Hear from Heaven," earlier in this chapter). As you undertake the next leg of your career journey, describe the actions you'll commit to for each of these factors.

Circumstances: What circumstances have you already seen that seem to have God's "fingerprints" on them? How will you keep a record of them?

_____

_____

Prayer: What changes might you need to make in your schedule to devote sufficient time to prayer? Who do you know who would be willing to partner with you in prayer? How will you connect? How frequently?

_____

_____

Peace: On a scale of 1–10 (10 is high), how would you rate your level of peace right now? If you want your score to be higher, what will it take to make that happen?

_____

_____

Godly Counsel: Proverbs 15:22 says, "Plans fail for lack of counsel, but with many advisers they succeed." Who are two or three mature believers you can confide in and confer with during your career transition? If you don't know of some, check with your church. It's also helpful to join a career change group—if one doesn't exist in your church, consider forming your own and working through the topics in this book (or contact Career Transition Ministries, mentioned below). Ideally, enlist the services of a Christian career/life coach who is experienced with career transitions and can incorporate God's Word and solid resources and transition systems into your situation. Write below whom you will enlist for support.

_____

_____

Start Your Own Career Ministry Group

The Career Transition Ministries Network (www.ctmnetwork.org) equips churches that want to start a ministry to job seekers. If your church doesn't have such a ministry and you'd like to see one started, contact the organization's Executive Director, Mr. Lynn Guillory (lguillory@etmnetwork.org), for details.

Career Choices: Door #1 or Door #2?

In the past, which door have you chosen when it comes to your career (Door #1 is the complete will of God for your life; Door #2 is the door of "I'll do it my way")?

- ❑ Door #1
- ❑ Door #2

If you haven't chosen Door #1 in the past, what would need to change for you to choose it now?

_____

_____

Ask God to remind you of a situation in which His love and faithfulness surprised you. How does this encourage you to choose Door #1—God's complete will for your life?

_____

_____

Progress comes one step at a time. Ask God to show you one small area of your life where you can trust Him today.

_____

_____

Pocket Prayer

Gracious God, You are the God who calls me by name. You called me out of darkness into Your marvelous light. Just as You called Abraham and his descendants to be Your chosen people, You have called me and chosen me as Your cherished possession. You called me to persevere and not be weary in doing good, promising that in due season I will reap. Thank You for Your calling on my life. Lead me to work that will build Your kingdom. Open my eyes to the new opportunity that You have hand-picked for me. Father, You say that the steps of a righteous man are ordered by the Lord. Show me the next step to take. As I begin to look at the "Master F.I.T." for my life, make clear to me how You have designed and equipped me to do the special works that await me. Help me press toward the mark for the prize of the high calling of God in Christ Jesus. Amen.

CHAPTER 3

RECONCILING YOUR MASTER F.I.T. WITH GOD'S MASTER PLAN

"The best vision is insight."

—*Malcolm Forbes*

When it comes to your career, do you believe there's a Promised Land waiting for you? Perhaps you're at a point in your work life where you readily relate to the Israelites who were enslaved in Egypt—you feel as though your job is a prison. You've been in so much pain that you can't even remember that God promised you a Promised Land. Maybe the Israelites' 40 years of wandering in the wilderness is the metaphor that best describes your situation— you've been in a desert experience. The waiting, waiting, and more waiting has caused you to doubt God or tempted you to turn back and not press on.

As Christians, the truth is that we have already been given a Promised Land. Here is what God might say to us today about this place we all long for:

> *"My people have crossed over from death to life, from slavery to freedom, from prison to the Promised Land, through belief in My Son, Jesus Christ. He is your Deliverer, Redeemer, Companion, and Keeper. The Promised Land is My presence, My provision, My promises. You possess all of this in Christ. You stand in a land that is good. Yes, there will be battles to fight. You're in one right now if you're feeling discouraged or confused. Be strong. Be courageous. I am here to defend you, to show you how to claim the territory that is yours, and to show you how to thrive in a land I want you to call home until I call you to your eternal home. No one can take the Promised Land away from you because it belongs to Me, and you belong to*

Me. I love you. I love your career. I love everything I created. And I want to use your career to cause you to prosper and to cause others to prosper. Abide in Me and allow Me to be at the center of everything. Amen."

God wants to give you a vision of walking victoriously in the Promised Land. To do that, you need to know Him (which is a lifelong process) and you need to know how He has wired you (which you'll tackle next). In this chapter, you will learn to do these things:

- Identify elements of your External Master F.I.T.™, including Function, Industry/Interests, and Things that Matter.
- Identify elements of your Internal Master F.I.T., including Fulfillment, Identity, and personality Type.

Ready to make progress on your journey?

Visioning and Planning

If you've recently read any popular books on personal success, you'll hear this common theme: Envision the ideal outcome, then plan accordingly. There is truth to the old adage "Fail to plan, plan to fail." And yet, how do we reconcile visioning and planning with admonitions like these:

- Proverbs 16:9: In his heart a man plans his course, but the Lord determines his steps.
- Proverbs 19:21: Many are the plans in a man's heart, but it is the Lord's purpose that prevails.
- Ephesians 1:11: In him we were also chosen, having been predestined according to the plan of him who works out everything in conformity with the purpose of his will....
- Philippians 2:13: ...for it is God who works in you to will and to act according to his good purpose.

God *does* want us to envision the future (Prov. 29:18) and, like faithful Boy Scouts, always be prepared. At the same time, we mustn't presume to know for certain where He will lead us because tomorrow, next month, or next year could bring a major development that we would never have considered!

We must be tenacious in following through on plans, but even more tenacious in listening to God to ensure that the vision is God-inspired. There may also be times when we need to let go of our investment of time and energy (and pride!) and change course. God's ideas will always be more strategic than ours!

The solution to blending personal action with spiritual accountability is found in Proverbs 16:3: "Commit to the Lord whatever you do, and your plans will succeed." In short,

Commit to your plan, but plan to commit everything to the Lord.

This requires the art of co-creating with God. It's a blend of talking to God, then taking action, and again talking to God, then taking action. Ultimately, as you "practice His presence," talking and taking action meld into one to produce a continuous consciousness of His presence.

> **Travel Tip:** For a deeper look at practicing God's presence, check out the classic book *The Practice of the Presence of God* (Revell, 1999) by Brother Lawrence, a 17th-century monk whose thoughtful writings influenced notable Christian authors such as A. W. Tozer *(The Pursuit of God)* and Hannah Whitall Smith *(The Christian's Secret to a Happy Life)*.

As you complete the steps in this chapter, practice God's presence and co-create with Him. It's the only way to find a masterful fit for your career!

If you're fairly clear on what your next career move will be and you want to commence with job search, consider skipping to the end of this chapter and using the 10 Quick Tips for Focusing on Your Master F.I.T. (figure 3.1), then moving on to chapter 5.

If you're not clear, read on! Your target *will* become clear because God promises to give you wisdom. James 1:5 tells us: "If any of you lacks wisdom, he should ask God, who gives generously to all without finding fault, and it will be given to him." What an amazing verse—God will not accuse, belittle, or humiliate when you ask for His wisdom. Instead, He gives it generously and graciously!

Identifying Your Master F.I.T.

Merriam-Webster defines the verb *fit* this way:

To be suitable for or to harmonize with

Let's add "God" to the end of that definition so that it reads "…to harmonize with God." When your work aligns with things that you are suited for and is significant to God, there is harmony and satisfaction. Instead of being a "square peg in a round hole," you can perform work that "fits like a glove."

Figures 3.1 and 3.2 give you a closer look at the Master F.I.T. model. Figure 3.1 shows a blank Master F.I.T. You'll note that there are two layers for each of the letters in F.I.T. The first layer shown in the left-hand column—Function, Industry/Interests, and Things That Matter—focuses on external elements that are easily observable. The second layer shown in the right-hand column—Fulfillment, Identity, and Type—homes in on internal elements that are less easily identifiable, but just as important. Each box has coaching questions, as well as relevant scriptures. Figure 3.2 shows a Master F.I.T. form that has been completed by "Alia," who was exploring a career move.

Career "Master F.I.T.™"

External "F.I.T." (the easily observable F.I.T.)	Internal "F.I.T." (the less observable, but equally important F.I.T.)
Function (<u>What</u> do you *want and like* to do? What strengths/talents/skills/passions have you excelled at in the past? What are your spiritual gifts? What would you like to learn to do? What job titles are associated with these functions? Conversely, what do you want to avoid? If there were one task you couldn't give up in your current career, what would it be? Job titles will often be associated with the <u>F</u>unction.) **Scriptures:** Rom. 12:6-8; 1 Cor. 12:7-12; Eph. 4:11-13; 1 Pet. 4:10; John 15:16a; Ps. 139:13-16; Heb. 2:4; Rom. 9:21; 2 Cor. 3:5	**Fulfillment** (<u>Why</u> do you work? What do you sense is God's purpose/destiny for your life? What difference do you want to make in the world? How would you describe your living legacy? Why will this be rewarding?) **Scriptures:** Jer. 29:11; Ps. 138:8; Prov. 16:9, 19:21; Eccles. 3:1; John 17:4; Eph. 1:11; Phil. 2:13; Acts 26:15; 2 Tim. 1:9 and 2:20
Industry/Interests (<u>Where</u> do you want to use your "function" skills? Where do your interests, knowledge, or experiences lie? What industries/companies/products do these interests represent? Conversely, what situations do you want to avoid?) **Scriptures:** Exod. 31:2-3, 35:10,31,35, and 36:2; 1 Kings 7:14b; 1 Chron. 28:21 and 34:12; Prov. 22:29; 1 Cor. 14:12b; 1 Tim. 4:14-15	**Identity** (<u>Who</u> are you? Who are you becoming? Who does God want you to be? What adjectives best describe your present and future you? How do you want others to perceive you? Who are your role models? Who have been your key supporters?) **Scriptures:** Prov. 22:1, 10:7; Eccles. 7:1; Phil. 2:7; Col. 3:3; 1 Cor. 1:30; 1 Tim. 3:7
Things That Matter (<u>Which</u> values and priorities—financial, work/lifestyle, environmental, intellectual, emotional, spiritual—must be present for you to be your best in your work?) **Scriptures:** Isa. 56:4b; Luke 42:10a	**Type** (<u>How</u> do you prefer to reenergize, take in information, make decisions, and orient your environment? For instance, are you more energized by people and things or ideas and concepts? Do you primarily trust information that is tangible and concrete or abstract and conceptual? Do you prefer to make decisions based on logic or how it will affect people? Do you prefer an environment that is more controlled and predictable or unstructured and variable? How do you learn best?) **Scriptures:** Prov. 22:6

Options:

Best Next Steps:

Figure 3.1: The Master F.I.T. model.

"Alia's" Career "Master F.I.T.™"

External "F.I.T." (the easily observable F.I.T.)	Internal "F.I.T." (the less observable, but equally important F.I.T.)
Function (What do you *want and like* to do? What strengths/talents/skills/passions have you excelled at in the past? What are your spiritual gifts? What would you like to learn to do? What job titles are associated with these functions? Conversely, what do you want to avoid? If there were one task you couldn't give up in your current career, what would it be? Job titles will often be associated with the Function.)	**Fulfillment** (Why do you work? What do you sense is God's purpose/destiny for your life? What difference do you want to make in the world? How would you describe your living legacy? Why will this be rewarding?)
Job titles: Instructor, project director, educator, program manager, trainer, director of educational programming. My spiritual gifts include leadership and teaching.	I work to learn, grow, and serve. My purpose is to help others reach their fullest potential in any way I can assist. My living legacy is to have helped others reach their personal educational goals—and gain freedom through learning. This is rewarding to me because I believe that in most instances, the "great" jobs in life require some type of formal training beyond the desire for that role. Many don't know how to get or access the education they need. Opening their eyes to the possibilities for their future through additional education makes me feel that they can touch/inspire others—thus spreading the "wealth" and improving their (and their children's) chance for success in life. I personally find the most joy in seeing women of color take the risk of using their time to further their education—seeing their success defies description as to what it means to me.
I would like to learn how to be more effective in building and retaining relationships.	
Random Thoughts: My passion lies in encouraging others to attain a greater level of education/learning. My greatest strength is in taking complex concepts/information and restructuring it for ease of presentation and learning. I sincerely believe that if I can "teach you to fish" you will be able to feed yourself, through learning, for the rest of your life. I have excelled at presenting information, coordinating activities, organizing tasks. Because I can do so many different things, I want to avoid being seen as a "flunky." I wouldn't want to give up searching for information that the employees need to help them further their education.	
Industry/Interests (Where do you want to use your "function" skills? Where do your interests, knowledge, or experiences lie? What industries/companies/products do these interests represent? Conversely, what situations do you want to avoid?)	**Identity** (Who are you? Who are you becoming? Who does God want you to be? What adjectives best describe your present and future you? How do you want others to perceive you? Who are your role models? Who have been your key supporters?)
Any organization that can see my value—ultimate goal is academia.	Present me: Task oriented, isolated, perceived as aloof
I want to avoid being in a sole IT role.	Future me: See the big picture, able to positively lead and effect change
	Want others to perceive me: Team player, helpful
	Role Models: Jesus Christ, Violet Greene
	Key Supporters: Friends
Things That Matter (Which values and priorities—financial, work/lifestyle, environmental, intellectual, emotional, spiritual—must be present for you to be your best in your work?)	**Type** (How do you prefer to reenergize, take in information, make decisions, and orient your environment? For instance, are you more energized by people and things or ideas and concepts? Do you primarily trust information that is tangible and concrete or abstract and conceptual? Do you prefer to make decisions based on logic or how it will affect people? Do you prefer an environment that is more controlled and predictable or unstructured and variable? How do you learn best?)
My values are faith-based: honesty, integrity. I'd like to have a salary of at least 150K/yr before I retire. I need autonomy, respect, and trust in the workplace for me to do my best. I also need to feel that my work is valued.	I reenergize by being creative and doing projects with my hands—building things, especially in my house, and painting pictures. Relaxing at a beach or just lying outside on a beautiful day. Both options energize me.
	I prefer to trust info that is tangible and concrete.
	Decision making—both options.
	I prefer a controlled, structured, and predictable environment.
	I learn best when it's information that I want to learn.
Options: Shift to a training/IT role at current employer (hospital); work in academia; work in IT/education-type consulting firm	
Best Next Steps: Create proposal for new/redirected position at current employer; apply for positions internally; apply for positions in academi a	

Figure 3.2: An example of a Master F.I.T. completed by a Christian exploring career options.

Use the form in figure 3.1 (or download a blank form from my Web site, www.ChristianCareerJourney.com/journey.html) to flesh out each Master F.I.T. item as it relates to you.

> **Travel Tip:** As you complete your Master F.I.T. and co-create with God, my prayer is that you get a glimpse of a larger, grander, and more fulfilling career.
>
> **Because you are God's chosen child, He has given you the potential to change the world, one life at a time!**

Step 1: Find the Right Function

Step 1 in the Master F.I.T. process begins with brainstorming functional areas (job titles and tasks) that fit with your skills and talents. Function is the "what" in your Master F.I.T. Answers always come by asking the right questions! To get started, pray! Ask God to reveal truth to you about the incredible gifts He has lavished on you and wants you to enjoy.

Review the coaching questions listed in the "Function" box of your F.I.T. form and jot down answers in the form as they come to you. Transfer any important results from assessments you have taken into the Master F.I.T. form, as well. Ideas for "Function" can also be generated by reviewing the Function Checklist with some 100 options at www.ChristianCareerJourney.com/journey.html. Before moving on to that checklist, you may find it helpful to review the topic of spiritual gifts and core skills.

Spiritual Gifts

> *"Each one should use whatever gift he has received to serve others, faithfully administering God's grace in its various forms."*

> *—1 Pet. 4:10*

Your spiritual gifts are presents to you from God. They represent the presence of God—an attribute of Him. Using your gifts is a little bit like giving God to others. It benefits your co-workers, colleagues, customers, and clients. The purpose of spiritual gifts is to share God's grace with others!

Three different types of gifts are mentioned in the New Testament, sometimes categorized as follows:

- "Motivational" gifts seen in Romans 12:6-8
- "Manifestation" gifts described in 1 Cor. 12:7-12
- "Ministry" gifts listed in Eph. 4:11

Motivational Gifts: The seven gifts listed in Rom. 12:6-8 include prophecy, service, teaching, encouraging, giving, leadership, and mercy. They are referred to by many as "motivational" gifts. According to the lexicon available at www.blueletterbible.org, the original Greek word for gift used in this passage is *charizomai,* with a root meaning of doing "something pleasant or agreeable." Indeed, when you use your spiritual gifts, you are motivated because the work is pleasant and agreeable.

Manifestation Gifts: The nine manifestation gifts of 1 Cor. 12 include the message of wisdom, message of knowledge, faith, gifts of healing, working of miracles, prophecy, distinguishing (or discerning) of spirits, different kinds of tongues, and interpretation of tongues. These are called manifestation gifts based on the Greek root word that Paul uses, *phanerōsis,* meaning "manifestation" or to make visible or known what has been hidden or unknown. (See www.blueletterbible.org for more information.)

Ministry Gifts: There are five gifts listed in Eph. 4:11, including apostle, prophet, evangelist, pastor, and teacher. These gifts are to be used to build up and equip other believers to do ministry—thus, the term "ministry" gifts.

Core Skill Areas

The skills required for the vast majority of careers fall into six core areas that were identified by Dr. John Holland, a respected career development theorist who spent much of his career at Johns Hopkins University. According to Holland's theory, people tend to choose environments that are consistent with their individual preferences and style. Referred to as the Holland Codes, the six styles are Realistic, Investigative, Artistic, Social, Enterprising, and Conventional.

One of the assessments recommended later to identify your interests is the Career Liftoff Interest Inventory developed by J.W. Lewis and Associates LLC. This inventory is available at www.careerliftoff.com (for more information on this assessment, e-mail info@careerliftoff.com or write P.O. Box 21772, Eagan, MN 55121). Figure 3.3 is a helpful excerpt from the Career Liftoff Interest Inventory (reprinted with permission) showing the six Holland Codes with examples of professions for each code.

ACTION STEP

Using the Master F.I.T. form in figure 3.1 (or the blank downloadable form at my Web site www.CareerAndLifeCoach.com/MasterFIT.pdf), enter your top choices for "Function" based on assessment results and the online checklist. Add any additional insights gained from your answers to the coaching questions on the F.I.T. form to uncover the "Function" fit.

REALISTIC - Likes to work with things, such as machines, tools, and plants; seeks technical or physical tasks and likes to work with one's hands. Often is practical and good at solving problems. Solves problems by doing. Typically values independent-mindedness, frankness, and physical activity and enjoys the outdoors.	
Protective Services	Enforcing the law, or guarding and protecting people or property, which includes police, military, corrections/prisons, security, or customs.
Skilled/Mechanical/ Technical	Working with tools and machines, fixing and installing products and equipment such as a machinist, electrician, plumber, or welder.
Production Services	Putting things together and assembling components or products involving such things as assembly-line work with machine tools.
Farming/ Environmental	Growing, caring for, or harvesting plants or animals, including farming, ranching, forestry, wildlife conservation, and pollution control.
Transportation	Transporting people or goods, including operating trucks, taxis, cars, buses, planes, helicopters, boats, or ships.
INVESTIGATIVE – Likes working with ideas, data, or observable facts and likes to watch, learn, analyze, and solve problems. Tends to be good at math and science, likes analyzing data, and likes to work independently. Solves problems by thinking. Typically values logic, caution, the creative process, science, intellectual freedom, and precision.	
Physical Sciences	Studying, researching, or applying the physical sciences, including physics, mathematics, engineering, meteorology, and astronomy.
Biological Sciences	Studying, researching, or applying the biological sciences, including biology, zoology, oceanography, and genetics.
Medical Sciences	Studying, researching, or applying the medical sciences, including surgery, pediatrics, neurology, and infectious diseases.
Behavioral Sciences	Studying, researching, or applying the behavioral sciences, including sociology, anthropology, and psychology.
Information Technology	Researching and developing computer systems, applications, and technologies, including designing new computer technologies.
ARTISTIC – Likes working in unstructured situations where creativity can be used. Enjoys writing, designing, performing (theater or music), and the visual arts. Solves problems by expressing feelings or ideas creatively. Is aesthetically sensitive and trusts intuition. Typically values novelty, unstructured conditions, nonconformity, and artistic freedom.	
Performing Arts	Performing before an audience, including interpreting a part or role, playing an instrument, singing, or dancing.
Visual Arts	Creating a tangible, visual, original expression in the areas of painting, drawing, or sculpture, or designing materials to achieve an artistic effect.
Crafts	Producing art and craft objects, including designing and engraving jewelry, bracelets, pottery, window displays, and sets for plays.
Creative Arts	Creating new ideas and concepts, including writing a book, story, play, poem, or music, or designing high-fashion items such as clothing.
Computer Graphics Design	Creating images on computers, including virtual reality, Web sites, commercials, Internet applications, or interactive video.

Figure 3.3: Excerpt from the Career Liftoff® Interest Inventory. (Reprinted with permission. This material is protected by copyright. All rights are reserved by the copyright owner, including the right to copy this material or any portion in any form.)

SOCIAL – Likes to work with other people rather than things; to instruct, advise, empathize, express, or assert feelings, or otherwise care for others. Enjoys training, instructing, counseling, or curing others. Solves problems by relating to others in a helpful way. Typically values genuineness and ethical awareness and has a strong sense of community.	
Personal Caring Services	Helping and caring for sick, injured, or mentally ill people, including children, the elderly, or people with chemical dependency.
Counseling	Helping others in understanding themselves, including relationships, crisis intervention, and identifying additional helping resources.
Education	Teaching and imparting knowledge to others by helping people learn through coaching, mentoring, presentations, or instruction.
Spiritual	Assisting people explore spiritual issues and beliefs, including ministering to the spiritual needs of others, or participating in religious services and study groups.
Customer Service	Assisting customers by providing information, listening to concerns, and helping resolve issues.
ENTERPRISING – Likes to work with people or data, have an impact, and achieve goals by persuading, selling, influencing, or directing others. Tends to be assertive and enthusiastic. Solves problems by taking the lead and taking risks. Typically values having influence on others, status, excitement, making decisions, and selling ideas.	
Sales	Selling products and services, including making presentations, persuading people to buy, and negotiating terms and conditions of a sale.
Politics	Participating in political activities, including debating political issues, participating in political rallies, campaigning for candidates, or seeking political office.
Hospitality	Providing services to the traveling public, including coordinating public relations events, or managing a convention center, resort, hotel, or restaurant.
Business Entrepreneurship	Starting, growing, and managing a business, including financing, marketing, and promoting a business.
Legal	Providing legal counsel, including advising clients on legal matters or presenting legal arguments on personal or public policy issues.
CONVENTIONAL – Likes working in structured situations and working with details or data. Is good at organizing, following procedures, learning regulations/rules, and calculating or budgeting. Solves problems by being organized. Typically values efficiency, self-control, social status, and respects the prevailing values of society.	
Business Administration	Providing business administrative management services, including accounting, purchasing, and the management of services/personnel.
Retail Sales	Providing sales support, including operating a cash register, taking inventory, and ordering and stocking products.
Government Services	Providing government services to the public by administering and interpreting governmental policies and regulations.
Administrative Support Services	Performing diverse office activities, including word processing, filing, bookkeeping, and answering phone calls.
Banking & Finance	Administering and monitoring financial information, including banking, finance, taxation, and currency exchange.

Step 2: Identify Your Ideal Industry and Interests

Step 2 helps you pinpoint industries "where" you can apply your functional talents. Review the coaching questions listed in the "Industry/Interests" box of your F.I.T. form and list answers in the form as they come to you. Transfer any important results from assessments you have taken into the Master F.I.T. form, as well. You can also generate ideas for this element by reviewing the 100-plus items on the Industry and Interests Checklist at www.ChristianCareerJourney.com/journey.html.

Rank your industry choices by order of preference. If your top choice is an industry where hiring is at a standstill due to transition conditions or economic factors, consider pursuing your second industry choice. In the Master F.I.T. form in figure 3.1, write the industry you're considering targeting. (You can include more than one industry preference if they are closely related.)

ACTION STEP

Using the Master F.I.T. form in figure 3.1 (or the blank downloadable form at www.ChristianCareerJourney.com/MasterFIT.pdf), transfer any assessment results or favorites from the online Checklist into the "Industry/Interests" box. Add any additional insights gained from your answers to the coaching questions on the F.I.T. form to uncover the "Industry/Interests" fit.

Step 3: Think About the Things That Matter

Step 3 identifies your "career needs." This element of the F.I.T. answers "which" things are matter most to you. When the "Things That Matter" are present in your work, your attitude can soar and your satisfaction can skyrocket. A chain reaction then occurs that benefits employers, customers, and shareholders. The Gallup organization, in a survey on the impact of employee attitudes on business outcomes, noted that organizations where employees have above-average attitudes toward their work had 38% higher customer satisfaction scores, 22% higher productivity, and 27% higher profits.

Review the coaching questions listed in the "Things That Matter" box of your F.I.T. form and write your thoughts in the form. Transfer any important results from assessments you have taken into the Master F.I.T. form. Ideas for this element can also be generated by reviewing the Things That Matter Checklist at www.ChristianCareerJourney.com/journey.html.

ACTION STEP

Prioritize up to 10 of your choices and list them in your Master F.I.T. form. To ensure a good job fit in your next position, you will evaluate whether each of these "Things That Matter" is available when considering new opportunities.

Step 4: Define Fulfillment

Step 4 will transform your job from "paycheck" to "purpose" as you write a fulfillment statement for your career. Fulfillment, or purpose, answers "why" you work. If the primary reason behind your work is simply to earn a paycheck, I propose with confidence that there can be much, much more. If you're wondering whether I'm advocating that you trade in your paycheck for purpose, the answer is *no!* Purpose and poverty don't need to go hand in hand. The secret is to pair your purpose with market demand—there must be employers or customers who will need and pay for your services or products. When this is the case, you can find profound fulfillment because you have identified your passion, which drives perseverance, enthusiasm, creativity, productivity, and, if important to you, income to peak levels.

> **Travel Tip:** To find what profoundly fulfills you, look for the "tingle factor." The tingle factor is that goose-bumpy feeling that comes from doing something you absolutely love. The tingle factor causes you to think, "I can't believe they pay me to do this!" Recognize that it is unrealistic to experience the tingle factor on a continuous basis. We're not in search of nirvana! Instead, your ideal work should allow you to experience the tingle factor randomly but fairly regularly.
>
> As a speaker, I experience the tingle factor when I see the Lord communicate liberating new truths to people and they come away encouraged, inspired, and confident. As a writer, I experience it after I've wrestled with and won the words that perfectly capture the concept I want to express.

Use the coaching questions in the Master F.I.T. Fulfillment box to begin drafting a fulfillment statement. It should be short, just one or two sentences, and resonate with you. Here are some examples that various professionals have penned:

- To encourage professionals to value their inborn talents and worth, and use their strengths to enrich the world (career coach).
- To cause students to think, examine their belief systems, and grow in their knowledge and understanding (teacher).
- To connect consumers with products and services that enhance their lives (salesperson).
- To provide technology solutions that serve, rather than restrict, business owners (IT sales liaison).

This recipe might help you in writing your own fulfillment statement:

Action Verb + Who and What + Benefit to Others

Using this format, table 3.1 illustrates how some of the previous examples can be broken down.

Table 3.1: Sample Fulfillment Statement Recipes

Action Verb	Who and What	Benefit to Others
To encourage	professionals to value their God-given talents and worth and use their strengths to	enrich the world
To cause	students to think, examine their belief systems, and	grow in their knowledge and understanding
To provide	technology solutions to business owners	that serve, rather than restrict

Use the blank rows in the following box to write a few drafts of your own fulfillment statement.

DRAFT YOUR FULFILLMENT STATEMENT

	Action Verb	Who and What	Benefit to Others
Draft 1:			
Draft 2:			
Draft 3:			

ACTION STEP

Use the preceding tools or the book resources listed later under "Career Assessments to Discover Your Master F.I.T." to draft your fulfillment statement. When you're comfortable with the wording, write your statement in your Master F.I.T. form. Feel free to come back to this and tweak it, as clarity on a fulfillment statement rarely comes in one sitting. Let it be a work in progress.

Step 5: Enhance Your Identity

Step 5 involves an assessment of "who" you are—who you see yourself as and what you believe you are capable of accomplishing (with Christ, of course). Assess this element periodically because God continually gives us life and work experiences that cause us to change and grow. It's obvious when children grow: They need a larger size of clothing. It's not so obvious when adults grow: It takes a very conscious examination of our thought patterns and level of confidence to recognize when it's time for us to try on a larger size of life—an enhanced identity.

In enhancing your identity, it's helpful to start with a simple list of adjectives that capture the essence of you. For instance, here's a 10-point list of how I view myself: loving, encouraging, inspirational, knowledgeable, leading, conscientious, thorough, intuitive, gracious, capable. I know that Christ inside me enables me to manifest these traits. Having these priorities in focus helps me to act in concert with them.

What characteristics describe your career identity? Review the coaching questions listed in the "Identity" box of your F.I.T. form and list your answers in the form. Transfer any important results from assessments you have taken into the Master F.I.T. form. Ideas for this element can also be generated by reviewing the Identity Checklist of 140-plus items at www.ChristianCareerJourney.com/journey.html.

ACTION STEP

Using information from assessments or the online checklist, write into your Master F.I.T. form the top 10 terms that capture the essence of your work identity. Add any additional insights gained from your answers to the coaching questions on the F.I.T. form to uncover the Identity fit.

Step 6: Know Your Personality Type

Step 6 allows you to better understand your personality type. It answers the "how" you prefer to operate, both on and off the job. The mother-daughter team of Katharine Briggs and Isabelle Myers developed an assessment to classify people's observable behavior. With this effort, the assessment known as the Myers-Briggs Type Indicator (MBTI) was born and is now administered to more than 2.5 million people each year. Briggs' and Myers' two-fold purpose for developing the MBTI was noble: (1) to better match people and jobs and (2) to contribute to world peace through a better understanding of people's type.

As with other elements of the Master F.I.T., when you understand yourself better, you can pursue positions that will complement, not clash with, your personality preferences.

Travel Tip: Although Type theory is well-researched and respected in both secular and Christian circles, it should not be the guiding light for making a career decision. God can trump your MBTI results and anoint you to do something outside of your ideal type (recall the example of Judy Santos in chapter 1).

The basic tenets of personality type measure four scales:

- **Energy:** The direction in which your energies typically flow—outward, toward objects and people in the environment (*Extroversion,* or its abbreviation *E*), or inward, drawing attention from the outward environment toward inner experience and reflection (*Introversion,* or its abbreviation *I*).

- **Perception:** Whether you prefer to take in information through your five senses in a concrete fashion, focusing on "what is" (*Sensing,* or *S*) or with a "sixth sense" in an abstract or conceptual manner, focusing on "what could be" (*iNtuiting,* or *N*).

- **Judgment:** Whether you make decisions based on facts and logic (*Thinking,* or *T*) or based on personal or social values (*Feeling,* or *F*).

- **Orientation:** Whether you orient your outer world in a methodical, deliberate manner, seeking closure (*Judging,* or *J*), or in a spontaneous, play-it-by-ear approach, remaining open to more information (*Perceiving,* or *P*).

The assessment yields a four-letter code, such as *INFJ* or *ESTP,* to indicate your personality preferences. These four preferences become the core of our attractions and aversions to people, tasks, and events.

Travel Tip: A relatively new personality type assessment called the Golden Personality Type Profiler (GPTP) has been developed by career assessment experts who helped create the original MBTI®. Like the MBTI, the GPTP is highly reliable and valid and yields a four-letter type code (the last letter in the GPTP measures one's preference for Organizing or Adapting, as opposed to the MBTI terminology of Judging or Perceiving). The GPTP provides you with a rich report that includes additional facet scales and has the advantage of a lower price tag than the MBTI.

The following examples shed light on the theory as it relates to career choice:

- People with a clear preference for "Extroversion" (E) will likely be attracted to work in which they can interact with people extensively or with large groups of people. People with a clear preference for "Introversion" (I) will be attracted to occupations in which they can interact one-on-one or with small groups, or concentrate quietly on ideas, impressions, or information.

- Those with a combined preference for "iNtuiting" and "Feeling" (NF) will likely be attracted to work such as advocacy, facilitation, or counseling; conversely, these same people would likely have an aversion to work that requires repetitive tasks, such as a production line job.

- Those with a combined preference for "Sensing" and "Feeling" (SF) often choose occupations that require work with details in a way that allows them to help others. Accordingly, professions such as health care (physician, nurse, medical records technician, therapist), management or administration (often in social services or education programs), data management (bookkeeping, librarian, secretary), or law enforcement (police detective, guard, site administrator) might be appealing.

- Those with preferences for "Sensing" (S), "Thinking" (T), and "Judging" (J) will likely be drawn to task-oriented work that might involve measurement, logistics, monitoring, or management.

- People with a combined preference for "iNtuiting" and "Thinking" (NT) will likely be attracted to work that involves problem solving, brainstorming, strategy, or leadership.

PERSONALITY TYPE CLEARLY IMPACTS CAREER CHOICE

On a national basis, only a small percentage of the population, 10.3 percent, has the NT preference (Source: *MBTI Manual,* 3rd Edition, CPP). Yet when this percentage of the population is compared with a sample of MBA students, the percentage of students reporting an NT preference is almost double that of any other type. Often, MBA graduate programs lead to an executive career track, something that's likely to be attractive for the NT group (although not a guarantee of excellence on the job).

Take one of the Personality Type assessments recommended under "Career Assessments to Discover Your Master F.I.T." Alternatively, use the Personality Type Checklist at www.ChristianCareerJourney.com/journey.html to identify your preferences for the four scales of energy, perception, judgment, and orientation. As a reminder, this is not a test—there are no right or wrong answers! This is about identifying your natural preferences, just as you have a natural preference for right-handedness or left-handedness. When responding, don't think about what is most socially acceptable or how you've trained yourself to be on the job. Instead, think about how you would naturally respond, with no one looking over your shoulder or judging you.

ACTION STEP

Write your preferences for each of the four scales in the blanks that follow, and then transfer those results into your Master F.I.T. form.

Energy (Extroversion or Introversion): _____

Perception (Sensing or iNtuiting): _____

Judgment (Thinking or Feeling): _____

Orientation (Judging or Perceiving): _____

Identifying your individual preferences for energy, perception, judgment, and orientation is only the first step in understanding type. Together these four preferences mesh to create a richly complex personality type, which can best be understood by completing the MBTI or GPTP. Two other resources for understanding type are the books *Do What You Are* (Little, Brown) by Paul D. Tieger and Barbara Barron-Tieger, and *What's Your Type of Career?* (Davies Black) by Donna Dunning, which provides detailed information about how type relates to career choice.

WILL MY TYPE LIMIT MY CAREER CHOICE?

Should an introvert avoid positions in sales? Absolutely not. One of my clients, a sales professional, identified his preference for introversion, yet he was the number-one sales representative in the nation for a Fortune 500 company and the number-one sales manager in the country for a national consumer packaged-goods company. When we explored this preference for introversion further, he noted that, although he loved being with people, the solitary driving time between clients was just what he needed to be able to reflect, process, and reenergize before he called on the next client.

Step 7: Set Your Salary Range

In addition to steps 1–6, you'll need to add one more item to your Master F.I.T. so that it truly FITS! That final item is *salary*. Identify the range that you're targeting for your next position. Of course, you won't be mentioning your salary requirements to many people at this early stage. However, it's important that you put pencil to paper to calculate what you would accept on the low end, what the industry average is, and what your ideal or dream salary would be.

Travel Tip: If you need help getting a handle on what your salary numbers should be, jump ahead to chapter 14, and review "Research Comparable Salaries."

List your three salary figures in the following box.

SALARY FIGURES

Low-end salary I would need to meet my financial obligations:
$ _____

Industry average:
$ _____

Dream-job salary:
$ _____

Career Assessments to Discover Your Master F.I.T.

Take advantage of career assessments to aid in the discovery process. Career and leadership coach Nancy Branton, a recognized expert in assessments (www.PeoplePotentialGroup.com), researched hundreds of instruments for this book and narrowed them down to a manageable list of highly validated and reliable assessments. Her top picks for comprehensive assessments are listed next. Assessments designed specifically for Christians are designated with a ✝. (For Branton's expanded list of career assessments with specifics on cost and helpful comments about each assessment, go to www.ChristianCareerJourney.com/journey.html.)

COMPREHENSIVE CAREER ASSESSMENTS

- The Call™ Vocational & Life Purpose Guide, available online at www.followyourcalling.com ✝
- Career Direct® Complete Guidance System, available online at www.careerdirectonline.org ✝
- Uniquely You Profiler Report, available online at www.uniquelyyou.net/giftedness/profiles.php ✝
- Keirsey Temperament Sorter®-II and Campbell™ Interest and Skill Survey® Bundle, available online at www.keirseycampbell.com

Don't rely on just one assessment to cover all the Master F.I.T. areas, even if it's a comprehensive assessment—taking more than one assessment can help confirm the results. If you are already clear about certain areas of the F.I.T., take only those assessments that will fill in the rest of the picture. Take assessments when you are fresh and rested, and allow plenty of time to finish without rushing. After receiving the assessment results, transfer significant highlights or insights into the appropriate box on your Master F.I.T. form.

Branton's suggestions for targeted assessments are listed by F.I.T. category here.

FUNCTION AND INDUSTRY/INTERESTS

- Career Liftoff® Interest Inventory, available at www.careerliftoff.com
- *Discover Your Spiritual Gifts* (Regal Books, 2005) by C. Peter Wagner ✝ available at amazon.com and other booksellers
- O*NET® Computerized Interest Profiler™ available at www.onetcenter.org/CIP.html

THINGS THAT MATTER

- O*NET Work Importance Profiler™, available at www.onetcenter.org/WIP.html
- Values Arrangement List (VAL™), available at www.harcourtassessment.com (click Talent Assessment in the left-hand navigation system, then choose Values/Culture under Assessment Type and click Find It)

FULFILLMENT

- *The Path: Creating Your Mission Statement for Work and for Life* by Laurie Beth Jones (Hyperion, 1998), and *The Path Workbook,* available at www.lauriebethjones.com (purchase The Path combo pac)
- *How to Find Your Mission in Life* by Richard Nelson Bolles (Ten Speed Press, 2001), available at www.amazon.com and major booksellers

IDENTITY

- 360°Reach, available at www.reachcc.com/360reach (click on 360°Reach for Career Advancement/Job Search)
- Work Behavior Inventory (requires administration by a WBI-qualified professional), available at www.hrconsultantsinc.com

PERSONALITY TYPE

- Myers-Briggs Type Indicator® Career Report Form (requires administration by an MBTI-qualified professional), available at www.cpp.com
- The Golden Personality Type Profiler® (requires administration by a GPTP-qualified professional), available at www.harcourtassessment.com
- Keirsey™ Temperament Sorter-II (KTS™-II), available at www.advisorteam.org (click on "Take the Keirsey™ Temperament Sorter-II (KTS™-II) Personality Instrument" at the top right of the home page)

For an expanded list of career assessments with specifics on cost and helpful comments about each assessment, go to www.ChristianCareerJourney.com/journey.html.

Chapter Wrap-Up

Remember that becoming a career conqueror (one who is walking in the Promised Land of all God has for them) is a process. It doesn't happen overnight. It requires honing in on and weaving together all six of the Master F.I.T. elements. Gaining a new awareness of each item puts you on the right path. The more you know, the more you grow.

An intentional focus on these F.I.T. elements will allow you to be "radically rewarded and enthusiastically engaged in work that adds value to God's kingdom." The words "adds value" contain an important truth. Of course, you want to add value to God's kingdom, but you also must bring value to others—specifically, your employer, colleagues, customers, and so on—so that your career is in sync with marketplace demands. Chapter 6 outlines how to add value so that potential employers will view you as a competitive candidate.

In the next chapter, we'll look at career decision making so that your Master F.I.T. fits with God's master plan!

---

10 QUICK TIPS FOR FOCUSING ON YOUR MASTER F.I.T.

1. **Commit to the Lord whatever you do, and your plans will succeed (Prov. 16:3).** Start your career discovery process with prayer, and then co-create your Master F.I.T. with God. Although there is a measure of truth to the saying "fail to plan, plan to fail," a better adage for Christians would be "commit to a plan, but plan to commit everything to the Lord."

2. **Step 1—Find the right Function.** Functions represent job titles, spiritual gifts, and tasks, such as engineer and graphic artist, or leadership and administration, or market research and product development.

3. **Step 2—Identify your ideal Industry and Interests.** Industry refers to where you will apply your functional skills, whereas Interests tap a specialty area that you connect with or are especially enthusiastic about. For instance, a nurse might target oncology as an Industry and then focus on pediatric oncology as a special Interest within oncology.

4. **Step 3—Think about the Things That Matter.** When what you do from 8 to 5 aligns with your values and needs, you will find greater energy, motivation, and career satisfaction. Employers value employees with energy and motivation. What motivates you? Autonomy? Authority? Influence? Monetary reward? Recognition? Teamwork? Variety? Know the top 10 things that matter most to you in your career.

(continued)

10 Quick Tips for Focusing on Your Master F.I.T. *(CONTINUED)*

5. **Step 4—Define Fulfillment.** Fulfillment transforms your job from paycheck to purpose. Fulfillment, or purpose, is the reason you work. To define fulfillment, pay attention to the "tingle factor"—that goose-bumpy, addictive feeling that comes when you do something you absolutely love. Be sure to pair your purpose with market demands to ensure that you don't compromise your paycheck for purpose!

6. **Step 5—Enhance your Identity.** Your identity, what you believe about yourself, is directly linked to the type of position you'll target. You are usually capable of accomplishing much more than you believe you can. Raise the bar on beliefs! Blast through self-imposed limitations. Adopt beliefs that serve you better and allow you to move forward in your career.

7. **Step 6—Know your personality Type.** Understanding your type allows you to pursue positions that complement, rather than clash with, your personality preferences. The basic tenets of personality type measure four scales: Energy—the focus of your energy and attention flows to the outer world or is directed toward inner experiences and reflection (Extroversion or Introversion); Perception—your preference for taking in information via "what is" or "what could be" (Sensing or iNtuiting); Judgment—your preference for making decisions based on facts and logic or personal/social values (Thinking or Feeling); and Orientation—your preference for coming to closure or remaining open to more information (Judging or Perceiving).

8. **Step 7—Set your salary range.** In addition to the six F.I.T. steps, your last step adds a final "S," for salary, so that your target truly FITS! Identify a range for your target position, listing the industry average for your position; a low-end salary figure that you would be comfortable with (one that won't make you feel as though you're being taken advantage of); and a top-end, dream-job number.

9. **Commit to the long haul.** Finding the perfect Master F.I.T. will take time. Keep an aerial perspective on your progress, proceed with small steps, and be patient with yourself. First, be clear about your functional strengths and gifts (step 1 in the process) and your purpose/fulfillment, and then systematically work through the remaining steps.

10. **Remember the benefits of the Master F.I.T.** An intentional focus on the F.I.T. elements will allow you to leverage your time by pursuing the right opportunities, to gain confidence by targeting positions you can be enthusiastic about, and, ultimately, to land a position that is radically rewarding.

MASTERFUL COACHING QUESTIONS

As you use the H.E.A.R. formula (mentioned in the preceding chapter) for hearing from heaven, what do you sense God is impressing on you about your Master F.I.T. and your next career move?

_____

_____

_____

Which of the Master F.I.T. elements had you already incorporated into your prior positions?

_____

_____

_____

Which Master F.I.T. elements will you focus on incorporating into future positions?

_____

_____

What system or reminder can you put in place to ensure that you weigh those new elements when considering new opportunities?

_____

_____

_____

Pocket Prayer

Heavenly Father, You are the God who reached down from heaven to transport Your children from death to life, from slavery to freedom, from prison to the Promised Land. Thank you for the Promised Land of Your presence, provision, and promises. Thank you that You have "career territory" already carved out for me. Open my eyes to understand how You have gifted me, the interests You have planted in me, and the purposes You have prepared for me. Help me see how You want to weave these Master F.I.T. elements together to be a part of your master plan. Lord, when I face battles on my journey, be my defender and source of strength. I stand on Your promise "the battle is the Lord's." Thank you for loving me and caring about my career. I pray You would bless my career in whatever way You choose, for I know I can trust a God who is able to do immeasurably more than all I ask or imagine. In Jesus' name, Amen.

CHAPTER 4

MAKING THE RIGHT CAREER DECISION

"When you get right down to the root of the meaning of the word 'succeed,' you find that it simply means to follow through."

—*F. W. Nichol*

To survive and thrive in the Promised Land, you must persevere. The enemy wants you to quit, shrink, or turn back. God wants you to advance, grow, and press on—He wants you to "persevere in the Promised Land" because there are great rewards awaiting you there.

The career of George Washington Carver epitomizes perseverance. The book *More Than Conquerors: Portraits of Believers from All Walks of Life* (Moody Press, 1992) captures highlights of his life. As an infant during the Civil War, he was stolen along with his mother by Ku Klux Klan night raiders. Ransomed by his slave owner for a race horse valued at $300, he was returned but would never see his mother again. A weak and sickly child, he became a Christian around the age of 10 and recalls from boyhood an insatiable desire to learn the secrets of nature and to apply them to benefit mankind. Prejudice repeatedly thwarted his attempts to pursue formal education. At one point he was accepted to a college via mail, only to be barred upon arrival because of his color. Disheartened but determined, he eventually found a college that would accept him and went on to earn a master's degree in botany. He was later asked by Booker T. Washington to join the faculty at Tuskegee Institute in 1896, where he taught for 47 years.

Around the turn of the preceding century, it was Carver who figured out why the Southern cotton crop was failing, along with its associated profits: Farmers had worn out the soil after more than a hundred years without crop rotation. His advice to plant peanuts and sweet potatoes restored the earth's nutrients; however, with no market for these crops, farmers were forced to leave the harvest rotting in the fields, sending them further into debt. Crushed that he had furthered their financial ruin, Carver cried out to God, "Mr. Creator, why did You make the peanut?" From this crisis, God led Carver back to his laboratory to eventually discover some 300 marketable products for peanuts.

Carver pushed on, and it brought success. If you're not sure what you want to do next or things just aren't making sense in your career, don't give up. In working with thousands of people in career transition over the past 20 years, I've come to realize that *the phase between uncovering the ingredients of your fit and discovering how to use them can seem daunting.* It's relatively quick and easy to take assessments or run through a checklist to learn what you're made of, but it's not always easy to confirm what God wants to make of those ingredients. As with Carver and his peanuts, God wants to show you how to bless others with what He's given you. Persevere!

> **Travel Tip:** Unclear about your options? As with wondering what's beyond a bend in the road, **you won't know until you move forward.**

In this chapter, you will learn how to do the following:

- Brainstorm ideas that will combine the most important elements from your Master F.I.T.
- Research and reality-test your options.
- Consider different options for getting where you want to go.
- Recognize the traps and temptations that can keep you from your calling.
- Commit to a new direction.

If you are ready to shift from career explorer (you want to uncover new options for your work life) to career hunter (you know what you want to do and are ready to plan your job search campaign), skip ahead to chapter 5.

MAXIMUM MIND-SET: IT'S ALL ABOUT TRUTH

As you prepare to brainstorm, recognize that there is a battle going on for your thoughts. God wants you to know the fullness of His love and calling on your life. Satan wants to dissuade you of God's love and faithfulness.

Have you ever had thoughts that question God's goodness? Thoughts such as

- God has abandoned me.

- This is unfair…I don't deserve this.

- God, why don't You bless me the way You bless other people?

- Lord, if You're really good, You'll make it easy for me to get this job.

The enemy's ultimate goal for you is death—spiritual, emotional, and physical. He wants to drag you down, discourage you, and disarm and disable you. God's ultimate goal for you is life, and life abundant. He wants to lift you up, encourage you, and arm and enable you to march victoriously in the Promised Land.

To maintain maximum mind-set, the single biggest factor you need is the Truth (yes, with a capital T)! God has given you the mind of Christ (1 Cor. 2:16) so that you can discern Truth. In John 8, verses 31-32, Jesus said: *"If you hold to my teaching, you are really my disciples. Then you will know the truth, and the truth will set you free."* Jesus reveals the secret for knowing truth: *"hold to my teaching."* Hold His teachings close. Love them. Write them on your heart. Obey them.

The truth will set you free. As the battle for your thoughts wages, ask yourself this key question: Does this thought align with God's truth? If it doesn't, it's a lie meant to sink you.

Did you know that bank employees can spot counterfeit bills quickly, not because they study the counterfeits, but because they handle the real thing all day long? The second they touch a counterfeit bill, they can feel the difference. The same holds true for our spotting "counterfeit truths." The more we handle God's Word of truth, the faster we'll discern the enemy's lies!

Brainstorming Options

We don't know what we don't know, so prepare to know something new! To begin brainstorming new options, you'll need your Master F.I.T. form. Make sure you have several ideas written into each of the six boxes on the form. Don't worry if the ideas are still "rough 'n' raw"—they will be refined as you move ahead.

If you took the online assessments described in the preceding chapter (highly recommended), avoid the temptation to look to the results as the silver bullet for instant career direction. Instead, review all the results together: Pay attention to areas with low scores, as well as high scores, and identify themes and patterns that emerge. If you haven't already done so, transfer highlights of the results into the appropriate boxes on your Master F.I.T. form.

Perhaps you're thinking you don't have enough ideas in your Master F.I.T. form at this point. To remedy this, take the time now to develop your Success Stories (described in chapter 6). Look for themes and patterns within your stories, and then transfer the highlights to the Master F.I.T. form before proceeding with the brainstorming process.

Brainstorming Is a Team Sport

Ideally, work with several people in the brainstorming process. You may want to enlist support from people in your church's career/job club, prayer partners, accountability buddies, colleagues who have a breadth of professional experience, friends who have a knack for coming up with creative ideas, and so on. Your brainstorming team can meet in person, by telephone, or even by Web conferencing.

To start, follow these steps:

1. Pray! Invite God to guide you through this process. (See the Pocket Prayer at the end of this chapter.)

2. Prioritize the items or ideas in the boxes of the Master F.I.T. form according to what is most important to you. Start with the Function box, then move to Industry/Interests, and Things That Matter. As an example, if in the Function box you have five ideas—corporate trainer, social work, motivating others, writing, human resources—order them according to your preferences. For example: (1) motivating others, (2) writing, (3) corporate trainer, (4) human resources, (5) social work.

   Don't worry about identifying formal titles for each of the ideas yet. For instance, "motivating others" could take a number of forms, from public speaker to soccer coach. You don't want to limit the creative process with hard-and-fast titles at this point.

3. After prioritizing the Function, Industry/Interests, and Things That Matter boxes, move to the Fulfillment box. Circle or underline the words that are most important to you in your fulfillment/purpose statement.

4. Prioritize the ideas in the Identity box. Finally, in the Type box, circle the items that are most important to your work style.

5. When you're finished prioritizing each of the boxes, review the entire form. Choose just one item that is an absolute must for your next career move and put a star by it. This is a nonnegotiable. In other words, you wouldn't take a position that didn't honor or include that item, even if you were offered a million dollars!

6. Remember Tinkertoys®? You'll want to use the Tinkertoys concept to mix and match elements from your Master F.I.T. For instance, if you're clear that preserving natural ecosystems is your mission in life (Fulfillment) and you excel at investigation (Function), consider a biologist position with the federal government. Or, if you are also passionate about ornithology (Industry/Interest), consider a research position with the Audubon Society.

7. Look for careers that hit the "sweet spot" in the F.I.T.—it's the place where Functional skills, Industry/Interests, Things That Matter, Fulfillment, Identity, and Type *all* overlap.

"God-Storming" Exercise

With God's help, what do you believe you are capable of? At 20 years of age, you will have a different answer to this question than you will at 30, 40, 50, and so on. The next opportunity you target will be directly linked to what you believe you are capable of tackling—what you have faith for.

It may be that God has whispered a tremendous vision into your heart—one that is overwhelming to your mind. All the better! If you think you can achieve it on your own, it probably isn't of God. God gives God-sized goals—goals that must be accomplished by His Spirit, and not by our might or power (Zech. 4:6).

In Mark 9, the father of a demon-possessed boy begged Jesus to heal his son, to which Jesus replied, "Everything is possible for him who believes." The father's response: "Help me overcome my unbelief!" Through Christ, you are capable of much more than you believe. Ask the Lord to increase your faith for what is possible!

Pocket Prayer

Father, You are the God of the impossible. Thank you that Your omnipotence is rooted in purposeful love. Increase my faith for what is possible in my career. Help me in my unbelief. Grow my trust in You. In Jesus' name, Amen.

The first person to brainstorm with is God! Take a moment now to answer the third question found in the worksheets at the end of this chapter.

Personal Brainstorming/Visioning Exercise

When was the last time you thought about the ideal vision for your life? Unfortunately, the demands of *managing* life often distract us from *living* life. In this exercise, take a sheet of art paper or poster board, gather some colored pencils or pens, and find yourself a favorite spot where you won't be interrupted. Draw, doodle, use stickers or cut out magazine pictures if you're apprehensive about your artistic abilities, or simply use keywords to describe the absolute ideal for each of these areas of your life (items are listed alphabetically rather than in order of importance):

- Career/Personal Ministry
- Community/Outreach/Volunteer
- Family/Marriage Relationships
- Finances
- Friends/Social
- Fun/Recreation
- Growth/Self-Development
- Health/Fitness
- Home/Physical Environment
- Other (Your Choice)
- Spiritual

I have created a similar tool to assess your current level of satisfaction in 10 aspects of your career. Use the following worksheet to complete the assessment.

CAREER ASSESSMENT

After reading each description, rate yourself on a scale of 1–10 (1 is low, 10 is high).

Rating (1–10)   **Description**

_____   **In Sync with Strengths:** Your responsibilities allow you to use your talents, gifts, strengths, and favorite skills the majority of the time; you wake up in the morning and look forward to work.

_____   **Career "Ministry":** Even if you work in a nonministry setting, such as the corporate world, small business, academia, or government, you sense that God is using you to bless others and further His kingdom.

_____   **Career Brand:** Others describe you in the way you want to be described; you have a reputation for a specific set of skills, work style, and solutions.

_____   **Industry & Interests:** You have a genuine interest in your professional field; you like the products or services that your organization is involved with.

_____   **Return on Investment/Value:** You bring bottom-line value to your organization, customers, and colleagues; you make an impact on others.

_____   **Income:** Your financial needs are met; your savings is growing; you have the means to support ministries that are important to you.

Rating (1–10)	Description
_____	**Work Environment and Schedule:** The location or commute is acceptable; your physical surroundings suit you; your work schedule allows you time for a balanced life.
_____	**Level of Responsibility:** You have the responsibility, authority, and flexibility you want; there aren't radical pressures or unethical demands placed on you.
_____	**Personal Growth & Career Development:** You are being stretched spiritually, emotionally, and intellectually and God is producing fruit in you; you are in a position or industry that allows as much growth as you want (in other words, opportunities for new learning, projects, or advancement).
_____	**Social/Relationships:** The social environment is satisfying; relationships are as positive as possible.
_____	**Your Choice:** Identify and rank an area that is personally important to you in your career.

First, give thanks for what is going right, and don't get down on yourself if you have low scores. The fact that you're taking steps to improve is most important. Transfer any essential insights from this assessment into your Master F.I.T. form. For example, if your score for Social/Relationships was lower than you want it to be and it will be important in your next career move, add "good social relationships" to the Things That Matter box in your F.I.T. form. Your Master F.I.T. form can be a work in progress that changes as you make new discoveries.

There is power in intention and being open to learning. "Alia," whose Master F.I.T. example is shown in figure 3.2 in the preceding chapter, landed her dream job in a different industry within six months of starting the career coaching process. During that sixth month, she sat down to write out some of the lessons she had learned during the past five years in dealing with a very difficult work environment. She notes, "I've finally been praying for understanding to see what I have learned—so far it's *strength* to come in every day; *prayer* to take this madness (knowing that He took much worse); *patience* to deal with the ungodly; *witnessing*, speaking His Word to others; *humility* to know that He is in control; and increased *faith* that He knows what's best for me. I've learned to stop looking back and to look forward to embrace Him *before* all things." She adds, "God answered my prayer for my 'dream' job about 30 minutes after I wrote this note. I guess that I needed to 'get it'—understand why He tested me—to prepare me for the next phase!"

Group Brainstorming Exercise

The purpose of this next exercise is to generate additional ideas and perspectives for your career direction.

1. Assemble a group of four to eight people. People who are miracle-minded, well-connected, and strategic thinkers are often helpful when it comes to this brainstorming exercise. Let them know that you are exploring a career transition and would value their input. Share this verse with them from Proverbs 15:22: "Plans fail for lack of counsel, but with many advisers they succeed." Make this a fun, upbeat time. I've even had some clients host a dinner party as the setting for this exercise.

> **Travel Tip:** If it's difficult to get your group together in person, consider using a telephone conferencing service. The service is free at www.FreeConference.com, although each individual pays the cost of his long-distance call.

2. To begin, share a copy of your prioritized Master F.I.T. form with the group (e-mail the form prior to the meeting if you're working via teleconference). Explain briefly what led you to prioritize items as you have and any other information that would be helpful. During this time, you are the only person allowed to speak. Everyone else in the group listens carefully and takes notes.

3. Next, allow members of the group to offer questions or suggestions. (Show them the sample questions that follow.) For example, if items on your F.I.T. form included bookkeeping, farming/environmental interests, love of animals, and entrepreneurism, the questions from the group might sound like these:

    *   What if you were to combine your love of pets and entrepreneurial spirit into your own mobile pet-grooming service or pet-sitting business?
    *   How about taking that idea—the mobile pet grooming—and turning it into a nationwide franchise?
    *   Have you thought about combining your love of animals and farming/environmental interests to become a veterinarian or veterinarian's assistant?
    *   Have you thought about starting your own bookkeeping service?
    *   Who do you know who has interests similar to yours and what do they do for a living?
    *   What about a bookkeeping position with organizations that focus on animals, such as zoos, pet food manufacturers, or animal rescue organizations?
    *   Would you consider contacting my friend Joe for more information on how he started a lucrative dog-training business?
    *   What if you were to move into an entrepreneurial bookkeeping venture by first working for a CPA firm, and then start the bookkeeping services on the side to give you time to build up a clientele?

- Have you thought about attending the monthly meetings of the Professional Association of XYZ where you could gather more information on that subject?

This suggestion phase lasts 10 to 15 minutes or until the group no longer has suggestions. During this time, you (or an appointed scribe) should log each comment and who made the comment, but you are not allowed to respond to the question or suggestion yet. As you get further into the questioning, your group may come up with what appear to be "off-the-wall" questions, and yet there may be some stroke of brilliance in these ideas!

4. After the suggestion/question period is over, review your notes and choose three to five ideas that seem to hold the most interest.

5. In following up on these ideas, consider pairing up with the person who posed the question as an accountability partner, or partnering with your coach. List specific action steps that you will take and timelines for completion.

If you are doing this exercise for more than one person in the group, repeat steps 2 through 5.

> **Travel Tip:** For those pursuing ministry opportunities, check out "Spiritual Gifts at Work in the Church" at www.ChristianCareerJourney.com/journey.html as an example of the many places you can use your spiritual gifts.

Friends, Family, and Fans Exercise

Gather input from loyal friends, family, and fans who admire and support you. You can interview people live (provide questions prior to your meeting so that they can give thought to their answers), send them a printed questionnaire to be returned by mail, or even set up a free online survey at www.surveymonkey.com. Ask them to provide answers to the following:

- Please list three tasks that you think I am good at, especially things I may take for granted; for example, "You know how to plan a party, and you make the best potato salad in the world" or "Few people know how to fix appliances as well as you do" or "You are a fantastic Civil War reenactor."

- Please list three attributes that you consider to be assets; for example, "creative, cheerful, people-oriented" or "perseverant, methodical, patient" or "detail-oriented, accurate, entertaining."

- If you were to choose the perfect career for me, what would it be (for example, "work at Whole Foods Market in catering/cooking" or "open your own handyman service" or "teach history")?

Take the highlights from your interviews and plug them into the appropriate box in your Master F.I.T.

A TIME FOR EVERY SEASON...A POSITION FOR EVERY SEASON

"To every thing there is a season, and a time to every purpose under the heaven" (Eccles. 3:1, KJV). What season are you in now? It might be a season to teach or to learn, to grow or to rest, to stretch or to convalesce, to move on or to wait. Perhaps one of these career situations sounds right for you at this time in your life:

- **Bridge job or stepping-stone:** A stepping-stone position is not a dream job, but it might lead to one. Perhaps your industry has encountered steep declines, and opportunities aren't plentiful. Maybe you need to remove yourself quickly from a situation that is causing you to sin (I'm reminded of a woman who was tempted toward an affair with a co-worker and needed to be away from seeing this person every day). Either way, a transitional position might be just the ticket.

- **High yield:** Looking for big rewards based on a significant investment of time and energy in your career? If you are a fast-tracker, you might be ready for a high-performance leadership position where God can stretch and challenge you to the extreme.

- **Incubator:** You might have recently endured a significant loss, illness, or setback. If so, an incubator position might be the place where God can help you heal and regain your strength. Incubator positions do require that you perform work of value, but the work might not be particularly challenging. Incubator positions are temporary and can serve a purpose for certain seasons of your life.

- **Life balance:** Life-balance positions appeal to those who previously sacrificed quality of life by pouring themselves into jobs that required 60-, 80-, or even 100-hour workweeks. Typically a lesser-paying position than what you've come from, a life-balance position can offer less tangible but more meaningful payoffs. It might even include a flextime or job-sharing arrangement.

- **Lobster:** Ever wonder how a lobster can grow to be so big? It has to shed its shell periodically. You might feel cramped or stifled in your current position. If so, it might be time to find a place where you can grow.

- **Circuit rider:** In the 1800s, a circuit rider was a clergyman on horseback who would spread himself among multiple towns. The concept of dividing time among two or three companies might be appropriate for you, especially if you're working in an industry that is cash-strapped and cannot afford a full-time arrangement.

- **Portfolio:** A portfolio position allows you to use and further develop a variety of special skills. This type of position is especially appealing to those who thrive on variety and a spontaneous, flexible approach to life and work.

It's obvious that "up and ahead" is not the only option when it comes to a new position. Instead, in enjoying your career journey, you should have as your goal progress, not perfection. Progress includes anything that God wants to teach you at this juncture in your life.

Investigate with Legwork

If you immediately identify a career track that looks promising at face value, proceed with the curiosity and objectivity of a detective. Prove it out through further investigation and make sure it is consistent with elements of your Master F.I.T. If you have a number of options that sound promising, begin to narrow them down to one or two preferred options to make your research more manageable.

Take time to thoroughly research your possibilities—your research will often turn up new ideas that will be an even better fit. Start your research online, tap into professional associations, read up on the industry, talk to people experienced in the field, and "taste-test" the profession.

Look for something wonderful about your preferred options; likewise, look for something wrong. This will give you a balanced perspective.

Check Online Resources

Here are a few online resources that may be helpful in researching occupations and industries:

- **Occupational Information Network (O*NET):** http://online.onetcenter.org. There are several ways to take advantage of this site:
  - Quick Search: If you know the occupational title you want to research, use the "Occupation Quick Search" box near the upper right of the page. From the results generated, select the occupation(s) you're most interested in and then view reports at the Summary and Detail tabs.
  - Find Occupations: At the "Find Occupations" link, browse by O*NET descriptor (knowledge, skills, abilities, work activities, interests, work values), by job family, by high-growth industry, or by STEM discipline (jobs requiring training in science, technology, engineering, and mathematics). To get started, I suggest selecting the "Skills" link under "Browse by O*NET Descriptor" and then starting with "Basic Skills." For example, a click on the basic skill of "Active Listening" reveals 30 professions that rely heavily on this skill.

- Skills Search: After selecting "Skills Search," checkmark skills that you have (or plan to acquire) among the six skill groups, then scroll to the bottom of the page and click "Go." You'll receive a report of possible occupations that use all or most of those skills.

- *Occupational Outlook Handbook (OOH):* www.bls.gov/oco/. The site recommends a variety of search methods.

- **Margaret Riley Dikel's The Riley Guide:** www.rileyguide.com. A well-established site for job seekers, Margaret Riley Dikel's Web site offers thousands of pages of career help. Check out the "Before You Search" link when you're in career exploration mode.

- **Hoover's:** www.hoovers.com/free. This site is helpful for gaining top-notch business analysis on an industry. Use the search box to enter your industry interest, such as "publishing," and select the drop-down area to search by "Industry Keyword" instead of the default "by Name/Ticker."

- **How to Learn about an Industry:** www.virtualpet.com/industry/howto/search.htm. This site is an interesting collection of industry links, from adhesives to woodworking.

- **Magazines by Industry:** www.newsdirectory.com/listmag.php or http://dir.yahoo.com/News_and_Media/Magazines/. Magazines will provide information on the latest trends for your profession or industry research.

If self-employment is figuring into your research, check out these resources:

- **SCORE (Service Corps of Retired Executives):** www.score.org. Providing free and confidential small business advice for entrepreneurs, SCORE's volunteers are working or retired business owners, executives, and corporate leaders who share their wisdom and lessons learned in business.

- **The U.S. Small Business Administration:** www.sba.gov/smallbusinessplanner/index.html. The U.S. Small Business Administration offers helpful planning tips for budding entrepreneurs.

- **Paul and Sarah Edwards:** www.workingfromhome.com. The Edwards are gurus on home-based self-employment, and the site offers a number of resources, including their best-selling books.

Tap into Professional Associations

Virtually every profession has its own association, from the American Trucking Association (www.trucking.org) to the American Association of Zoo Keepers (www.aazk.org). Two reference books containing extensive listings are

- *WEDDLE's Guide to Association Web Sites: For Recruiters and Job Seekers* (WEDDLE's, 2005)

- *National Trade and Professional Associations of the United States* (Columbia Books Inc. Publishers, 2004)

Although not as comprehensive, there are also online resources to find professional associations:

- WEDDLE's: www.weddles.com/associations/index.cfm
- The Internet Public Library: www.ipl.org/ref/AON/

When you find an association for your area of interest, here are some actions to take:

- Comb its Web site for information. Depending on the size of the organization, contact the executive director or a regional representative.

- Ask about local, regional, or national meetings that you can attend. If appropriate, offer to come early to a local meeting and help set up or hand out name badges, because this is a great way to get to know people.

- Inquire about trial memberships or ways to learn more about the association before spending the money to join.

- Subscribe to relevant print or online newsletters.

Read Up on the Industry

Visit your local library (and make friends with the reference librarian) or the nearest well-stocked bookstore for these resources:

- *EZ Occupational Outlook Handbook* (JIST, 2007). This book contains one-page descriptions of every career—nearly 270 in all—described in the Department of Labor's *Occupational Outlook Handbook*.

- *WetFeet Insider Guide* (WetFeet, Inc.). This series contains titles such as *Careers in Marketing and Market Research, Careers in Biotech and Pharmaceuticals,* and *Careers in Investment Banking.*

- *VGM Careers for You Series* (VGM Career Books). Titles in this series include *Careers for Perfectionists and Other Meticulous Types, Careers for Travel Buffs and Other Restless Types,* and *Careers for Scholars and Other Deep Thinkers.*

- *Guide to Your Career,* 5th Ed. (Princeton Review, 2004). Find insider profiles on more than 200 popular careers.

Connect with People

After your preliminary online and print research, talk with people, preferably face to face. This will give you a feel for what the industry is really like. Line up field interviews based on contacts you've uncovered in your preliminary research or through referrals from your network. Three to seven interviews is ideal. Choose association representatives, industry veterans, and even newbies who can give you a fresh perspective on what it's like to enter the field. Suppliers, vendors, and customers can also add perspective.

To request an interview, try this language:

> *Hello, Mr. Smith! This is Jane Doe and I'm calling at the recommendation of your colleague, Jim Dokes, who assured me that you would be the perfect person to speak with to learn more about the field of _____. I'm looking at a career in your field and wondered if you'd have a few minutes to answer a few questions that would help me confirm the research I've done thus far.*

Convey sincere appreciation to the person taking the call. If you're able to meet in person, all the better. When speaking with your contact, choose several (not all) questions from the following list—you don't want to overstay your welcome with too many questions:

- How did you get started in this career?
- What does your typical day look like?
- What do you like best/least about your career?
- How do you see the Lord using you in your work?
- What causes the greatest stress in your profession?
- What did you learn on the job that can't be taught in school?
- What do you know now about this career that you wish someone had told you at the outset?
- What do you recommend in the way of books…training…professional associations to join?
- How would you suggest people taste-test this type of career?
- If you had to name five or six skills that make people truly successful in this field, what would they be? How are those skills put to use? (Tip: This is a critical resume-builder question, so be sure to get it into the conversation somewhere.)
- How do your bosses measure your performance? (Another resume-builder question.)
- Would you say that a particular personality (for instance, social and gregarious, or analytical and quiet) is better suited for this profession?
- Who makes it to the top fastest in this career, and why? Conversely, why do people leave the field?
- Where do you (or others) go from here…what would be your next step? And then where?
- What changes or trends are happening in the industry?

- How might I combine my interest in _____ with this profession?
- My research on salary ranges for someone starting out in this career shows salaries of $xx to $xx, with a range of $xx to $xx after about five years in the field. Are those numbers realistic?
- What have I *not* asked that I should have?
- Based on what we've talked about, what do you think my next steps should be?
- Who else would you recommend I speak with?

At the end of your meeting, do the following:

- Ask for permission to check back and let your contact know how you've followed up on the recommendations made.
- Ask for a business card so that you have correct contact information.
- Give back! Ask, "Based on what you know of my background, might there be some way that I could be of assistance to you?" (One college graduate was able to be of assistance to her contact by setting up an introduction to a business friend of her father's.)
- Thank the person sincerely for the time spent.

Taste-Test the Job

There is no substitute for experience, so whenever possible, taste-test the position or field you're considering. Of course, if you're looking into a career as a neurosurgeon, you won't get anyone to turn over a scalpel to you, which is why thorough informational interviews are important. Whenever possible, find a way to do the job you're interested in. Here are some options for that:

- Volunteer (in your church, community, or business community).
- Take a temporary, part-time, or evening position in the field.
- Job-shadow someone in the field.
- Take a class or training program that will give you a better feel for the profession.
- Ask for reassignment to a similar position with your existing employer.
- If you have some vacation time accrued, spend it immersed in the area you're considering.

Jumping into a new career without giving it a good taste test is reminiscent of getting married after spending only a few hours with a blind date. You can avoid many unpleasant surprises by doing your groundwork!

Consider the Steps to Get There

When traveling from point A to point B, you are never magically transported for instantaneous arrival. Between those two points, there are miles to walk, bike, drive, or fly. It may be that there are several legs of the journey to get to your desired career goal.

For example, leg 1 in your journey might start by adding a part-time position in your new area of interest. The second leg might have you scaling back on your original position while you ramp up the new career. The third leg could be dropping your original position and going full-time in your new career. If your career goal seems like a very big leap, use table 4.1 to break down your journey into manageable phases. You'll see in chapter 5 that having a realistic goal will also shorten your job search.

Table 4.1: Steps to Get There

Position Path	Key Skills Needed	Training Needed	Wins Needed	People I Need to Know	Time Frame
Put current position in first row, then use each additional row for positions/ steps to get to the goal.	Technology, Soft Skills, Hard Skills, Technology Skills	Soft Skills, Hard Skills, Technology Skills, etc.	What results or accomplishments do you need in order to gain experience, competence, credibility?	Clients, Internal Management, Industry Contacts, etc.	Anticipated time for this position in months or years.

Weigh the Pros and Cons

Answer these questions when weighing the pros and cons for your number-one career option:

- Does the career align with the direction in which God seems to be leading you? Do you have a sense about how He can use you in this work? Looking back to chapter 1 and God's Four Key Purposes for Work, how does the choice you're leaning toward intersect with these purposes?

- Is it in sync with your motivated skills (Master F.I.T. Function), interests (Industry/Interests), and values (Things That Matter)? How about purpose? Will it stretch you in how you see yourself (Identity)? Is it a good match for your personality type (Master F.I.T. Type)? What are the salary ranges, including salaries for the top 5 percent of performers?

- Does the organizational culture of most companies in the industry match your profile and values? Is the industry in an up or down trend?

- Will additional education be required? If so, what are the pros and cons and the options for obtaining and financing it? Do the time, cost, and difficulty of training outweigh the benefit?

- What career paths are available beyond your entry point? If this is a stepping-stone toward something bigger, what time period do you see yourself committing to this position (for example, "I'm willing to do tech support for one year because I need a job, but if there aren't opportunities for promotion at the end of that time, I will consider moving elsewhere")?

- What will the ramp-up time be? How long before you're productive and being compensated at the level you need?

- What implications will this career move have on your network? Will it connect you with people who could be important to your influence and impact down the road…and with people you could be a blessing to, as well?

- What's the worst-case scenario if things don't work out? Loss of money, time, pride? What safety nets can you put in place to minimize risk? What will be the rewards of having taken a calculated risk?

CALCULATED RISK OR RED FLAG?

Making a career change requires taking a calculated risk. If before you make a move your thinking is, "I want a 100% guarantee that I'll get a $70,000 salary and insurance benefits," you may never take action. Life rarely offers us 100% guarantees!

I've also heard people say, "I need the Lord to give me a really clear sign before I move," when He has, in fact, been giving very clear signs. It reminds me of the joke about the man atop his roof with floodwaters rising who prays for a miracle, then goes on to reject offers of rescue from several boats and a helicopter, insisting that God will grant him a miracle. On arriving at the gates of heaven with broken faith, he says to Peter, "I thought God would grant me a miracle and I have been let down." St. Peter chuckles and responds, "I don't know what you're complaining about—we sent you three boats and a helicopter." God's hand of grace is ever present in your life, always watching, always loving, always providing.

You must develop discernment to know the difference between a calculated risk and a red flag. Red flags are those warning signals from God that He wants you to stop and inquire of Him and perhaps change course. To determine whether you're yielding to God or bulldozing your own path, refer to "Clues That You May Be Ignoring God" in chapter 2.

See table 4.2 for how to evaluate your options based on the elements of your Master F.I.T.

Table 4.2: Comparing Your Career Options Example

Career Options:	Option #1: Occupational Therapist	Option #2: Grant Writer	Option #3: Filmmaker
Function Fit/Skills Required	Seems to match up with my high scores of "Social" and "Realistic" in the Career Liftoff® Interest Inventory assessment. Uses skills I love but would require a new degree; would allow me to be a good steward of the gifts God has given me.	Good fit with my business writing and research skills; may require business development skills if I go the self-employed route.	Requires additional training.
Industry/ Interests Fit	I've also been interested in helping people gain skills for independence after they've had an accident or have been disabled in some way; it reminds me of the good feelings I had as a child going with my mother to see my Aunt Mae when she was in a rehab hospital after a bad car accident.	This is a new area of interest for me, but my research has confirmed my interest.	I've always been a movie buff, specifically a documentary movie buff, and this would be a cool way to put those interests to work.
Things That Matter Fit	Great fit.	Can be a home-based business, so it would work great with my schedule and allow me to be home with my kids in the afternoon.	Not sure I'd be comfortable with the culture.

Career Options:	Option #1: Occupational Therapist	Option #2: Grant Writer	Option #3: Filmmaker
Fulfillment/ Purpose Fit	Would feel like I was really making a difference in people's lives, giving them ability to be independent; fits beautifully with my life purpose statement.	Would fit well if I could write only for people seeking faith-based grants.	This sort of fits, but it feels too removed from, say, the people connection I would have in other careers.
Identity Fit	Fits well with my key brand attributes of caring and competent.	Doesn't seem to fit my identity/brand.	Not sure this fits too well for my identity/ brand.
Type Fit	Seems to fit within my ISFJ type profile; allows for one-on-one, practical work with people, which would be nice.	Fits well; would work especially well with my preference for introversion.	As an ISFJ, this may require that I do more "big-picture" work than I prefer.
Salary Fit	$55k	$50k+	$40k to millions if you hit it big.
Market Situation	Good demand; projected industry growth of 21%–35%.	Good demand.	Jobs are rare as hen's teeth; very risky.
Pros	I'm really drawn to this. I could have a fairly flexible schedule to also be with my children. This has great insurance and health-care benefits, as well. And I can see using these skills on the short-term missions that my family does each summer.	Schedule flexibility.	Very creative environment, which would be enjoyable.

(continued)

Table 4.2: Comparing Your Career Options Example *(continued)*

Career Options:	Option #1: Occupational Therapist	Option #2: Grant Writer	Option #3: Filmmaker
Cons	The biggest drawback is that I'd have to return to school.	Doesn't seem as meaningful as the OT option.	Very difficult to break into; need connections; takes years to get career rolling; would need to find a mentor.

Create your own comparison tool using table 4.2 as a template (or download a blank form, "Comparing Your Career Options," under the Decision-Making Tools at www.ChristianCareerJourney.com/journey.html).

Wait or Faith?

If after thorough research you're still not crystal clear on the right path for you, one of two things may be the case: God wants you to wait or He wants you to step out in faith. These stories illustrate those points.

God wants you to wait. "Caroline" was an executive in a firm but was not happy with her position after a merger with another company. She had already published her first book three years prior to this merger and felt God calling her out of corporate into a consulting role that would allow more time to focus on her natural gifts of writing, speaking, and teaching. After her second book was published, she knew that the time was right but explained that she had to "wait for God to convince my husband. It took two years for that to happen, and then I moved out and have been having quite an adventure!"

God wants you to step out in faith. "Jenny" writes of the importance of moving out in faith. "My husband passed away after only nine years in our new life with Youth With A Mission (YWAM). Had he waited to join YWAM until he retired, many ministries that have started all over the world would not have been started. His life and decision to leave his comfort zone has had lasting, eternal value!"

Provided there are no "Do Not Enter" signs flashing in your head, it may be that you simply need to step out and trust God. If so, choose the career direction that most aligns with your skills and gifting (Function), purpose (Fulfillment), and values (Things That Matter). You can fine-tune the fit as time goes on.

Commit to a Decision

After sufficient research and field testing, you will eventually need to make a decision. One of the first questions you should ask yourself is this:

What do you need to know to be comfortable with your decision?

In other words, how much information do you need to have? And how will you measure whether you have peace about your decision? Review your answers to the questions listed earlier in this chapter, under "Weigh the Pros and Cons." Do the pros outweigh the cons? What is your decision? Use the line below to commit your decision to God in a written statement.

_____

If you're not yet quite clear on your commitment, see the handout "Decisions, Decisions" at my Web site (www.ChristianCareerJourney.com/journey.html).

Create Your Focus Statement

After writing out your commitment, let's finalize it by creating a focus statement for your next career move. The benefits of doing so are threefold:

- **Motivation:** Your focus combines the unique ingredients that will energize and motivate you throughout your transition.
- **Meaning:** Your focus homes in on what God wants for you, as opposed to striving after the dreams of someone else (be it parents, spouse, friends, or co-workers).
- **Map:** Your focus will keep you on course as you make decisions about what interview opportunities to pursue.

"Jeff's" sample focus statement will help get you started:

> I am committed to targeting opportunities that will use my branch management skills in the field of financial services, specializing in mutual funds, where I can develop management and marketing strategies that will allow me to be a good steward in ethically growing shareholder value and investors' net worth. This type of position is in sync with my personality preferences for "intuiting" and "thinking" (seeing the big picture, brainstorming, making decisions based on logical facts) and is consistent with my self-image as a leader and my core values, such as intellectual stimulation, logic, and financial stewardship (with salary in the range of $75,000 to $90,000).

Here's how the target statement relates to the Master F.I.T.:

I am committed to targeting opportunities that will use my

[step 1, Functional abilities] <u>branch management skills</u>

[step 2, Industry] in the field of <u>financial services</u>, specializing

in [step 2, Interests] <u>mutual funds</u>, where I can

[step 4, Fulfillment] <u>develop management and marketing strategies that will allow me to be a good steward in ethically growing shareholder value and investors' net worth.</u>

This type of position is in sync with my personality preferences for

[step 6, personality Type] <u>"intuiting" and "thinking" (seeing the big picture, brainstorming, making decisions based on logical facts)</u>

and is consistent with my self-image [step 5, Identity] <u>as a leader</u> and core values [step 3, Things That Matter], such as

<u>intellectual stimulation,</u>

<u>logic</u>, and

<u>financial stewardship</u> (with salary in the range of <u>$75,000</u> to <u>$90,000</u>).

In the following template, write your own focus statement (refer to prioritized items in your Master F.I.T. form if needed).

I am committed to targeting opportunities that will use my [Functional abilities]

_____

[Industry] in the field of _____, specializing

in [Interests] _____, where I can

[Fulfillment] _____

_____ .

This type of position is in sync with my personality preferences for [personality Type]

_____

_____

_____

_____

and is consistent with my self-image [Identity] as [a] _____,

and core values [Things That Matter], such as _____,

_____ ,

_____ , and

_____, as well as my salary needs in the range

of $_____ to $_____ .

When networking, you might want to use just the first sentence in your focus statement to help others know what you are looking for. (Omit the second sentence and reserve salary for discussions with hiring managers.) In chapter 6, we'll look more closely at developing "sound bites" for networking and interviewing. In the meantime, this focus statement will help keep you on course as you evaluate new job opportunities.

Chapter Wrap-Up

When it comes to making the right career decision, I have good news for you. You can't make a mistake in your journey! Why? Because God weaves everything together for His good purposes. Yes, there will be times when you fall short of His best. Yes, there will be times when you wish you had made a different choice. But God offers forgiveness and is able to use every circumstance to draw you yet one step closer to Him and His eternal purposes. So take your time in brainstorming options, investigate thoroughly with legwork, consider the steps to get there, and then commit your decision to the Lord.

10 QUICK TIPS FOR MAKING THE RIGHT CAREER DECISION

1. **Prepare to persevere.** Exploring career options requires tenacity and time. During this phase, be open to new things—we don't know what we don't know.

2. **Brainstorming is a team sport.** Enlist the support of people who are miracle-minded, well-connected, and strategic thinkers to help expand your career options. Stretch your vision of what's possible by looking through the lens of God's perspective.

3. **Play Tinkertoys with your Master F.I.T.** Mix and match key career elements, such as Function and Interests, or Function and Fulfillment, or Interests and Things That Matter. Use sources such as the Occupational Information Network (O*NET, at http://online.onetcenter.org) for additional ideas.

4. **Narrow it down.** If you have a number of options that sound promising, begin to narrow them down to one or two preferred options to make your research more manageable. If you immediately identify a career track that looks promising at face value, proceed with the curiosity and objectivity of a detective.

(continued)

10 QUICK TIPS FOR MAKING THE RIGHT CAREER DECISION *(CONTINUED)*

5. **Investigate with legwork.** Take time to thoroughly research your preferred options. Your research will often turn up new ideas that will be an even better fit than you thought possible. Look for something wonderful about your preferred options; likewise, look for something wrong. This will give you a balanced perspective.

6. **Check online resources and read up on the industry.** Start your research on the Web with free resources such as the O*NET, the *Occupational Outlook Handbook (OOH),* The Riley Guide, and Hoovers. Visit your local library and make friends with the reference librarian to learn about other resources for researching industries and occupations. Tap into professional associations. Find an association that represents your preferred options and comb its Web site for information. Attend association meetings and industry events to learn more about the profession.

7. **Connect with people face to face.** There should be a law against making a career change without first interviewing people in your target field! Three people is minimum; seven is even better. Choose association representatives, veterans of the field, and even newbies. Suppliers, vendors, and customers can also add perspective.

8. **Taste-test the job.** There is no substitute for experiencing the job. Whenever possible, look for opportunities to volunteer, consider a temporary or part-time job, job shadow, or take training classes to get a feel for the good, the bad, and the ugly of your preferred option.

9. **Weigh the pros and cons.** Evaluate your preferred option against your Master F.I.T. preferences and the direction God seems to be leading. List the pros and cons. Do the pros outweigh the cons?

10. **Commit to a decision.** Determine what needs to be in place to make a decision, and then make it. Commit to a career that is radically rewarding and adds value to God's kingdom!

MASTERFUL COACHING QUESTIONS

When it comes to "persevering in the Promised Land," how would you rate yourself on a scale of 1 to 10 (1 = completely stalled, 10 = unstoppable)? What payoff (whether negative or positive) do you receive for not persevering? What would life be like if you were to persevere just a degree or two more?

_____

_____

With God's help, what do you believe you are capable of? Write a few sentences that raise the bar on what you believe God might want to accomplish through you in your next position.

_____

_____

_____

_____

_____

Who would you love to have on your brainstorming team?

_____

_____

Would you describe your career options as God-sized? If not, what would it take to make them bigger?

_____

_____

As you do your research, what do you need to know to make an informed decision?

_____

_____

Who will you approach for your informational interviews? Are you stretching your comfort zone and reaching out to people you wouldn't normally network with?

_____

_____

_____

Who needs to be a part of your decision-making process (spouse, family members, friends)? What support do you need to ask of them during this period?

_____

_____

In what time frame do you want to finish your career exploration and come to a commitment? Create a timeline with action steps. Who will help hold you accountable?

_____

_____

Pocket Prayer

Father, you are the Master Creator, the originator of great ideas and grand thoughts. Your ways are higher than my ways and Your thoughts are higher than my thoughts. Thank you for giving me the mind of Christ. Guide my thoughts as I brainstorm new options. Impress on me the ideas and visions You want me to see. Your Word tells me in Jeremiah 33:3 to call on You and You will show me great and mighty things that I do not know. So show me, Father, the great and mighty things that I do not know about the gifts You've given me and how to use them to please You and bless others. And, if there is an idea You have for me that I am resisting, reveal that to me also. Show me how to take every thought captive to the obedience of Christ. Shine a flashlight on the areas that You want me to pursue, and close the doors to areas I should avoid. I commit this journey to you. In Jesus' name, Amen.

PART 2

PLANNING YOUR CAMPAIGN AND CREATING YOUR CAREER MARKETING DOCUMENTS

CHAPTER 5

GETTING YOUR JOB
SEARCH PLAN TOGETHER

"In his heart a man plans his course, but the Lord determines his steps."

—*Prov. 16:9*

"If you want to make God laugh, tell Him your plans."

—*Anonymous*

I'll admit it. After several decades of working with people in career transition, I have succumbed to a sobering truth: I don't have the perfect success formula when it comes to finding your next position. In fact, no one does. Do I know of systems and strategies that lead to success? Yes. Can I share a few insider secrets most people aren't aware of that can help expedite your job search timeline? Yes. Can I guarantee that you'll land your dream job in exactly 29 days, 17 hours, and 8 minutes if you apply them? Unfortunately, no.

Our current culture typically defines success as getting what we want quickly and avoiding embarrassment or failure in the process. God's definition is quite different. I imagine that terms in His lexicon of success include *trust, obedience, perseverance,* and *humility.* In the first chapter of Joshua, verse 8, God reveals to us that to have success we must continually speak of and meditate on His ways. In other words, every word and thought is to align with God's thoughts. True success means thinking like God. This *is* possible, because God has generously given us the mind of Christ (1 Cor. 2:16)!

As you approach this chapter on planning, keep in mind that God is the one who has your perfect formula for success. And revisit the scriptures on planning from chapter 3. My favorite is Proverbs 16:9: "In his heart a man plans his course, but the Lord determines his steps." The first part of this verse implies that we are to use our reasoning powers to devise a plan—a plan to do good and please God. The second part of the verse makes clear that our plans are subject to God's master plan.

If we are off course, God might delay, detour, or completely redirect our plans. In fact, we can be *on* course and still experience a delay, detour, or redirection. God wants to entrust us with an ever-deepening experience of His love and power, and He uses our present circumstances as the object lesson for instruction. The depth of knowing Him is unfathomable—we can be assured that these lessons will last a lifetime, because He will be faithful in finishing the good work begun in us (Phil. 1:6).

Another favorite verse on planning is Proverbs 16:3: "Commit to the Lord whatever you do, and your plans will succeed." Matthew Henry, the famous preacher whom God used to help bring about the Great Awakening of the 18th century, offers a memorable commentary on this commitment: "We [must] resolve that whatever pleases God shall please us." Now there's a definition of success.

So now that you have a sense of where you're headed based on your work in the prior chapters, let's put a plan in place that pleases God!

> **Travel Tip:** Know your strengths and weaknesses. Are you the ultimate planner? If so, plan with aplomb, but leave room for God to move. Do you loathe planning? If so, play it by ear, but be sure you have the structure of daily priorities and goals.

12 Tips for the Road to Self-Employment

Is God drawing you toward self-employment? Although the remainder of this book focuses on landing a job with another employer, you'll continue to find helpful career tools in the chapters to come. Many personal/career marketing strategies are relevant to small business marketing, networking, and sales. In fact, Richard N. Bolles, author of the classic *What Color Is Your Parachute?* (Ten Speed Press), insightfully points to the irony that working for yourself puts you into the state of perpetual job hunter. He notes, "If you are running your own business, you will have to *continually* beat the bushes for new clients or customers—who are in fact *short-term employers.*"

Before jumping in to the entrepreneurial fold, make sure you've done plenty of research and talked to lots of people regarding the ups and downs of business ownership. Brian Head, Economist with the SBA Office of Advocacy, noted that "as a general rule of thumb, new employer businesses have a 50/50 chance of surviving for five years or more."

Here are 12 tips to help you beat the odds:

1. **Be in it for the right reasons:** Many businesses fail because the principals suffer from the "I-Had-No-Idea Syndrome," a term coined by David Birch, former head of a research firm specializing in studying small business data. Some common misconceptions about working for yourself include thinking you'll get rich quick (you won't), you'll have tons of free time (businesses are demanding), or you'll be able to call your own shots (you'll answer to your customers and, of course, to God).

   If, on the other hand, you have a passion for serving people with your product or service, thrive on finding solutions to problems, and are above average when it comes to self-initiative, stamina, and stick-to-it-iveness, you'll do fine (Prov. 6:10-11, 10:4, 23:4, 28:19-22)!

2. **Get a business coach:** An experienced business coach who can combine business know-how with Biblical principles is worth his or her weight in gold (Prov. 20:5). Visit www.ChristianCoaches.com to search for a business coach or www.LeadershipCoachAcademy.com to search for a leadership coach.

3. **Start small:** The Lord may have given you a grand vision for your business, but don't hesitate to start small. That includes starting part-time, growing the business slowly, and getting financial reserves in place.

   For example: Don't rent expensive office space if you can accomplish what you need from a home-based office (caveat: If your business success is dependent on ease-of-access and high-traffic patterns, do not pinch pennies on location). Don't add staff until you have fairly consistent cash flow from month to month. Don't buy an expensive new piece of equipment just because you want to grow; try waiting until you've outgrown your existing equipment.

   See Zechariah 4:8-10a for words of wisdom on laying a foundation and never underestimating the seemingly insignificant.

4. **Don't skimp on getting good counsel:** Use a business attorney for any legal agreements you'll enter into. If you're purchasing a business, get an appraisal from an accountant who specializes in business valuations. Talk to an accountant about your business plans and set up your accounting systems correctly from the start. Consult with specialists in Web marketing for your online presence. Take advantage of organizations such as SCORE at www.score.org or the U.S. Small Business Administration at www.sba.gov/smallbusinessplanner/index.html (Prov. 15:22).

5. **Create a business plan:** At minimum, outline your mission statement, products/services, marketing plan, competition, operating procedures, key team members, and financial data with budget, income projections, break-even analysis, and so on. Business plans are a work in progress and are meant to be updated as circumstances change (Luke 14:28).

6. **Manage your money:** Pay attention to where your money is going. Talk to your accountant or business attorney to make sure you aren't undercapitalized. Advice will vary on whether you should incur debt—some say to avoid loans entirely, whereas others approve of short-term debt. Do your best to follow the adage from the Great Depression: "Reduce, reuse, make do, or do without" (Prov. 22:7).

7. **Price your products or services realistically:** The tendency of many newbie business owners is to underprice their wares. Make sure you're calculating in all your business costs, especially hidden costs, such as unexpected computer repairs, technology upgrades, quarterly taxes, city/county business taxes, conferences and other professional development, and so on (Prov. 16:11, 28:8).

8. **Learn how to manage:** You must manage yourself and your time well, as well as other people. If you've never managed other people, consider starting with a "solopreneur"-type business that can be run on your own (Prov. 29:11).

9. **Master your marketing:** Most people go into business because they're good at something—catering weddings, editing thesis papers, restoring furniture. Far fewer go into business because they're good at marketing and selling, yet if this skill isn't mastered, it will quickly sink your entrepreneurial ship. As with the proverbial light hidden under a bushel, you must let your light shine. Network, get a Web site, write a blog, advertise, send out press releases, and more. And don't neglect marketing after the business starts to roll in (Matt. 5:15).

10. **Surround yourself with support:** Join the professional association representing your chosen industry and network with like-minded people. Stay in touch with friends who will keep you covered in prayer and be available for an occasional lunch, movie, or game of tennis (Rom. 12:4-5).

11. **Commit to becoming excellent at your craft:** "Whatever you do, work at it with all your heart, as working for the Lord, not for men" (Col. 3:23). Get really good at what you do. Customers love to work with entrepreneurs who are good at what they do and also treat them well in the process.

12. **Get a life:** I'm confident you already have a life—I just want to make sure you don't lose it to your business! You'll soon discover that the demands of self-employment can become all-consuming if you're not careful. Don't let your new business subtly steal more and more time from devotions, family, church, self-care, and other nourishing activities (Luke 10:42).

Executive coach Shandel Slaten (www.truelifecoaching.com), a committed Christian, has coached hundreds of entrepreneurs, executives, and small-business owners to take their businesses, and their lives, to the next level. Shandel shared her wisdom for new business startups: "Do the right thing in the right way, while staying focused on relationships." She also advocates assessments, advising that "every entrepreneur will get farther faster with three types of assessments: behavioral and communication style, internal motivators, and personal skills and talents. These tools really help you understand how you operate and relate, what drives you, and where your strengths lie."

Slaten also shared with me her list of top-10, "must-read" books for budding entrepreneurs who want to succeed in business while putting Christ at the center of their operating systems:

1. *Now Discover Your Strengths* by Marcus Buckingham and Donald O. Clifton (Free Press, 2001)*

2. *The Dream Giver* by Bruce Wilkinson and Heather Kopp (Multnomah, 2003)*

3. *The E-Myth Revisited: Why Most Small Businesses Don't Work and What to Do About It* by Michael E. Gerber (HarperCollins, 1995)

4. *Leading from Your Strengths: Building Close-Knit Ministry Teams* by Dr. John Trent and Rodney Cox (B&H Publishing Group, 2004)

5. *Spiritual Leadership: Principles of Excellence for Every Believer* by J. Oswald Sanders (Moody Publishers, 2007)*

6. *The Prayer of Jabez* by Bruce Wilkinson (Multnomah Publishing, 2001)*

7. *Good to Great: Why Some Companies Make the Leap…and Others Don't* by Jim Collins (Collins, 2001)

8. *The Five Dysfunctions of a Team: A Leadership Fable* by Patrick Lencioni (Jossey-Bass, 2002)

9. *Leadership and Self-Deception: Getting Out of the Box* by The Arbinger Institute (Berrett-Koehler Publishers, 2002)

10. *Streams in the Desert* (devotional) by L. B. Cowman (Zondervan, 1999)*

I've used an asterisk in the preceding list to indicate books that will be helpful to anyone's career, not just entrepreneurs. In fact, it's helpful for everyone to think of their career as an entrepreneur does. The buck stops here—with you—when it comes to making sure you have what you need to succeed. Never rely on your employer to lay out a training plan for you, or your manager to tell you what you should be doing next. Instead, think about what training you might take next, or what you should be doing next, and then confirm it with your employer or manager. Self-initiative is a hallmark of successful employees.

Break Your Job Search Plan into Small Steps

You may be familiar with the movie *What About Bob?* starring Bill Murray and Richard Dreyfuss. Murray plays Bob Wiley, a troubled but lovable therapy patient who has phobias about everything. Bob makes great progress with noted psychiatrist Dr. Leo Marvin (Dreyfuss), thanks to the advice found in the doctor's latest self-help book, *Baby Steps*. The book title is a fun metaphor for taking small steps when approaching any goal, whether it be conquering fears or tackling an important project, such as your next career move.

Without a plan, your job search may seem overwhelming or beyond your control. Yet the very act of creating a plan helps put you back in control with the simple steps to stay focused. Plans make dreams materialize. They move desires from your head and heart to your hands and feet. To help make your God-driven dreams reality, do the following:

- **Write About It:** Put pen to paper or start a file on your computer and detail your goal and action steps. Fine-tune your purpose statement for your career. Describe your future success in full-sensory detail. Write a letter dated several months in the future congratulating yourself on your new position, the focused work you accomplished to get there, and all you learned from the Lord in the process. Send the letter to one of your support partners.

- **Talk About It:** God spoke the universe into existence. Jesus is described as the Word. We're told that if you confess with your mouth, "Jesus is Lord," and believe in your heart that God raised him from the dead, you will be saved…it is with your mouth that you confess and are saved (Rom. 10:9-10). There is power in spoken words. Share your vision with people who wholeheartedly support you. Practice describing your passion and value to networking contacts and employers. Learn how to strike up conversations with strangers who can share their mutual interests, ideas, tips, and leads.

- **Act on It:** Get moving! Results come when you put yourself in motion.

Big dreams are realized in small steps. Your first small step is to develop a plan. Before you do that, let's get an overview of the phases of your job search.

> **Travel Tip:** No matter how small the step, start walking toward your dream today! Do you dream of one day managing a large business venture? Start by managing yourself—your time, finances, priorities, relationships. Do you dream of one day writing inspirational books that will be read by millions? Start by writing an article and sharing it with one person. Take a step. Journeys require movement!

Five Phases of a Job Transition

The five phases of your transition can be described by the memorable vowels A-E-I-O-U, as table 5.1 shows.

Table 5.1: Five Phases of a Job Transition

Phase I: Analyze	Phase II: Express	Phase III: Investigate	Phase IV: Orchestrate	Phase V: Uncover
Career success starts with self-analysis and market analysis; you've already completed this step in earlier chapters.	Package strengths and bottomline value through a career brand, including resumes, verbal networking scripts, and interviewing responses.	Identify a list of target companies; research and target specific companies in a phased approach; learn TOP (Trends, Opportunities, Problems/ Projects), identify contacts, and investigate how to add value to the company.	Blend targeted/ active and traditional/ passive search strategies; in addition to resume posting, make 20 to 30 contacts daily to get to the 5 to 10 people who have the authority to hire you; continue with Investigate Phase. Calendar daily goals to stay focused.	Uncover employer's priorities, needs, and motivation to hire; clarify key deliverables of target position; prove you can do the job in the interview. Employers are typically focused on three factors: competency (can you do the job?); chemistry (will you fit in?); and compensation (can we afford you?).
Duration: A few days for Career Hunters; weeks and possibly months for Career Explorers (see "Career Explorers, Career Hunters, and Career Conquerors" later in this chapter).	Duration: One or two days with focused effort; a week or more is not unusual.	Duration: A few hours to get you going; continue with weekly research.	Duration: One to two weeks to gain momentum; this phase continues throughout your search.	Duration: Depends on company that's hiring—in rare cases, firms hire in a few days; many take weeks; and some take months.

Travel Tip: There's a spiritual "I" that applies to the "Investigate" phase (as well as all the other phases): Inquire. Joshua 9:14 describes a situation in which the Israelites had entered into the Promised Land but neglected at one point to inquire of God. This lapse in total dependence on God led them to be tricked by the Gibeonites. During your job search, you'll have success if you are continually inquiring of the Lord, asking for His wisdom and guidance every step of the way.

ACTION STEP

Grab a calendar! It's very important that you sketch out timelines and general steps for your search. Without timelines, it's hard to stay focused. Use a calendaring system that works best for you, whether it is software such as Microsoft Outlook, Act!, or Franklin Covey PlanPlus™ that interfaces with Microsoft Outlook, or a low-tech system such as a pocket day planner or a calendar dry-erase board.

Refer to table 5.1, and pencil into your calendar a timeline along with the general steps you will complete in each phase. For example, in the Express Phase, you might write that you will spend approximately two days on completing your resume. In addition, write into your calendar a weekly meeting time (preferably with one of your accountability partners). At these meetings, evaluate your progress on each step for the week, congratulate yourself on the ground covered each week, and make adjustments to the upcoming week's schedule.

Set daily goals for yourself—what must absolutely be accomplished each day—and then follow through.

Now, let's focus on getting your job search plan together.

Plan A–Create a SMART Goal

Front and center in any plan is a compelling goal—one that truly stirs your soul, stimulates your mind, and is significant to God. This goal can align with the SMART acronym, widely used in business to create great goals—whether for big-picture, lifetime goals or for immediate, short-term goals. SMART stands for

> S = Specific
>
> M = Measurable
>
> A = Attainable (or Achievable)
>
> R = Relevant (or Realistic)
>
> T = Time-specific

Following is a description of each of these components as they relate to landing a new position. After reviewing them, you'll have a chance to write your own SMART goal using the blank form (My SMART Goal) that appears near the end of this chapter.

Specific

Write your new career goal in present tense, as if it were true today. This will help you internalize the goal. For instance, a Web developer might state his goal this way:

> *I have a challenging position in Web development with a prestigious tech firm, where I am creating amazing Web sites!*

If you're not yet clear on your next move, consider this kind of a specific goal, again written in present tense:

- *I loved completing the process of learning about my gifts and strengths. I have uncovered ideas on how to make a living at something I'm passionate about. Now I'm ready to home in on target opportunities that will be an ideal fit.*

CAREER EXPLORERS, CAREER HUNTERS, AND CAREER CONQUERORS

Paul reminds us that in all things "we are more than conquerors through Him who loved us" (Rom. 8:37). What does it look like to be a conqueror in your career? I propose the definition of a **Career Conqueror** as this:

> *Being radically rewarded and enthusiastically engaged in work that adds value to God's kingdom.*

How do you become a Career Conqueror? Start by being a Career Explorer.

Career Explorers (also known as career changers) are taking the time to analyze the best F.I.T. (Functional skills, Industry/Interests, Things That Matter, and so on) before they hunt for specific opportunities. Explorers are still getting clear on the "what," "where," and "why" of their next career move.

Career Hunters, the next step in the process, have clarified their Master F.I.T. and are now on the hunt for specific opportunities that are a good match. Career Hunters are simply in a different place in their professional journey than Career Explorers. And, all too often, people think they are Hunters and jump into a job search without a careful analysis of the best F.I.T. The end result is a frustrating position that is an occupation rather than an Occupassion™.

As an Explorer, how much time should you budget for the exploration process? I'd love to tell you that you'll have an epiphany in the next 24 hours, but that doesn't seem to be the pattern. My experience is that it takes a few weeks or even several months to uncover a totally new career direction (not bad, given the grand scheme of things). If you accomplish it in less time, wonderful.

(continued)

CAREER EXPLORERS, CAREER HUNTERS,
AND CAREER CONQUERORS *(CONTINUED)*

Ideally, you should go through the Career Explorer process every few years to stop and take stock of new skills, passions, priorities, and opportunities that God is presenting to you.

Measurable

A measurable goal has a result that can be evaluated on either a success-failure rate or some sort of graduated scale. The following examples describe a measurable goal using a graduated level of attainment, from exceptional to unsatisfactory:

- **Exceptional:** *A position as Web Developer with one of my "dream" employers.*
- **Expected:** *A position as Web Programmer with opportunities to expand my technical and leadership skills.*
- **Could do better:** *A Web Programmer position on a short-term contract that doesn't include benefits; or a different position that will be a stepping-stone to my desired position.*
- **Unsatisfactory:** *A position with a salary below my "reality" number.*

Be prayerful and flexible about establishing measurable goals. God's best plan for us doesn't always align with our expectations!

Attainable

An attainable goal is one that is reasonable given various factors. In job search, there are 10 factors that affect attainability: skill set, industry experience and education, motivation, social skills, support systems and network, search strategy, computer skills, target salary, amount of time available for your search, and potential obstacles. The last of these can include anything from conducting a long-distance search to being handicapped by a history of job-hopping. Before we address the 10 factors, let's look at the ultimate job search factor.

God's Will Is the Ultimate Job Search Factor

Of course, if God wants you in a position, He will move heaven and earth to make it happen, even if you are "unqualified."

"Tina" tells the story of getting hired in a sales position at a respected engineering firm without a shred of sales experience. In fact, her boss, when hiring her, stated, "I don't know why I'm doing this. I think you're here for another reason." Tina is convinced the reason God put her there was to be a witness of Christ's love to her boss. She confides, "When I was first hired, I would come in with big sales orders that were unheard of. This was especially surprising, given my lack of sales experience. My boss would ask, 'How did you do that?' and I'd reply, 'I prayed and the Lord helped me.' At first, this angered my boss. In fact, he even retorted, 'Don't you think you can do anything on your own?' But I could only reply, 'No. I can't. Jesus is my strength.' Even though there have been some challenging times in the job, I know that the Lord is with me and allowing me to bring His presence into my workplace."

The 10 Job Search Factors

The following examples illustrate how one job seeker used the 10 factors to evaluate whether his goal for a technology job was attainable:

- **Skill Set:** *I have 80% of the skills, education, and experience needed for my target position. I have a solid knowledge of Internet technologies and programming (C/C++, Perl, PHP, Python, ColdFusion, ASP, Visual Basic & VB.net, SQL, Java, JavaScript, and HTML). I need more hands-on time with PHP, but I could get up to speed quickly.*

- **Industry Experience and Education:** *I have five years of experience developing and maintaining department-level applications, components, Web and desktop clients, and back-end data services. I'm currently working for an advertising agency, building Web sites for their clients. I did work on one Web site for a technology start-up, but I don't yet have experience working inside technology companies. I don't have a four-year degree, but I do have my IWA Certified Web Professional (CWP) Site Designer certification and am working on certification as a Microsoft Certified Application Developer (MCAD). I'm also looking into the Sun Certified Web Component Developer for the Java 2 Platform certification.*

- **Motivation:** *I am determined to get this position and willing to work hard to move ahead. My parents instilled a really strong work ethic in me, and I don't expect things to be handed to me on a silver platter.*

- **Social Skills:** *I've been told I'm a bit of a recluse, which may affect my networking and interviewing.*

- **Support Systems and Network:** *My wife supports me completely in making this move. I also have a buddy who promised to be my accountability partner. I know a few people who have ties to my target companies.*

- **Search Strategy:** *I have five specific companies that I'm targeting, and may add more later. Since I'm in the tech field, I'm using primarily online methods for my search (e-portfolio, blog, online networking), and will also do face-to-face networking through one of my professional associations.*

- **Computer Skills:** *I have above-average computer skills and all the equipment I need to work at home.*

- **Salary:** *I researched www.salary.com and am realistic about my salary goals.*

- **Time Availability:** *I'm putting in 60-hour workweeks on my current job and I have a 1-year-old, so I can devote only a few hours a week to face-to-face networking. I will do a lot of my online networking in the evenings.*
- **Potential Obstacles:** *I have a couple of tattoos from my B.C. (before Christ) days, which might put some people off if I have to interview with traditional corporate types.*

The stronger you are in each factor, **the faster your search will be.** Likewise, if you come up short in some areas, it will take longer to get where you want to go.

How Attainable Is Your Goal?

Table 5.2 will help you assess each of the factors that affect goal attainment. Using a scale of 1 to 10 (1 is low/false, 10 is high/true), circle a rating for each factor and then total your scores. Get a reality check on your scores by asking a trusted colleague to also rate you—compare your scores and calmly explore any differences.

Table 5.2: Assessing the 10 Factors That Affect Search Success

Factor	1–10 Rating (1 = low/false; 10 = high/true)
1. **Current Skill Set:** Do you have the majority of the skills employers want for your target position? Can you get up to speed quickly? Are your skills above average? (This is especially important if the number of openings for your target position is limited.)	1 2 3 4 5 6 7 8 9 10
2. **Industry Experience and Education:** Do you have recent, hands-on experience in your target position? Do you have the number of years of experience most employers are looking for? Is your target industry hot and hiring? Are you experienced in your target industry? Have you researched your target company thoroughly? Are you familiar with its competitors? Do you have the degree or certifications required for the position?	1 2 3 4 5 6 7 8 9 10

Factor	1–10 Rating (1 = low/false; 10 = high/true)
3. **Motivation:** Do you *really* want this career change? Are you willing to make some sacrifices to get what you want? Do you have an accountability mentality (in other words, "if it's going to be, it's up to me") vs. an entitlement mentality (in other words, "the world owes me because I've been dealt some hard blows"). Are you resilient, able to delay immediate gratification, and perseverant?	1 2 3 4 5 6 7 8 9 10
4. **Social Skills:** Are you personable and well-groomed? Do you have good communication and relational skills? Are you reasonably self-confident? Can you clearly and persuasively articulate your target and your return-on-investment in networking and interviewing situations?	1 2 3 4 5 6 7 8 9 10
5. **Support Systems and Network:** Are you enlisting the support of others during your search? Do you have goal-oriented accountability and prayer partners? Can you tap into a reasonably strong professional and personal network, or can you resurrect one quickly? Do you know people in the industry? Do you know how to build reciprocal networking relationships? Is your spouse or family behind you 100 percent in this transition? Are you familiar with the benefit of working with a career coach during this critical time?	1 2 3 4 5 6 7 8 9 10
6. **Search Strategy:** Do you have a clearly defined position target and company/ministry target, giving consideration to geographic area, company size, organizational culture, and so on? Are you using the wisest job search strategy for your situation? Are you working smart as well as hard? Are you leveraging time and not just being busy?	1 2 3 4 5 6 7 8 9 10

(continued)

Table 5.2: Assessing the 10 Factors That Affect Search Success *(continued)*

Factor	1–10 Rating (1 = low/false; 10 = high/true)
7. **Computer Skills:** Are you proficient with the technology needed for the target job? Do you have a computer and Internet connection at home for job search activities?	1 2 3 4 5 6 7 8 9 10
8. **Salary:** Is your salary goal in line with market realities and current salary surveys?	1 2 3 4 5 6 7 8 9 10
9. **Time Availability:** Can you devote 30 to 40 hours or more each week to your search if you're unemployed and 10 to 15 if you're employed?	1 2 3 4 5 6 7 8 9 10
10. **Potential Obstacles:** Are you free of any of these potential obstacles: a long-distance search; poor employment record; disability; appearance; "silent" discrimination for reasons of race, sex, religion, or age; language barriers; criminal record; health problems; heavy smoker; emotional problems; anything else?	1 2 3 4 5 6 7 8 9 10
Total your points (100 possible):	_____

Although there may be some gray areas in scoring, this quick assessment will give you an idea of whether your goal is attainable. If your total score is in the 80 to 100 range, you should be set up for a relatively smooth and quick search. If your score is in the 50 to 80 range, concentrate on the factors that need shoring up. If your score is below 50, change your target to a "bridge" job if you want to be in a new position quickly.

Travel Tip: Working full-time already and need more time for your search? One of my favorite resources for negotiating a flexible work schedule is Pat Katepoo's www.WorkOptions.com. Pat, a successful entrepreneur who honors Christ in all her business dealings, offers free tips and low-cost proposal templates for presenting the business case to your boss for fewer or flexible hours on the job.

How Long Will Your Search Take?

That's the million-dollar question! Be assured of this: The higher your score in the "10 Factors That Affect Search Success" (table 5.2), the greater your appeal to employers. The greater your appeal, the faster you'll be hired!

The two most common factors for initial screening of applicants are functional skills and industry experience. If you don't score high in these two areas, your search can stall in a hurry. Figure 5.1 illustrates how the combination of functional skills and industry experience affect the length of a search.

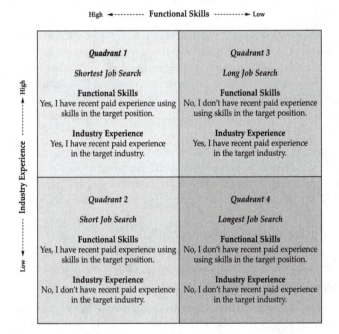

High ◄---------- Functional Skills ----------► Low

Quadrant 1 *Shortest Job Search* **Functional Skills** Yes, I have recent paid experience using skills in the target position. **Industry Experience** Yes, I have recent paid experience in the target industry.	**Quadrant 3** *Long Job Search* **Functional Skills** No, I don't have recent paid experience using skills in the target position. **Industry Experience** Yes, I have recent paid experience in the target industry.
Quadrant 2 *Short Job Search* **Functional Skills** Yes, I have recent paid experience using skills in the target position. **Industry Experience** No, I don't have recent paid experience in the target industry.	**Quadrant 4** *Longest Job Search* **Functional Skills** No, I don't have recent paid experience using skills in the target position. **Industry Experience** No, I don't have recent paid experience in the target industry.

(Industry Experience: High ↑ → Low ↓)

Figure 5.1: Length of job search related to functional skills and industry experience.

Which of the four quadrants does your search fall into?

- **Quadrant 1 Search, the Shortest Search:** Targeting a similar position in the same industry.
- **Quadrant 2 Search, a Short Search:** Targeting a similar position in a different industry.
- **Quadrant 3 Search, a Long Search:** Targeting a different position in the same industry.
- **Quadrant 4 Search, the Longest Search:** Targeting a different position in a different industry.

An example of a Quadrant 1 Search, the shortest job search, might involve a customer service representative in the utilities industry who is targeting a similar customer service position in the utilities industry. Here, the functional skills and industry are the same, so the search should be relatively easy and short.

In a Quadrant 2 Search, the customer service representative might target a customer service position (similar position) in the healthcare industry (new industry), also typically a short search but not as easy given the new industry.

In Quadrant 3, the customer service representative might target a sales position (new skill) in the utilities industry (same industry). Assuming that the candidate has no history of sales, this search will be long in comparison to a Quadrant 1 or 2 search.

Finally, in a Quadrant 4 Search, the customer service representative might target a sales position (new skill) in the health-care industry (new industry). This type of search will take the longest because it appears that there are neither functional skills nor industry experience related to the target position. Is a Quadrant 4 search impossible? No, but it definitely requires a strategically written resume, great communication skills, extensive networking, lots of confidence, oodles of action and perseverance, and plenty of prayer.

Of course, deficits in any of the 10 job search factors listed in table 5.2 can affect the length of your search. If any of your scores needs bolstering, visit www.ChristianCareerJourney.com/journey.html and download "Strategies to Shorten Your Search" for an extensive list of strategies to enhance your candidacy.

When God Delays Your Search

You may score high in all of the 10 job search factors but still be stalled in your search. If so, it may be that God wants to accomplish something else first. Consider whether any of these four factors might relate to you. God may want to…

- **Move other puzzle pieces into place:** There may be people or circumstances that need to be aligned before He moves you into a new position. If so, persevere in doing what is right as you wait. Continue to do good (1 Pet. 4:19)!

- **Bear more fruit in you:** You may be doing everything right but feel like God has abandoned you. If so, consider the possibility that He simply wants to see you remain faithful, even when things don't seem to be going your way. Your faithfulness to trust and obey during these times will not go unnoticed because He rewards those who earnestly seek Him (Heb. 11:6).

- **Teach you something new:** God may want to develop or sharpen life skills through the process of job search. For instance, if you're extremely shy, He may want you to break out of that insecurity and gain more self-confidence. If you're a take-charge, gotta-be-in-control person, He may want to teach you to "let go and let God." Or it could be something as simple as learning the self-discipline of setting daily action goals or putting off immediate gratification for a longer-term goal. (I've often wondered if self-control, the last of the fruits of the Spirit mentioned in Gal. 5:22-23, is last because it's the hardest one to master!)

- **Curb sin:** Ask God to reveal anything unpleasing in your life to Him. It could be that He wants to see a change in how you handle money, treat your spouse, or use your time. There may be hurts He wants to heal or habits He wants to break. Maybe it's one of those secret places that no one else sees, but God does. Whatever it is, He will not overwhelm you; instead, He patiently reveals only to the degree that you're able to receive from Him. And recall that "no discipline seems pleasant at the time, but painful. Later on, however, it produces a harvest of righteousness and peace for those who have been trained by it" (Heb. 12:11).

As we wrap up the "A" in the SMART acronym, remember that an Attainable goal directly affects the length of your search and degree of success. Those who proactively address the 10 job search items and the four factors of a delayed search are better off than those who passively bury their heads in the sand!

Relevant

Relevant goals are aligned with your purpose and the Big Picture of your life. This example shows how the job seeker's goal has been a long-term desire and is aligned with his natural talents:

For the past 10 years, I have wanted to be part of a Web development team at a leading tech company. From as far back as I can remember, I have been fascinated by technology. I sense that my purpose is to use my technical skills to create Web experiences that inspire, educate, and empower people.

Time-Specific

Your goal needs a realistic deadline. For example:

I anticipate accepting an offer within 90 days.

ACTION STEP

To help clarify your goal, write about it using the following form. The wording doesn't need to be perfect at this point. It's more important that you move the ideas from your head to paper. Seeing your thoughts written out helps you commit to the goal. Remember to write the first section (Specific) in present tense, as if it were already true. If you need ideas, refer to the examples for each of the SMART elements. When finished, read each item aloud to further internalize the goal. Pay attention to the Holy Spirit's leading as you read them, noting if something needs to be adjusted or changed.

MY SMART GOAL

Specific:

_____

_____

_____

Measurable:

Exceptional: _____

_____

Expected: _____

_____

Could do better: _____

_____

Unsatisfactory: _____

_____

Attainable:

Skill Set: _____

_____

Industry Experience and Education: _____

_____

Motivation: _____

_____

Social Skills: _____

_____

Support Systems and Network: _____

_____

Search Strategy: _____

_____

Computer Skills: _____

_____

Target Salary: _____

_____

Time Availability: _____

_____

Potential Obstacles: _____

_____

Relevant:

_____

_____

_____

Time-specific:

Plan B–Give Yourself Options

Think of Plan B as creating options. Options help us adjust our expectations to anticipate and accept whatever God might bring. Life is unpredictable, and there are variables beyond your control that may affect your success with Plan A. Better to prepare an alternative now rather than later, when you may be disappointed and not thinking as clearly.

Plan B often works out for the best. A business development client of mine who was targeting an executive position with a Texas-based company was disappointed when his Plan A didn't work out. He went to Plan B, which involved transitioning from part-time consultant to full-time executive for an East Coast company. A few months later, he was accepted to the Wharton Executive MBA Program at the Philadelphia campus. The employer in Plan B was located in an area much closer to the campus, freeing up dozens of hours in commute time for this rigorous academic program. Although Plan B wasn't his first choice, God knew what he would need in the future and orchestrated accordingly.

Write your Plan B (and even a Plan C) here:

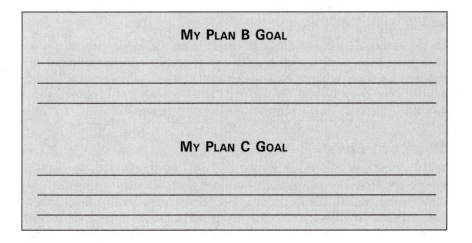

MY PLAN B GOAL

MY PLAN C GOAL

Job Search Resources and Budget

When the Israelites were preparing to cross over the Jordan to enter the Promised Land, Joshua told them to "get your supplies ready" (Josh. 1:11). A job search plan requires that you get your supplies ready. Resources should include computer setup, resume stationery and envelopes, networking business cards, note cards for follow-ups and thank-yous, a calendaring system, professional wardrobe, and so on. Note that business cards are a must in your networking, and you can obtain them free at www.vistaprint.com. Also, take a look at your monthly budget and adjust for necessary job search expenses.

One of my favorite tools to help organize and manage your job search is JibberJobber (www.JibberJobber.com). Designed by a software professional while unemployed to help manage his job search, the system allows you to keep track of networking contacts, job leads, resume distribution, follow-up tasks, and much more. The site offers a free account with basic services, as well as an upgrade for premium services.

Your Support Team

Job search is a team sport! You learned this in earlier chapters, and it's driven home as one of the factors that affect goal attainment. Support is critical. Please do not attempt your transition alone. You might think that this book will give you all the support you need. It is definitely one form of support, but it's not enough! *Nothing* replaces the powerful synergy created when believers connect (Matt. 18:20). God wants us to be together (Heb. 10:25), so pull out all the stops when it comes to enlisting support.

Do you have trouble asking for help? If so, chances are you don't want to be a bother, or you perceive asking for help as a sign of weakness. If you adopt either line of thinking, it prevents you from being your best and prevents others from the blessing of being a part of the body of Christ (Rom. 12:5). The truth is that two (or more) are better than one (Eccles. 4:12)—you are stronger with support.

Whom to Enlist

Whom should you recruit for your support team? In the "My Support Team" box that follows, jot down names that come to mind. If you can't fill in each space right away, try this "antenna exercise" (aptly named because it puts you in a heightened state of awareness). In your notebook or computer, outline the categories in the "My Support Team" worksheet and leave space to fill in names later. Next, say this pocket prayer aloud:

Pocket Prayer

Father, in Psalm 139:4 You tell me that You know everything, even before there is a word on my tongue, so thank you for knowing my need. In order to use Your gifts and be a blessing to others, I need help from the types of people listed on my support team worksheet. In the hours and days to come, please make me aware of who they are. In Jesus' name, Amen.

Carry your outline with you and be ready to fill in names and ideas. You'll be surprised at what will come to you.

MY SUPPORT TEAM

Prayer partners and goal-oriented accountability partners (more than one is okay) who will hold your feet to the fire on job search tasks and celebrate with you when you've gotten closer to your goal (choose someone with a style that works best for you—you may want a gentle but firm friend, or a military-like commando, or an enthusiastic cheerleader who keeps reminding you, "You can do it!"):

_____

_____

Well-connected colleagues who know virtually everyone (these should be a few people whom you know fairly well; later, you'll identify a longer list of networking contacts):

_____

_____

A savvy researcher who can help you uncover important company information (this may be your local librarian):

_____

_____

One or more trusted friends with whom you can be transparent when you hit a low spot:

_____

_____

A job search group where you can help one another stay focused (these are often sponsored by churches or affiliated with quasi-governmental or community groups—as a reminder, if you can't find one in your area, start your own using resources from Career Transition Ministry, www.ctmnetwork.org):

_____

_____

(continued)

MY SUPPORT TEAM *(CONTINUED)*

Outplacement assistance (typical in larger corporations, outplacement is offered to employees affected by a RIF [reduction in force] and paid for by the corporation; if you get an outplacement package, take advantage of it. If you have the option of selecting your own outplacement services, select a career expert experienced in career transition and job search):

_____

_____

A professional career coach or job search expert who has strategies that will fast-forward your progress (a trained coach is well worth the investment, supporting you as a catalyst, strategist, collaborator, resource person, cheerleader, and more):

_____

_____

Be Courteous

Remember that people feel good when they help others, so you're providing them an opportunity to feel good. Just be mindful to limit two things:

- **Time**—the amount of time you'll need from them
- **Pressure**—the extent you look to them for answers or emotional support

Don't look to just one person for too much time, too many answers, or too much emotional support. And avoid the temptation to look to other people first before looking to God for answers. He should always be your starting point!

Avoid the Traps, Temptations, and "Yes, Buts" That Keep You from Your Calling

Your journey will have its share of traps and temptations because there is an enemy prowling about who wants to keep you stuck and spinning your wheels. At the root of every trap is a lack of belief that God can and will help you. Succumbing to temptation is simply longing for something other than God's best. God wants to give you a hunger for His best, and He can and will help you no matter how insurmountable the obstacle. In fact, the bigger the obstacle, the bigger the opportunity for Him to show you His incredible power and faithfulness.

A side effect of traps and temptations is a malady I refer to as the "yes, buts"! "Yes, buts" are those valid-sounding excuses we can all come up with to justify not moving forward. God wants to turn our "yes, buts" into "yes, ands." In other words, "Yes, and I'm going to show you how to get beyond that." Let's look at some of the traps, temptations, and "yes, buts" you may be facing.

Fear

For most of us, the known is more comfortable than the unknown. The old acronym for FEAR—Ealse Expectations Appearing Real—helps us to examine those expectations and find ways to take action. Name your fears:

- ❏ I'm afraid that the new work God is leading me to will require sacrifices on my part.
- ❏ I worry about having the resources I need to make my transition (finances, networking connections, affordable training).
- ❏ I'm afraid of others having negative opinions about my new career direction.
- ❏ I'm afraid I won't make enough money in the direction I want to go.
- ❏ I don't know if I can do the job well enough to be successful.

Get comfortable with not knowing. God doesn't guarantee us all the answers up front, but it delights Him when we come to Him daily for wisdom and courage. Fight fear with the truth of God's promises to provide for your every need.

The Time Trap

Life's most precious commodity these days is time. Our calendars are crammed with commitments—some good, some not so good. If you're working, career commitments take up the majority of each weekday, which is extended for many people by a horrendous commute. Then there's the business of staying alive and healthy, so include grocery shopping, meal preparation, sitting down to eat (or dining on your commute!), exercising, devotions, getting to the doctor and dentist regularly, and so on. Add to that some home maintenance and repair activities—running the vacuum occasionally, mending the fence, paying the electricity bill on time, and so on. If you have school-age children, add in getting them to school on time, picking them up from school on time, helping with homework, supervising chores, reading to them, and taxiing them to sports practice, friends' houses, Awana/youth club, and so on. The list is growing and I haven't even gotten to friends, recreation, or church responsibilities.

With the busyness and breakneck speed of life, the thought of making a career change could send you over the edge with thoughts of "I don't have time!" Do any of these statements ring true?

- ❏ The thought of finding time to pursue a new career direction seems overwhelming and impossible right now.
- ❏ I want my transition to be quick and painless.
- ❏ I'm running so fast that I can't even hear from the Lord.
- ❏ Although my calendar is full, I'm asking God to show me what I can let go of, turn from, or put on hold.
- ❏ I have already developed a strategy to prioritize my career transition.

The reality is that we make time for what's important. When a busy working mother is given the news that she has cancer and needs daily radiation treatments to beat the disease, she finds time in her schedule. This is an extreme example, of course, but it illustrates that you *can* make changes in your schedule.

Ask God to give you a strategy for finding time today—first, find time to be with Him (alone, without multitasking!), to ponder His Word, to tell Him how much you love Him, and to listen to the treasures that He has to say to you. In your prayer time, thank Him that He knows every second of your day and what priorities He wants for you to accomplish. Expect Him to give you ideas about what to cut back on or let go of to free up the time needed for your career.

Perhaps your transition will require a phased approach. Don't buy into the quick-fix mentality that is so pervasive in our society. If it takes a few months or even a few years to get where you want to go, you'll be exactly where you're supposed to be every step of your journey. Think long-term. God does!

> **Travel Tip:** Take thoughts captive! 2 Cor. 10:5 reminds us, "We demolish arguments and every pretension that sets itself up against the knowledge of God, and we take captive every thought to make it obedient to Christ."

Finally, some Christians don't move ahead because they haven't sensed clear direction from God. If this is the case for you (and you don't sense God holding up a bright red stop sign!), do what you know to be right. Like the good and faithful servants in the parable of the talents (Matt. 25:14-30), they "went at once" (v. 16) to put their talents to work—their master wasn't there directing them in how to use their talents day-in and day-out. Instead, they acted as responsibly as they knew how. When the master returned, he was happy that they had made progress.

Finances

Money can be one of the biggest obstacles to career freedom. Which of these statements do you relate to?

- ❑ My new opportunity will require me to take a cut in pay, which I (or my family) cannot afford.
- ❑ My new opportunity will require me to lower the lifestyle to which I have become accustomed.
- ❑ My new opportunity requires an investment in retraining and I can't afford the tuition.

❏ I'm going after this position primarily because of the high salary it pays, even though it will cost me in terms of having life balance or pursuing what I truly feel called to.

❏ Salary isn't my primary consideration. The Lord has always provided for me, and I know He will in the future.

If finances are frustrating you, take advantage of the planning resources at Crown Financial Ministries (www.crown.org). Talk to a financial planner. Develop a strategy to create financial reserves. Consider a phased transition. Look at work options such as a flexible part-time or temporary position to financially cushion your transition.

Identity

The topic of identity can range from feeling insecure to struggling with pride. Check the statements that you most relate to.

❏ I just don't have the confidence to move ahead. I can't imagine myself doing something new—I've been a _____ [fill in the blank] my whole life.

❏ I have feelings of unworthiness—I just don't deserve to pursue this new direction. People will likely think I'm being presumptuous and wonder, "Who is she to think she can do that!"

❏ I am being pressured by parents, family, or colleagues to pursue a career course that just doesn't fit with who I am.

❏ I'm avoiding the direction God seems to be leading because it seems beneath me—I've paid my dues and shouldn't have to lower myself to that level.

❏ My ego is itching! I have to admit that I'm pursuing this opportunity because people will be impressed with the title/company/perks.

❏ I have a "spiritual itch" to be more for God. This new opportunity appears to be a direction that will allow me to obey God, stretch and grow, and serve Him more fully.

As human beings, we are meant to grow throughout our lives. Only when our identity is rooted in Christ and our thoughts are fixed on first pleasing Him can we make the personal progress that He desires for us.

Isolation

God designed us to be connected with one another. From the beginning of Genesis to the end of Revelation, we see that God wants us with Him and walking in unity with each other. Which of these statements do you relate to?

❏ I prefer to do things on my own.

❏ I'm too busy to network or get together with a support group.

❏ I've already taken steps to hook into a strong support network.

❏ I'm also reaching out to support others.

Christianity is a contact sport, and so is your career! If you don't have a support network, start your own career club in your home or a coffee shop using this book as an outline. Form a Career Conqueror's group at your church. Find a job club in your city. Get connected!

Chapter Wrap-Up

Your plan should be taking shape at this point, making hopes and dreams become the new reality. Remember to break tasks into small-step phases if things look overwhelming and set daily goals for yourself that involve networking, research, interview practice, and so on.

10 QUICK TIPS FOR GETTING YOUR JOB SEARCH PLAN TOGETHER

1. **Big dreams are realized in small steps.** The first small step in any career change is to develop a plan. In your plan, understand the sequence of a job search and outline timelines according to these five "A-E-I-O-U" phases: Analyze, Express, Investigate, Orchestrate, and Uncover. Analyze your skills and the market and settle on one or two targets for the focus of your search. Express your skills in resumes, verbal scripts, and interviewing responses. Investigate by assembling a list of 50 to 100 companies and identifying their TOP issues and key contacts. Blend targeted/active and traditional/passive search strategies (in addition to resume posting, make several dozen contacts daily to get to the 5 to 10 people who have the authority to hire you). Finally, uncover the employer's priorities, needs, and motivation to hire; clarify the key deliverables of the target position (the tangible outcomes expected as a result of your work) and prove you can do the job.

2. **Set a compelling goal.** Front and center to any plan is a compelling goal. This goal should align with the SMART acronym, meaning it should be Specific, Measurable, Attainable, Relevant, and Time-specific.

3. **Know the 10 job search factors.** There are 10 factors that affect attainability in a job search: your skill set, industry experience and education, motivation, social skills, support systems and network, search strategy, computer skills, target salary, amount of time available for your search, and potential obstacles. Using a scale of 1 to 10 (10 is high), rate yourself on each of these 10 factors. Shore up any areas needed to speed up your search. If your score is below 50, change your target to a "bridge" job if you want to be in a new position quickly. Remember that God's will is the ultimate job search factor.

4. **Hone in on functional skills and industry experience.** The two most common factors for screening applicants are functional skills and industry experience. If you don't score high in these two areas, your search can stall in a hurry.

5. **Motivation is another big factor to success.** If your goal isn't thoroughly enticing, there won't be sufficient motivation. You must first find the right carrot. If the goal is right but you're still not taking action, examine potential fears or beliefs that might be blocking you. Break through limiting beliefs with God's truths.

6. **Think beyond Plan A.** After creating a SMART goal, give yourself some options by identifying a Plan B or Plan C goal. Options help us adjust our expectations to anticipate and accept whatever God might bring. Better to prepare an alternative plan now rather than later.

7. **Create a budget for your search,** taking into consideration the cost of distributing your resume through online vehicles, membership in professional organizations, networking expenses, travel expenses, relocation expenses, hiring a career coach, and so on. Take stock of your resources (from printer cartridges and resume paper to a professional wardrobe suitable for interviewing).

8. **Job search is a team sport.** Assemble your team with people like these: prayer partners and goal-oriented accountability partners (more than one is okay) who will hold your feet to the fire on job search tasks and celebrate with you when you've gotten closer to your goal, a few well-connected colleagues who know virtually everyone, a savvy researcher who can help you uncover important company information, one or more trusted friends with whom you can be transparent when you hit a low spot, a job search group where you can help one another stay focused, outplacement assistance (if available), and a professional career coach or job search expert who has strategies that will fast-forward your progress.

9. **Avoid the traps, temptations, and "yes, buts" that keep you from your calling.** For example, face the fear of the unknown, get control of a crowded schedule, deal with finances, grow your identity, and avoid the trap of isolation or going it alone. God wants to use every obstacle to show you His faithfulness. Filter lies from truth. If God delays your search for some unknown reason, walk in humility and perseverance.

10. **Keep your plan on track.** To keep your plan on track, write into your calendar a weekly time to evaluate your progress, congratulate yourself on the ground covered each week, and make adjustments to the upcoming week's schedule. Set daily nonnegotiable goals to accomplish priorities.

MASTERFUL COACHING QUESTIONS

If you haven't already done so, by what date will you have sketched out your SMART goal, your job search plan, and timelines for the A-E-I-O-U phases? To whom will you be accountable?

_____

_____

Which of the 10 factors of job search success can you focus on improving? What action will you take to do so?

_____

_____

What motivates you? How will you build this motivation into your daily routine?

_____

_____

What fears or limiting beliefs might block your success?

_____

_____

What is one action step you will take today to boost your job search momentum?

_____

_____

What traps, temptations, or "yes, buts" might be in your path? Use a concordance or an online Bible tool such as those found at www.BlueLetterBible.com or www.BibleGateway.com to search for the words "fear," "anxiousness," and "impossible." What do God's truths state in relation to these words?

_____

_____

_____

Pocket Prayer

Father in heaven, You are the ultimate planner. Your plans are good, righteous, and just. No plan of Yours can be thwarted. You are the one who determines my steps, and the one who has promised to lead me in paths of righteousness for Your name's sake. As I prepare my plan, show me how to align it and all the details with Your purposes. If I have a tendency to rush ahead of You, help me wait for Your perfect timing. If I have a tendency to hesitate, help me to step out and take action. I commit my plans to You, Lord. And, Father, if there are traps or temptations or "yes, buts" in my life that are causing me to not enjoy the fullness of all You want to give me, take me beyond them according to Your grace and mercy. I resolve to do whatever pleases you. In Jesus' name, Amen.

Capturing Your Value with "Smart" Success Stories

"The basic building block of good communications is the feeling that every human being is unique and of value."

—*Author Unknown*

The apostle Paul wrote in Philippians 2:15 that as children of God we "shine like stars in the universe" for holding out the word of life. That brilliance ought to pervade every area of our lives, including the way we conduct ourselves when managing a job search campaign. The familiar equation $E = MC^2$ captures Einstein's brilliant theory of relativity. I've translated that memorable formula into job search terminology so that *you* can be brilliant in your quest for new employment!

To shine in the realm of job search, $E = MC^2$ will read like this:

Employment = Mechanics × Commitment-Squared

Let's explore what each of those terms means to you:

- **Employment:** Working in a role that God has hand-picked to add to your life story, grow your faith, increase your capacity and influence, and allow you to reflect His love and purposes to others.

- **Mechanics:** Applying wisdom-centered strategies, systems, and tactics—the ins and outs—of job search.

- **Commitment-Squared:** Maintaining faith, optimum mind-set, emotional energy, and intelligent attitude throughout the job search process.

If you've purchased this book, I'll assume that different employment—a career of significance—is your goal. To get that, you'll need to put into practice the nuts and bolts of job search and interviewing, which I've referred to as "mechanics." Add to that a double portion of commitment. Together, these ingredients translate not just to employment, but to a kingdom career—one that adds value and brings blessing to others, one in which you can be enthusiastically engaged and radically rewarded.

In chapter 3 you began to apply some of the mechanics of job search by honing in on your Master F.I.T.™ exercises. This was the first step on your job search journey. Some of the next steps that you're now ready to walk through include these:

- Developing success stories and sound bites for your job search campaign
- Targeting companies and networking to identify opportunities and openings
- Communicating your value and return on investment (ROI) to hiring managers as you network and interview

Chapters 6 and 7 are devoted to the mechanics of preparing the success stories and sound bites that will make you stand out with style, as well as creating and communicating a strong career brand. I'd like you to feel fresh when tackling this chapter because it will be the *foundation* for preparing your networking scripts and interview responses. The work you do now will enable you to avoid the most common downfall of many candidates: talking to networking contacts and interviewers unprepared.

Conveying Value to Employers

Offering value—contributions to the bottom-line goals of the organization—should be at the heart of your job search message. Use it to describe how you'll work in a manner that will make your employer a better, stronger, more profitable company. Value can be woven into your interview responses at every turn. Three methods for conveying value include the following:

- Linking your past successes and future solutions to employer buying motivators
- Demonstrating a return on investment
- Emphasizing benefits instead of features of your qualifications

Let's look at each of these three methods more closely.

The Employer's 10 Motivations to "Buy"

"Love your neighbor as yourself." When asked by His disciples what was the greatest commandment, Jesus' response was to love God with all your heart, soul, and mind. He followed that with the second commandment to love our "neighbors." In other words, bosses, coworkers, clients, customers, vendors, suppliers…anyone whose lives we touch as we go about doing our work.

Often paraphrased as "do unto others as you would have them do unto you," this commandment can help you adopt an employer-focused mind-set. You would probably like to be "done unto" with good compensation, respectful treatment, and opportunities to achieve your goals. Employers want the same: good profit, respectful treatment, and opportunities to achieve their goals.

Numerous "Employer Buying Motivators" drive business. These 10 buying motivators are key to why hiring decisions are made:

- Buying Motivator #1: Make Money
- Buying Motivator #2: Save Money
- Buying Motivator #3: Save Time
- Buying Motivator #4: Make Work Easier
- Buying Motivator #5: Solve a Specific Problem
- Buying Motivator #6: Be More Competitive
- Buying Motivator #7: Build Relationships, Brand, and Image with Internal/ External Customers, Vendors, and the Public
- Buying Motivator #8: Expand Business
- Buying Motivator #9: Attract New Customers
- Buying Motivator #10: Retain Existing Customers

In subsequent chapters, you'll have a chance to explore how you can link your resume and networking/interviewing language to these 10 buying motivators.

What's Your ROI?

ROI, short for *return on investment,* is a business term widely used by companies to determine how quickly their decision to invest in new equipment, advertising, or an expansion will pay for itself. In the case of a hiring decision, the employer is investing in salary, benefits, training, work space, and equipment.

In the corporate world, savvy career professionals concentrate on generating a return on investment for their employers. For instance, a top sales performer can show that a $125,000 salary will be justified by her ability to bring in $500,000 in new sales contracts. A materials manager might find methods to reduce waste or recycle scrap, which may add up to a six-figure savings. A production line worker might make a suggestion that, when implemented, leads to a spike in productivity, which can be tied to the bottom line. An assistant to a pastor can show how she has fielded calls to free up time for the pastor's priorities. Whatever your role, challenge yourself to look for ways to boost your employer's success, and then document that success.

Benefits vs. Features

As with most people, hiring managers are tuned to radio station WIFM, or "what's in it for me?" Benefits are the key to clarifying "what's in it for them"! High-paid advertising copywriters know that benefits sell, whereas features can put you to sleep. Let's compare features and benefits for a minute by using career coaching services as an example.

Here are a few features that a career coach might have:

- Certified Professional Christian Coach
- Certified Career Management Coach
- Nationally Certified Résumé Writer
- Founder of Career Coach Academy

You'll note that the features are title-oriented. Yawn. Features might carry some weight, but they don't really describe the benefit of what a career coach can do.

On the other hand, these statements describe benefits:

- Partnering with people who feel stuck in their careers to discover God's plan and provision for their lives.
- Equipping job seekers with insider strategies that shorten the time it takes to find a new job.
- Sharing strategies that eliminate the guesswork and frustration from career transition and job search.
- Supporting job seekers who wish networking would just go away to find self-marketing methods that are both comfortable and compelling.
- Lighting a fire under the dream you've relegated to the back burner, standing with you to break through roadblocks and find meaningful life-work…purpose produces passion!

The preceding benefits use carefully chosen language to address needs that a prospective client might have. Part of your goal in writing success stories is to address the needs, or pain points, of a prospective employer. To do so, concentrate on knitting in benefit-oriented words such as these:

Accelerate	Equip	Help
Build	Find	Honor
Create	Formula	How To
Decrease	Free	Improve
Discover	Gain	Increase
Eliminate	Grow	Less
Enhance	Guarantee	More

Numbers	Save	Techniques
Proven	Secret	Tips
Reduce	Steps	Uncover
Relief	Strategies	
Relieve	Strengthen	

How many of the words from the list did you see in my benefit statements?

S.O.S.

The familiar Morse code of S.O.S. stands for *Save Our Ship*. Although most companies that you will target aren't necessarily sinking, they will likely need some help bailing out from an overflow of work or plugging a hole caused by someone's absence.

When writing your success stories and sound bites, offer your own S.O.S. Response, in the form of *Solutions Or Services*. Organizations want to know how you are going to help them solve problems or get things done. Positioning yourself as a provider of solutions or services will give your candidacy favored status.

In the remainder of this chapter, you'll see how each of these three techniques—linking to buying motivators, demonstrating a return on investment, and focusing on benefits—is woven into sample success stories and sound bites.

Inventorying Your Success Stories

William Barclay, past professor of divinity at Glasgow University and author of dozens of commentaries, offers an insightful look at the parables of Jesus in his book by the same name. In the book's introduction, he explains why Jesus used stories to teach: "If Jesus had argued purely abstractly, using only ideas, few might have understood Him. But He knew what was in man; and He gave us these cameo-like pictures we call parables so that the great ideas He wished to teach might become comprehensible."

Your SMART Stories—cameo-like pictures of your experiences—will help others to comprehend how you can be of value. In this section, you'll take stock of your successes to create stories for networking and interviewing. When I give the upcoming exercise to my clients, I sometimes hear, "I don't have any success stories." They assume that if they didn't single-handedly initiate and execute a project of monumental proportions, they have no success stories. However, *any* information that helps support your candidacy qualifies as a success story. And to argue that you have no successes implies that God has not provided for you or helped you over the years, which we know is not the case!

> **Travel Tip:** Proverbs 27:2 says, "Let another praise you, and not your own mouth; someone else, and not your own lips." How do we reconcile this verse with developing success stories for job search purposes? This verse implies that we mustn't do works only to be seen, but to do them for the sake of blessing others. The motive for sharing success stories must be pure—**not to be a show-off or a superstar, but to be a servant,** humbly conveying value and a desire to meet the employer's needs.
>
> And, to act upon this proverb, when you're developing your SMART Stories, quote what others have said or written about you in performance appraisals, "attaboy" letters, kudos, and so on. These third-party endorsements add to your credibility.

Although you'll want the majority of your success stories to have a positive outcome, it's also acceptable to include a few anecdotes that describe an unsuccessful attempt or lesson learned. Employers will be suspicious if you can't exhibit humility and admit to having met with some failure or disappointment over the course of your career. Later, you'll identify and think through your response to potential negatives so that you're ready with a positive response in the interview. The key is to *leverage the lessons learned*. In doing so, the situation can be categorized as a success!

What Is a Success Story?

Everyone can uncover success stories, especially when this definition is adopted:

> **Success Story:** An anecdote or account providing evidence that you have the knowledge, hard and soft skills, and motivation to excel in the target job. Let's expand on the elements in this definition.

- *Anecdotes*—short descriptions of a relevant incident—can be interesting, amusing, or biographical in nature.
- *Knowledge* can be gained through employment, education (class activities, group projects, case studies), and unpaid experience (internships, work study, job shadowing). Even community service, team or sports involvement, and parenting can contribute to your knowledge bank.
- *Hard skills* refer to your technical skills and talents, whereas *soft skills* are those less-tangible but often-important interpersonal and communication skills. Beyond knowledge and skills, employers today are also interested in whether you have the inner drive and ambition to do the job.
- *Motivation* stems from being rewarded and engaged by work that aligns with your Master F.I.T. (see chapter 3).

- The verb *excel*—the final part of the definition of a success story—implies that you are bottom-line oriented, with a commitment to delivering results that help add revenue, reduce costs, or boost productivity.

Each of these examples illustrates a success story that conveys value:

- **Materials Management Success Story (materials coordinator describing a reduction in order-cycle time):** In my last position as a materials coordinator at Lanco Foods, I participated on a team that cut our order cycle time by about 75 percent. We analyzed turnkey processes and identified two key areas for improvement: order placement and payment closure. I then took the lead on writing new procedures for order placement and taught our customer service team how to implement the procedures. Within six months, our order cycle was shortened from 45 days to 11 days.

- **Marketing Success Story (retail marketing specialist for Christian bookstores describing an increased return on trade spending):** I inherited a retail marketing specialist position in which the return on investment on trade spending was below the target of 10:1—it was actually at 8:1—and we ended up delivering a 50 percent increase. After analyzing syndicated data and interviewing marketing specialists at other stores to learn what they were doing to get higher returns, I initiated a campaign to increase the displays in some of our top customers. I prepared proposals and accompanied sales reps as they made presentations to store managers. Within three months, my action plan allowed us to exceed the benchmark in trade spending with a return ratio of 12:1 versus the target of 10:1.

- **Teacher Success Story (kindergarten teacher describing her success with language arts):** I was challenged by teaching a kindergarten class at Washington Elementary, where 80 percent of the students were from non-English–speaking homes. I addressed the needs of emergent readers through phonemic awareness, phonics, concepts of print, decoding, guided reading, and shared reading. Writing skills were cultivated through modeled, shared, interactive, and journal writing, and I introduced spelling at the appropriate developmental level. By the end of the year, all of the students were at or above grade level in their reading scores, excited about "graduating," and confident about entering the first grade. My success with these students led to my principal asking me to share my strategies with the other kindergarten teachers.

Travel Tip: To what (or whom) do you attribute your growth and success? In Genesis 32:10 Jacob prayed to the Lord, attributing his increase in family and wealth to God: "I am unworthy of all the kindness and faithfulness you have shown your servant. I had only my staff when I crossed this Jordan, but now I have become two groups."

Questions to Elicit Success Stories

Answers come when you are asked the right questions. Here are 20 questions to ask yourself that will help percolate great ideas for your success stories:

1. What are you most proud of in your career?

2. What are you most proud of in each of your past positions?

3. What challenge or crisis did you face on the job, and what was your approach for solving each situation?

4. In what way did you help your employer generate more revenue?

5. In what way did you help your employer save money?

6. In what way did you help your employer increase productivity?

7. What was the most interesting suggestion or project you initiated?

8. When were you complimented by a supervisor, co-worker, or customer?

9. What positive comments (or ratings) were documented in your performance evaluations?

10. When do people say to you, "You are amazing!" or "You make it look so easy!" or "How do you do that?"?

11. What skills or talents are you especially known for?

12. What kinds of work activities cause you to lose track of time?

13. What special projects or teams have you worked on?

14. How were goals and productivity measured on the job?

15. When did you go above and beyond the call of duty?

16. What do you do that your co-workers don't do? What would happen if you weren't on the job?

17. What would others point to as evidence of your success?

18. When did your actions motivate or influence others to do something that they initially did not want to do?

19. Under what circumstances did you display character and integrity?

20. When did you use your verbal communication skills to influence or improve a situation with a co-worker or team?

> **Travel Tip:** *Service* is at the heart of offering value. Christ reminds us that He did not come to be served, but to serve (Mark 10:45).

Network Meeting
Saturday, August 29, 2009

The Career Transition Ministry will conduct a
Network Meeting on August 29, 2009
at Parkhills Baptist Church.

Network meetings are held monthly at the church for facilitated
and informal networking, expert speakers on career
search topics, and access to local employers.

Everyone is welcome to participate.

Networking meetings offer encouragement, contacts and ideas to help
find a job, change careers and discover God's calling. The meeting
connects people at a crossroad in their career with one another and
with speakers and volunteers who can help them in their transition
process.

The meeting, beginning at 9:00am, will last 2 - 3 hours and features:

- Presentation of the 6 steps to walking through a
  crossroads in your career
- A career expert speaker
- Live testimony of someone who has
  experienced a career transition
- Facilitated networking time with other attendees
  and volunteers.

Participants will share ideas and exchange leads with others who are
going through career transitions while developing networking skills.

Contact Gary Shelton for more information
Email: shelton.gary01@gmail.com

To participate, please register at the Welcome Center
in the outer foyer or call the church office @ 494-5219.

Using the SMART Format to Answer Behavioral Interview Questions

Many interviewers prefer that you deliver your responses to behavioral interview questions using a format that first outlines what was happening, then what you did about it, followed by what resulted from your actions. Common variations on this format include the following:

- **STAR:** Situation/Task, Action, Result
- **CAR:** Challenge, Action, Result
- **PAR:** Problem, Action, Resolution

In coaching people for networking and interviewing, I've found that a variation on this format called the SMART Story™ works well. SMART stands for

- Situation and More
- Action
- Results
- Tie-in or Theme

A SMART Story will allow you to craft your interview responses with a definitive beginning, a middle, and a dynamite ending and provide the many details that interviewers are hungry to hear about. It also is unique in that the final step positions you to neatly link the response back to the employer's competency question, inquire further into the employer's needs, and focus the conversation on how you can *do* the job instead of simply *auditioning* for the job. Here's how it breaks out:

- **Situation and More:** Frame the story with contextual details, offering specific numbers about the situation. What was the specific situation you were faced with? Use numbers to describe who and what was involved. Where and when did it occur? What was the impact of the situation? What was the timeframe for the story?

- **Action:** What specific action did you take to tackle the task, overcome the challenge, or resolve the issue? If others were closely involved, how did you interact with them? What were your thoughts or decision-making processes? What was your specific role in relation to the team?

- **Results:** Essential to your success story are numbers-oriented, bottom-line results. They will help you convey your return-on-investment value and give you leverage in salary negotiations. Draw from the following questions to help identify your bottom-line results:

    - What measurable outcome was achieved? Think beyond your own work role to how others were impacted, including your boss, your team, your department, your company, your customers, your community, or your industry.

- If it was a group effort, what measurable outcome did the group achieve or contribute to? Did you contribute to a 5 percent increase in productivity; support a team that met or exceeded its goal by 9 percent in a difficult economy; participate in an effort that improved customer satisfaction scores; collaborate with team members to accomplish work with 25 percent less staff; or provide ideas that halted a conflict or impasse that had held up progress?

- If the outcome wasn't rosy, what conclusions did you reach or what positives did you learn from the experience?

- Compare your performance. You can make comparisons to a variety of numbers, including your prior work performance, the company's past record, the industry standard, or your competitor's average.

- **Tie-in or Theme:** Use a question or statement to link this story back to important issues or link it to a theme of key competencies sought by the employer. Statements such as these might convey enthusiasm or knowledge gained:

  - "I found that I thrive in these sorts of situations, as they give me a chance to use my problem-solving skills," or

  - "I learned that it's important to regularly communicate progress status to the various departments of the church, especially when the campus is so spread out and people don't see each other regularly," or

  - "From the conversation I had with one of your vendors, it sounds like my strengths in vendor relations would be of help."

An occasional question can also be effective in tying the story back to the employer's needs. For instance,

- "Would you like additional detail or another example?" or

- "How will this experience relate to your current needs?" or

- "Is the department encountering opportunities [or challenges] similar to the one I just described?"

The SMART Story format will help you structure your writing. It will take an investment of time to develop these stories, so keep in mind the payoff:

- Interviewers will be impressed because you offered tangible evidence of your success stories.

- Interviewers will remember you over other candidates who provided vague, unspecific responses.

- You will feel more comfortable and confident during interviews because you have tip-of-your-tongue evidence that documents your ability to do the job.

- You will be fully prepared to answer behavioral interview questions, which require tangible, step-by-step details about your behavior in past situations.

Note the numerous facts and figures included in the following SMART Stories:

SMART Story

Situation and More:	My role: *Production Worker*
	Where: *Wamco Manufacturing, my current employer*
	When/Timeframe: *January through March of this year*
	Who else was involved or impacted: *Production shift team of 10 and maintenance mechanic*
	What was the task or challenge: *I managed to work with outdated equipment that continually broke down and caused long downtimes. The company had been hit hard financially due to industry issues and didn't have the funds to invest in new equipment or even special maintenance.*
Action:	What was your thought process? What steps did you take? What decisions were made? Describe the sequence. *At first, we waited for the maintenance mechanic to come to fix things—sometimes that took a while because this guy had to cover our facility and another facility across town, since they had laid off the mechanic for the plant across town. If he was working on a problem at the second facility, it would take him hours to get to us. Sometimes, the boss would let us go home for the day. I hate waiting around, so after about the third or fourth breakdown, I talked to the maintenance mechanic and asked him if I could help. At first he said no. Then I asked him if I could just watch what he did. He said yes. It wasn't too complicated. So the next breakdown, the mechanic let me work with him on the repairs. Later on, when things broke down on the vacuum-seal line, I was able to work on it.*
Results:	Use numbers to relate your results. *There were at least three times this past month that I had the problem fixed, and we were back up and running in less than an hour. In the past, it might have taken two or three hours to fix it. Our manager wants a goal of 300 units per day, so in a few cases, we kept our production numbers up even with the breakdown. This past month, we made our production goals, which was the first time in several months. Some other factors came into play as well, but part of it was the repair work I did.*
Tie-in/Theme:	*I know that productivity is key to a profitable operation. Are your productivity numbers where you'd like them to be?*

(Competency Theme: *Initiative, problem-solving, teamwork, mechanical ability*)

SMART Story

Situation and More:	My role: *Vice President, Business Development Manager* Where: *State Bank & Trust* When: *The current calendar year, June 200x–May 200x* Who else was involved or impacted: *A 30-branch Northern State Community Banking District* What was the task or challenge: *I enjoy telling my "how I went bald" story! It started with being given the charge by my Senior VP to turn around a two-year history of double-digit declining revenues for the district. At the time, the district was ranked last among 17 for revenue performance and had been through four business development managers over the course of three years.*
Action:	What was your thought process? What steps did you take? What decisions were made? Describe the sequence. *Here's the storyboard. I piloted a new business-development program for the district, which included creating sales strategies for a full complement of products and services (commercial loans, trust and investment services, cash management services, retirement and depository accounts, government guarantee programs, computerized banking, and alliance banking). I scheduled a two-day meeting for the 30 branch managers in the district, and I used a very motivational "All-Star" theme. At the meeting, I created a vision for what could be accomplished, laid out the program, and then used interactive train-the-trainer systems so that they could teach the strategies to 150+ sales reps in the district. I laid down the challenge, telling them that if we reached our goal early, I would shave my head! I had already cleared this with the Senior VP.*
Results:	Use numbers to relate your results. *Bottom line, we secured 44 new customers with $16+ million in loan commitments approved, added nearly $4 million in deposits, and secured first-time fee revenue of $162,000 from establishing new international business. We broke all records for loan and deposit growth in the district's 30-year history and boosted the district's ranking from #17 among 17 to #2 in less than two years. And, yes, I was proud to be bald for a time!*
Tie-in/Theme:	*In visiting some of your branches, I had a few ideas about how fee-based revenue could be introduced.*

(Competency Theme: *Leadership, motivator, innovation, strategic, analytical, communication*)

SMART Story

Situation and More:	My role: *Mother*
	Where: *Home*
	When: *The past six years*
	Who else was involved or impacted: *Children, husband.*
	What was the task or challenge: *Adapting to my new role as mother after having had a record-setting career in sales.*
Action:	What was your thought process? What steps did you take? What decisions were made? Describe the sequence. *I remember the mind shift I had to go through when I first had my daughter. It felt odd to be out of the business world, where I had been regularly recognized for my sales abilities. Being so goal-driven, I knew that I had to have goals in place for myself. The goals I started with may not sound too exciting, but they were appropriate goals for that time of my life—things like not losing my patience when the baby had a fussy night, no small feat when you're seriously sleep deprived. A few years later, I graduated to bigger, more lofty goals, like "selling" broccoli to my 4-year-old!*
Results:	Use numbers to relate your results. *Bottom line, I recognized that an innate value for me is performance—setting and achieving goals—for every aspect of my life, whether personal or professional. It's what allowed me to rank among the top 10 percent in a region of 46 while in my last position at Cosamar, Inc.*
Tie-in/Theme:	*I know that my initiative and problem-solving skills will serve me well in the position you need to fill. Could you tell me a little more about the types of challenges I'd be tackling in this outreach position for your ministry?*

(Competency Theme: *Initiative, problem-solving, goal-oriented*)

Writing Your Success Stories

Use the blank forms that follow to capture your stories. Be generous with the contextual details. In the form, you'll see a Keywords & Competencies area. Leave it blank for now. You'll come back later to complete this section. Don't be concerned about finding the perfect wording or magic words at this stage. And remember that you'll be delivering these stories in verbal rather than written format. That means you don't have to be concerned about perfect punctuation or syntax as you write. Spoken language is far more flexible and forgiving than written language.

Before you get started on your stories, I want to make a somewhat unusual request. I'd like the first SMART Story that you write to be about your current job search situation. Write about the Situation and More in past tense, such as: "I conducted a job search while still employed, working a 60-hour workweek," or "I conducted a job search during a time when my industry had experienced a severe downturn." The Action, again in past tense, might include this: "I read *The Christian's Career Journey*, developed a solid set of success stories, networked beyond my comfort zone, enlisted the support of a job search group, and said 'no' to certain activities so that I could devote as many as 15 hours a week to my job search while I was also working full-time." The Result will be written in present tense. Make it a vision statement, such as this: "God brought me an employment situation in which I can be a witness of His love and work with a godly boss, performing radically rewarding work that is in sync with my gifts, interests, values, purpose, and personality." And, finally, tie it to a Theme: "The experience underscored my self-initiative and perseverance, gave me the ability to learn new research strategies, and sharpened my communication skills. In addition, I have an acute understanding that career success is all about tapping into God-inspired purpose and walking in obedience while providing value to employers."

After you've written about your current situation, you can then dive into your other SMART Stories.

Some Points to Guide You

These points will guide you in the writing process.

- **Use the "it's about them, not me" perspective when describing your stories.** This means that, ultimately, your SMART Stories must be related to "them"— the employer—and *their needs*. Think in terms of what will motivate the employer to buy, the return on investment you offer, and your benefits vs. features.

- **Use the same standards of quality that a judge or jury would accept.** Choose vivid examples, weave in expert testimony (for instance, from customers, co-workers, vendors, or supervisors), and incorporate appropriate statistics.

- **Write SMART Stories about your work for each of your past employers.** The heaviest concentration of stories should be about your current or most recent experiences. Pen a SMART Story for each recent accomplishment on your resume.

- **Assign themes to your SMART Stories that underscore competencies needed for the target position.** For instance, competencies for a customer service rep might include customer-focused orientation, interpersonal judgment, communication skills, teamwork, problem solving, listening skills/empathy, and initiative.

- **Write SMART Stories for nonwork experiences.** It is fair game to draw on volunteer work, school experiences, and general life incidents. (If you sense you need additional experience, identify and quickly act on how you can best prepare yourself through reading, attending a course, job-shadowing, volunteering, or taking a relevant part-time job.) Regardless of what point your career life is at, *everyone* should recollect influential or life-altering events throughout youth and adulthood. Write SMART Stories about these times.

- **Numbers speak louder than words!** Load the stories with numbers, dollar amounts, productivity measurements, comparisons, and the like. (Be cautious about conveying proprietary or confidential company information. In these cases, use year-to-date or quarterly comparisons and translate the numbers into percentages.) Be specific and offer proof. Instead of saying, "I learned the program quickly," make it crystal clear with language like this: "I studied the manual at night, and in three days, I knew all the basic functions; in two weeks I had mastered several of the advanced features; and by the end of the month, I had experienced operators coming to me to ask how to embed tables into another program."

- **Include emotions and feelings.** Yes, feelings. When describing the situation, don't be afraid to include details such as these: "The tension among the team was so serious that people were resigning"; "the morale was at an all-time low"; or "the customer was irate about receiving a mis-shipment that occurred because of our transportation vendor." When writing about emotions or feelings, be mindful *not* to whine or disparage anyone, even through a veiled reference.

- **Avoid personal opinions.** You can, however, include the opinion of a supervisor or another objective party. Instead of saying, "I believe my positive outlook really helped keep the customer happy," rely on someone else's opinion: "My supervisor commented in a memo how my outlook helped us save a key account that was in jeopardy of being lost. I have a copy of that memo if you'd like to see it."

- **Choose your words carefully.** There might be a tendency to say, "I was chosen to lead this project" when it would be more powerfully worded as, "The VP sought me out, from among 12 eligible specialists, to spearhead this critical project."

- **Pace the stories so that each is approximately two to three minutes in length.** Set up the story briefly with facts, place the greatest weight on the action portion of the story, wrap it up with numbers-driven results, and tie it back to the interviewer's needs. Occasionally, vary the delivery by dropping in a result at the front end of the story.

- **Make the stories relevant.** You have myriad experiences in your background. Sift through them and select the stories that best substantiate your competencies, knowledge, skills, and motivation to excel in the target job.

Remember to review the 20 questions listed earlier in case you encounter writer's block. Enjoy the process…and may you gain a clearer picture of your value and grow in confidence as the stories emerge!

TWO HEADS ARE BETTER THAN ONE!

If you prefer to collaborate on your SMART Stories, enlist the support of a colleague, mentor, or trusted friend. If you'd like to benefit from working with a professional coach who is also a Christian, see the list of coaches in Appendix A.

Catalog Your SMART Stories

I'd like you to develop a *minimum* of 10 stories. Sound like a lot? I want you to feel fully confident and completely prepared! DBM, a leading global workplace consulting firm, revealed that job seekers participated in five to seven interviews per job opportunity. Ten stories will get you started; however, if you anticipate in an extended series of interviews, consider writing 20 or more stories so that you have enough "ammunition" to shine throughout the process.

Complete the Situation and More, indicating your role, where (what company), when (what time period and for how long), who was involved or impacted, and what the specific situation was. Describe the Action taken, as well as the Results. Leave the Keywords & Competencies and Potential Interview Questions sections blank for now. You'll fill them in later as you link job postings or job descriptions to your various success stories. (You may make multiple photocopies of the SMART Story Worksheet or download the form from www.ChristianCareerJourney.com/journey.html.)

SMART STORY WORKSHEET

Situation and More:

Your role: _____

Where: _____

When: _____

Who else was involved or impacted: _____
_____

What was the task or challenge: _____
_____
_____
_____

Action:

What was your thought process? What steps did you take? What decisions were made? Describe the sequence.

_____

_____

_____

_____

_____

_____

Results:

Use numbers to relate your results.

_____

_____

Tie-in/Theme:

Keywords & Competencies:

_____

Potential Interview Questions:

_____

_____

_____

Rate Your Stories

After you've completed writing your SMART Stories, you can rate each one. For each story, give yourself a point for every item you can say "yes" to on this 10-point quiz.

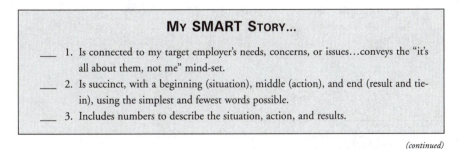

MY SMART STORY...

____ 1. Is connected to my target employer's needs, concerns, or issues...conveys the "it's all about them, not me" mind-set.

____ 2. Is succinct, with a beginning (situation), middle (action), and end (result and tie-in), using the simplest and fewest words possible.

____ 3. Includes numbers to describe the situation, action, and results.

(continued)

> **MY SMART STORY...** *(CONTINUED)*
>
> ____ 4. Documents specific competencies relevant to the position.
>
> ____ 5. Uses keywords common to the target job or industry.
>
> ____ 6. Frames the situation/task with contextual clues, such as the who, what, when, and where, as well as emotions or feelings present (without disparaging or blaming anyone).
>
> ____ 7. Provides interviewers with insight into my decision-making process and details the sequential steps I took.
>
> ____ 8. Is devoid of my personal opinions or intentions that I did not act on.
>
> ____ 9. Is specific, avoids vague phrases, and uses the active rather than passive voice.
>
> ___ 10. Is relevant to my career field, giving evidence that I can excel at meeting the deliverables the employer needs.

How did you score? If most of your SMART Stories earned a 9 or a perfect 10, reward yourself. If your stories scored in the 7–8 range, this is a great start. They will probably require the addition of a few details or numbers to become 9s or 10s. If most of your stories scored 6 or less, take a break and rest your brain a bit. When you come back, look at the pattern of the stories to determine where they can be reinforced, and edit wherever appropriate.

Chapter Wrap-Up

The Lord wants you to experience success—He made you to be the head, not the tail (Deut. 28:13)! You *can* cooperate with Him in that success by always being prepared. You should be feeling like the proverbial Eagle Scout by now! Know that the work you've completed in this chapter is key to "controlling the controllables"—the systems and steps that you can control in the job search process. Evidence-based success stories are at the heart of your interview message. When you're ready to move on, chapter 7 will help you convert your success stories into a cohesive career brand…one that can position you as a trusted expert, attract your ideal employer, and communicate the value of hiring you.

10 QUICK TIPS FOR CAPTURING YOUR VALUE

1. $E = MC^2$ in a job search context refers to Employment = Mechanics × Commitment-Squared, meaning that a job offer is gained through mechanics (strategies, systems, tactics) multiplied by a double dose of commitment (mind-set, emotional energy, attitude). Focusing on providing value to the employer is an essential employment strategy.

2. Avoid the most common mistake of candidates—going unprepared to interviews. A critical step in preparation is to craft relevant success stories.

3. Use the SMART Story method to structure relevant success stories, remembering to include contextual situational clues, sequential actions, numbers-driven results, and a tie-in to the employer's needs.

4. Translate your value into ROI (return on investment).

5. Tap into the 10 reasons employers are motivated to buy (hire you).

6. Focus on benefits rather than features to inject value into your stories.

7. Load your stories with numbers, such as year-to-year comparisons, records, past highs, past lows, target goals, size of project, number of persons involved, and budget or project figures (when not confidential).

8. Add flavor to your stories using emotion, humor, and metaphors.

9. Write S.O.S. responses that provide solutions or services. Keep humility and servanthood as the motives for all your stories.

10. Remember the mind-set mantra "them, not me" when writing your stories. Employers will filter everything they hear through the screen of "Will the candidate's skills help me?"

MASTERFUL COACHING QUESTIONS

As you review your success stories, where have you seen God's faithfulness? How does His faithfulness impact your walk during this period of career transition?

_____

_____

_____

Recall Proverbs 27:2, explained earlier in this chapter, and the importance of developing success stories from a servant perspective rather than a show-off or superstar perspective. Put a check next to the following statement that best reflects your thinking on this subject.

(continued)

MASTERFUL COACHING QUESTIONS *(CONTINUED)*

___ I don't give God much credit for my success because I'm the one who has gotten out there and done the work.

___ I serve, but my motive for serving is often to gain attention and be recognized for my abilities.

___ I continually seek God to maintain a heart of humility and give Him credit for any successes.

For further study on humility, read Philippians 2:5-8, Genesis 32:9-10, Psalm 18:27, Psalm 25:9, and Proverbs 3:34.

Jesus used parables to help people understand a kingdom truth and then apply it to their lives. Read the parable of the seed growing secretly or spontaneously in Mark 4:26-29. What truths do you see in this parable? How will you apply them to your life?

Pocket Prayer

Heavenly Father, thank you for being the Author of my ultimate success story, for You have redeemed me from a life of not knowing You and taken me to a place of provision and prosperity in Your presence. As I go about writing my SMART Stories, I acknowledge that You have punctuated my life story with many wonderful successes, along with some painful scenes. Thank you for those low points, as well as the high points, for all of them are learning opportunities for me to experience Your love and become more of who You want me to be. Bring to mind the successes I will write about for the exercises in this chapter. Remind me of how You have been there all along the way, faithfully helping and guiding me. May these SMART Stories honor You and Your faithfulness to me. In Jesus' name, Amen.

CHAPTER 7

COMMUNICATING YOUR VALUE VIA A CAREER BRAND

"Reputation is character minus what you've been caught doing."

—*Michael Lapoce*

"A good name is more desirable than great riches; to be esteemed is better than silver or gold."

—*Proverbs 22:1*

Great branding makes it easier to land new opportunities. With a strong brand, your reputation will precede you. It speaks of what you do well, and how you do it. It makes clear to employers that there are significant advantages to hiring you!

As we discuss branding in this chapter, let's start by looking at your reputation from God's perspective. What kind of reputation do you think God wants you to have?

One of my colleagues (not a follower of Christ) loves to discuss politics and religion. In a recent conversation, he was criticizing statements made by a prominent televangelist. I knew that trying to defend the televangelist would suck me into an argument that would be a lost cause. Instead, I calmly responded to my colleague with a suggestion that if he wanted to criticize Christians, he should do so by comparing their behavior to that of Christ, and not to that of other Christians. In fact, I laid down a light-hearted but serious challenge: I invited him to be blunt with me if he saw me doing *anything* that didn't align with Christ's teachings. (I know he will, but then we can talk about godly sorrow and forgiveness!) The only condition I asked of my colleague was that he study the life of Jesus in order to compare my shortcomings accurately.

Your co-workers may never darken the doorway of a church, but they will go to work every day. God wants your reputation to be Christ-like because you may be the only expression of Christ that people experience. As God's representative in the workplace, you should ensure that your career brand has attributes of Christ at its core: ethics above reproach, selflessness, servant leadership, humility, agape love, joy, initiative, productivity, and a depth of excellence to all you do. These and similar attributes of Christ should be the foundation on which all of Christ's followers build their brand.

As you build your brand, ask yourself these two questions:

- What abilities, attributes, and advantages do I want to be known for?
- What kind of employer do I want to connect with?

Your answers will capture the essence of what branding is all about: reputation and connection. Think of your brand as a distinctly individual image with a magnet attached to it. What unique combination of skills or competencies do people recognize in you? Why do people in the work world trust you? What value do you want to contribute to your world of work? What kind of employer will be drawn to, connect with, and pay a premium for that?

How Can a Career Brand Help?

Perhaps you're thinking, "I don't need a brand…I just need to land a job!" You might be surprised to learn that a brand *will* help you land a job because many of the same dynamics behind why a consumer chooses Crest over Colgate also apply in hiring.

The benefits of a brand are numerous. A compelling career brand can

- Make you more attractive to employers, even when there are no formal job openings (see the information in chapter 11 on networking)
- Control what interviewers remember most about you
- Elevate you from the status of commonplace commodity to one-of-a-kind, value-driven service
- Guide you in your decisions about which interviews to pursue
- Create employer desire to buy (hire)

What happens if you don't create a brand? Obviously, the opposite of everything in the preceding list. Worse yet, potential employers will determine your brand for you, and it might not be the brand you intended to project! With a few sound bites that bring your brand into focus, the employer is more likely to concentrate on the strengths or value you want him to see.

The Elements of Your Brand

No longer reserved for corporate giants, brands are now applicable to career-minded individuals with a commitment to excellence. For your brand to accomplish its purpose, it must knit together these three A's:

- Authentic Image
- Advantages
- Awareness

The good news is that you have already put in place the first two of the three A's. Your Authentic Image is the genuine you—not costumed to play the part of someone else, but cast in the role that God hard-wired you for—a role that allows you to be enthusiastically engaged in work that adds value to others. Your Master F.I.T. work in chapter 3 pointed you toward your Authentic Image. The second A, Advantages, is synonymous with benefits and value. You concentrated on identifying benefits and value in chapter 6, especially in writing numbers-oriented results for your SMART Stories™. The final A, Awareness, refers to communicating your brand in a manner that makes people attentive and responsive to it.

Authentic Image, Advantages, and Awareness add up to one word: *Marketing*. In a job search, you are the product and your employer-to-be is the consumer.

JOB SEARCH = MARKETING

In earlier chapters, the focus was on your gifts and what you can offer to an employer—your product, so to speak. Now it's time to look at your product through the eyes of consumers (employers) and their awareness and perception of your product. In this and future chapters, the focal point will be what the employer needs and whether the employer perceives that you can meet those needs better than others who are applying for the same position.

The Essence of Branding

The focus of this chapter is on how to make employers aware of, and how to communicate (or market), your career brand. We'll do that in two ways:

- Verbal branding
- Visual branding

Verbal Branding: Creating Your Sound Bites

Sound bites, like success stories, will help you feel prepared to meet any networking or interview situation. To be prepared for these and other job search conversations, equip yourself with three key sound bites:

- **Three-Point Marketing Message:** A succinct sound bite, less than 30 seconds, used to convey your unique key strengths and integrated throughout your resumes and cover letters, networking, informational interviews, and job interviews.
- **Verbal Business Card:** A succinct sound bite, less than 30 seconds, used in networking, informational interviewing, and job interviewing to articulate your goals and the benefits you offer.
- **Mini-Bio:** A short message, between one and two minutes, the elements of which can be mixed and matched to offer a relevant career capsule in networking, informational interviewing, or job interviewing.

Companies often communicate their brand in as few as three or four words with a pithy tagline (e.g., FedEx's "The World on Time" or Nike's "Just Do It"). Luckily, in job search, you'll be able to use more than a few words. Let's look at what those words should be.

Your Three-Point Marketing Message

A Three-Point Marketing Message is the most recyclable sound bite you'll use when networking and interviewing. You can use it again and again. The three-point message should be part of your response to the age-old interview request, "Tell me about yourself." It's also a great way to wrap up the interview and leave the interviewer with a clear message about your qualifications. You can weave the three points throughout your job search communications, including resumes, inquiry/approach letters, and follow-up letters. The following example is especially memorable because of its catchy alliteration:

Sound Bite of Three-Point Marketing Message:	As a sales representative for the hotel industry, my strengths lie in the areas of Research, Relationships, and Revenue Enhancement.

> **Travel Tip:** Ideally, your Three-Point Marketing Message should be customized for each employer. Remember, it's not about you; it's about them. Always connect your strengths to what the employer needs most.

Combining Your Three-Point Marketing Message with Other Job Search Tools

Figure 7.1 shows an example of how to integrate the three points into your resume. The strengths are listed under the Strengths subheading near the top of the resume.

You can also vary the wording on your Three-Point Marketing Message and combine it with a SMART Story:

Variation on Three-Point Marketing Message:	The reason I've exceeded quota in all my positions—and the reason I'm confident I would generate similar results for you—is that I home in on the three Rs of sales: Research, Relationships, and Revenue Enhancement.
SMART Story:	In my last position, where we were faced with stagnant revenues, my research skills helped me unearth a prospect list that included Fortune 1000 companies, including ABC Company, DEF Company, and GHI Company. I turned that cold data into warm leads, and gained access to decision makers at 9 of the 10 target companies. Bottom line, our revenue increased 45 percent during my tenure and our average sale increased 17 percent. Based on what you've told me about your operation, it sounds like research might be an area that you'd like to concentrate on first.

What Your Three-Point Marketing Message Should Include

Your Three-Point Marketing Message should convey your three most marketable selling points (if you use more than three, people won't remember them!). They are likely common themes in your SMART Stories or the focus of your resume. These three points might be functional strengths, unique experiences, or even soft skills. This social work case manager identified two functional strengths (counseling and teaching) and one soft skill (client advocacy) as part of her Three-Point Marketing Message:

Sound bite of Three-Point Marketing Message:	As a case manager with more than 15 years of experience, my greatest assets for this position are counseling, teaching, and client advocacy.

CHRIS CABALLERO

555 East Serena
Los Angeles, CA 90000

Relocating to Chicago

(555) 555-5555
c_caballero@hotmail.com

SALES / BUSINESS DEVELOPMENT

Hospitality ◆ Convention ◆ Meeting ◆ Visitors Bureau

Strengths:

Research—Developed qualified business leads using traditional and online research methods.
Relationships—Quickly established loyal and trusting relationships with key accounts and networking contacts.
Revenue Enhancement—Set new records for group and convention business at major-brand and boutique hotels.

PROFESSIONAL EXPERIENCE

Assistant Director of Sales—MAJOR HOTEL, Los Angeles, California 1/00–Present
(396-room property, with 42,000 sq. ft. of function space)

Manage more than $2 million in group business. Prospect and book national and state association accounts. Attend national and regional trade shows to increase market share. Travel 4–6 times per year for sales trips and trade shows. Coordinate familiarization trips with Bureau and hotel for lead generation. Exclusively sell and coordinate Rose Bowl group business. *Contributions:*

◆ Increased revenue 45% during tenure, with average sale up 17%.

◆ Delivered record group bookings first year in position, with 25,000 group room nights in 2000.

◆ Increased total bookings each subsequent year (despite challenge of post-9/11 market)…on track to close 32–34,000 group room nights this year.

◆ Maximized Rose Bowl business by working closely with Tournament of Roses Association and targeting Fortune 500 companies that sponsor floats and host VIPs. This year, sold out before July (in past years, sell-out occurred as late as December for this New Year's Day event), while also increasing minimum stay and rates.

◆ Expanded communications and working relationships with Convention & Visitors Bureau, gaining more business from special events such as the People's Choice Awards, Emmy Awards, and major Broadway shows.

National Sales Manager—GRAND HOTEL, Los Angeles, California 9/98–12/99
(800-room property, with 40,000 sq. ft. of function space)

Recruited to manage convention and group business within the Southeast Region. Prospected new business and expanded existing accounts. Traveled 6–8 times per year for sales trips and national trade shows. *Contributions:*

◆ Met and exceeded quota, earning maximum bonus for revenue increases.

National Sales Manager—EXCLUSIVE HOTEL, Los Angeles, California 11/96–9/98
(84-room boutique hotel located inside historic private club)

Developed and executed marketing plan to capture untapped group business. Established relationship with Bureau, offering niche-market services for convention-goers desiring full workout facilities in an upscale setting. *Contributions:*

◆ Grew group business from virtually nil to more than 2,500 room nights per year (record still unsurpassed).

Prior Experience with major brands—management trainee, convention service manager, sales manager.

EDUCATION, PROFESSIONAL DEVELOPMENT & AFFILIATIONS

BA, Sociology—Northwestern University (1995)
Seminars—Dale Carnegie, Professional Selling Skills (PSS), Professional Sales Negotiation (PSN), Hilton Sales College
CSAE (California Society of Association Executives)

Figure 7.1: A resume with a Three-Point Marketing Message integrated into it.

Travel Tip: When preparing your branding messages, follow the advice of Ecclesiastes 6:11: "The more the words, the less the meaning, and how does that profit anyone?"

Creating Your Message

What will your Three-Point Marketing Message be? Here's an easy two-step process to create your marketing message. First, select an introductory phrase. You can choose one of these or write your own:

- ❏ I've always been recognized for…
- ❏ My background is unique because…
- ❏ Throughout my career as a _____ [functional title], I've always been drawn to…
- ❏ At the heart of my experience are these three strengths…
- ❏ I am passionate about…
- ❏ Clients or co-workers frequently compliment me for…
- ❏ I'm very good at…

Second, add your three key points to the introductory phrase. Write them here:

1. _____
2. _____
3. _____

Now, combine the introductory phrase you selected previously with your three key points and write it here:

_____

_____

_____

Speak the Three-Point Marketing Message aloud. Make any adjustments needed until it feels comfortable and sounds strong.

Your Benefit-Driven Verbal Business Card, or "What's in It for Me [the Employer]?"

Similar to the focus statement you developed in chapter 4, a benefit-driven Verbal Business Card helps networking contacts or employers recognize both the type of opportunity you want and the benefits you bring to the table. Hiring managers are tuned to radio station WIFM, or "what's in it for me?" Now's your chance to tell them. In the preceding chapter, I listed 10 employer buying motivators (also known as benefits), each of which addresses the employer's profit need or pain point—a situation in which the employer is hurting and needs help solving a problem. When you focus on benefits, you

- Appear business-savvy
- Connect with the employer
- Indicate your understanding of the need for profitability and productivity
- Demonstrate a track record for contributing to the bottom line

What benefits do you bring to a prospective employer? What are you better at than others who have similar credentials? What "invisible" factors might be behind your success? The answers to these questions will strategically reposition you from run-of-the-mill to out-of-the-ordinary.

I'd like you to brainstorm ideas on how you can benefit an employer in each of the 10 buying motivations. To illustrate that this exercise isn't just for people in executive or sales positions, table 7.1 shows examples for an administrative assistant who worked in a small real estate office.

Table 7.1: Examples Tied to Employer Buying Motivators

Employer Buying Motivator	Example of Brainstorming on Solutions or Services That Benefit My Target Employers
Buying Motivator #1: Make Money	Worked overtime to help boss close a multi-million-dollar real estate transaction that generated $240,000 in commission.
	Developed administrative systems that supported a new fee-based consulting line of business for the company. Revenues on this grew from start-up to $60,000 in one year.
Buying Motivator #2: Save Money	Shopped for better pricing on office supplies.
	Cut costs on key expenses by approximately 10 percent.
Buying Motivator #3: Save Time	Wrote and cataloged standardized word-processing clauses to speed document processing and project completion. System saved an average of 20 percent time.

Now it's your turn. Take a blank sheet of paper and create your own table based on "The Employer's 10 Motivations to 'Buy'" listed in chapter 6 (or download the blank form "My Benefits That Relate to Employer Buying Motivators" at www.ChristianCareerJourney.com/journey.html). List as many benefits as come to mind for each of the Employer Buying Motivators. Remember to make it an S.O.S. (Solutions Or Services) response whenever possible (see chapter 6).

To finalize your Verbal Business Card, combine your Master F.I.T.™ Function and Industry targets from chapter 3 with the benefit ideas you just created. Table 7.2 shows how the Verbal Business Card elements relate to each of the elements from chapter 3:

Table 7.2: Elements and Wording of a Verbal Business Card

Element	Sample Wording
Function	I'm a communications professional targeting director-level opportunities with…
Industry	industrial manufacturers…
Benefit (linked to Buying Motivators #1 and #7)	where I can leverage my track record for developing award-winning creative teams and delivering record returns on marketing communications.

Use the following worksheet to create your Verbal Business Card.

MY VERBAL BUSINESS CARD

Element	Draft Wording
Function	I'm a _____ targeting _____ opportunities
Industry	in the _____ industry
Benefits	that will allow me to _____ _____ _____ _____

Your Mini-Bio

The final sound bite to be crafted for your verbal branding is a short biography, which we'll call a Mini-Bio. Also known as an "elevator pitch," this is another sound bite you'll need to have down pat. Some (but not all) of these elements will appear in your bio:

- Three-Point Marketing Message
- Number of years of experience

- Prestigious employer(s)
- Title or functional area
- Scope of responsibility (budget, staff, special projects)
- Verbal Business Card
- Key selling points or strengths
- Key accomplishments
- Impressive educational degree or credentials
- Fulfillment/purpose/mission statement
- SMART Stories
- Tagline
- Inquiry/call to action

Building on the communication professional's example cited previously, let's look at how these elements can come to life. In table 7.3, the left column notes the element, whereas the right column breaks down the Bio.

Table 7.3: Elements and Wording for a Mini-Bio

Element	Sample Wording
Verbal Business Card	I'm a communication professional targeting director-level opportunities with industrial manufacturers where I can leverage my track record for developing award-winning creative teams and delivering record returns on marketing communications.
Number of years of experience	Over the past 10 years,
Prestigious employer(s)	I've worked with the region's leading lighting manufacturer
Title or functional area	in senior-level positions as an Advertising Manager and Director of Communications
Scope of responsibility	with charge of a staff of 25 and six-figure project budgets.
Sound bite of Three-Point Marketing Message	Throughout my career as a creative director, I've been recognized for my expertise in advertising strategy, project management, and creative development.
Key accomplishments (tied to Three-Point Marketing Message)	I can offer some examples if you'd like. As an advertising strategist, I delivered an ROI of 15:1 on marketing funds, which, as you know, is well above average.

Element	Sample Wording
	As a project manager, I have numerous contacts with artists, copywriters, and printers and have a track record for bringing projects in on time and on a shoestring budget. It wasn't unusual for me to save $5,000 on printing costs when our total budget was $25,000.
	And, because of my strong creative background, many of the campaigns I directed earned national advertising awards.
Tagline	I'm known for turning ideas into dollars.
Inquiry/call to action (use when speaking to a networking contact)	What companies come to mind that might benefit from someone with my background? OR What companies are you aware of that are doing interesting work with their marketing communications?

You're allowed some wiggle room with the length of your Mini-Bio. It can be about a minute or two. Keep in mind that if it's too short, you won't be able to give people a good sense of who you are, what you're looking for, and what you can do for others. If it's too long, you'll confuse people and risk sounding long-winded.

Travel Tip: Get a tagline! Some job seekers borrow (with appropriate credit) company taglines or corporate references to describe themselves. For instance, a project manager conveyed his track record in this way: "My boss likes to call me Mr. FedEx because I have a reputation for delivering projects on time."

Create your Mini-Bio using the outline of elements in table 7.3 (or download the blank form "Elements of My Mini-Bio" at www.ChristianCareerJourney.com/ journey.html). At this point, develop material for each element; however, you do *not* have to use every element when you introduce yourself. In fact, it will sound too wordy if you do. Instead, you can mix and match the different elements so that you have some variety when speaking to people. This should be a fairly simple exercise because you have already developed much of the information needed.

Practice delivering your Bio. Start by practicing alone in front of a mirror. Then ask someone to critique you. Know the material inside and out, backward and forward. Make adjustments until you can comfortably deliver it without feeling like you're a telemarketer following a script!

Travel Tip: Need help with branding? Check out the Reach Certified Personal Brand Strategists at www.reachcc.com. Professionals committed to assisting you excel, these strategists exude a passion for personal branding and understand the power that branding has to enhance your career.

Visual Branding: Look and Act the Part!

In chapter 5, when describing the Uncover phase of a job search, I tipped you off that you would be judged on three dimensions: competency, chemistry, and compensation. The second dimension, chemistry, requires a reciprocal connection between you and the company (watch for that "goose-bumpy" feeling, also known as "Godbumps," described in chapter 3!). Yes, *your* opinion of the company does count in this matter! You must connect with the company, its people (especially the hiring manager), and its customers. The converse is also true. The company's people (again, especially the hiring manager) must connect with you. In visual branding, we'll concentrate on how your visuals—image and dress—can create some good chemistry.

Your Image

Entering a room to meet a new employer can be like walking into a whole new chapter of your life. At that moment, you can influence the employer's perception of you based on your actions, attitudes, and attire. Of course, God can also grant you favor in the eyes of the employer, as illustrated in Daniel 1:9. I like to coach my clients to act with humble confidence, "as if" they are already doing the job they are targeting.

To confidently act the part, you'll need a clear description of the image you want to project. One of the best ways to do this is to look for role models. Who in your industry do you admire? Who is successfully doing the type of work you want to do? Even better, who is a notch above the role you'd like to be in?

Travel Tip: Role models are important! When employers are ready to interview, the first place they go to is the desk of their top performers. Hiring managers painstakingly analyze top performers to determine the behaviors and competencies that make them so successful. In turn, those behaviors and competencies will be the high-water mark you're measured against. Find and emulate a successful role model and you'll see your career move forward faster.

After you've identified a role model or two, study them and respond to the questions in the column "What I Admire About the Role Model," in table 7.4. It's sometimes difficult to see yourself as others perceive you. To give you a fresh perspective, compare yourself with your role model(s) by completing the column "Success Traits I Already Possess." In the final column, itemize some of the choices you can make to enhance your image. In approaching this exercise, make sure that your self-talk is inspirational and encouraging (your language should sound like the words of God), not critical and disapproving (your language should not sound like the words of the enemy).

If needed, enlist the support of a trusted colleague on this role model exercise. If you do solicit a support partner, make sure you choose someone who will be respectful and kind, yet direct and honest—someone with a heart for helping people become all that they can be. First, ask the person to tell you what you're doing right. Then, give the person permission to tell you things you might not want to hear. Further, give permission to point out where this person senses you're resisting change. We cannot change until we are aware of what we need to change!

Finally, let me make perfectly clear that I'm *not* asking you to become a clone. God intricately designed you so that you would be unique, one-of-a-kind. Instead, I'm suggesting that you adopt elements of what you like best from others to enhance your own individuality and marketability.

BUGGED BY BEING COMPARED TO OTHERS?

It is frustrating to think that people are judging you based on your image. However, the reality is that image does factor into the hiring process—even if it isn't supposed to. In the hiring game, when two candidates have equal skills and one has an image that fits better with the company, the candidate with the right chemistry will get the job. Candidates who don't examine this topic with fresh eyes put themselves at a disadvantage.

Your Wardrobe

Remember that corporate America uses colors and visual images as part of its branding. In career branding, your colors and visual images are communicated through your wardrobe. As we discuss wardrobe, consider that your attire for the interview shouldn't be an anomaly, like a one-night tuxedo rental for a special occasion. One candidate dressed beautifully for an interview and, once hired, didn't don a suit coat again, much to the chagrin of the executive team. Your interview attire should be part of who you are, as well as who you are committed to becoming.

 Travel Tip: Modesty is becoming a lost art, sad to say, even in churches. Avoid clingy, see-through fabrics and low-cut blouses. Even if it's in fashion to show some tummy, don't do it in the workplace. And wear the right size—squeezing into snug clothing will make you look heavier than you really are!

Table 7.4: Positive Traits of Role Models

Questions	What I Admire About the Role Model	Success Traits I Already Possess	Choices I Can Make to Enhance My Image
How would you describe this person?			
What action does he or she take that causes success?			
What does he or she do that grows his or her walk with the Lord?			
What do you like about the way your role model treats others?			

Questions	What I Admire About the Role Model	Success Traits I Already Possess	Choices I Can Make to Enhance My Image
What is this person's mind-set and attitude?			
Who does he or she associate with?			
How does your role model dress? (style, colors, and so on)			
What is this person's posture like? How does he or she stand, walk, sit?			

(continued)

Table 7.4: Positive Traits of Role Models *(continued)*

Questions	What I Admire About the Role Model	Success Traits I Already Possess	Choices I Can Make to Enhance My Image
How does your role model communicate with others? What, and how much, does he or she say? Not say?			
Is there something about the way this person spends his or her lunch or free time that feeds success?			
What does your role model *not* do (for example, making excuses, blaming others, stretching the truth, and so on)?			

With business attire across the board these days, a one-size-fits-all recommendation on this subject won't fit. Use good judgment. Assess the type of companies you'll be targeting and dress to their standards. Image experts offer varying advice regarding dressing for interviews. Some counsel you to dress a little nicer than the norm for the business; others advise you to dress the same as your interviewer, just cleaner! Either can work.

NOT-SO-EXTREME MAKEOVERS

If you're in the market for an image update, enlist the support of an expert. One of my trusted authorities on the subject is Mary Ann Dietschler (www. CoachMaryAnn.com), a Christian coach who is able to work long-distance around the areas of image and visual branding.

Chapter Wrap-Up

With the work accomplished thus far, I can guarantee that you will shine and stand out. Why? Because many job seekers have tunnel vision when it comes to job search—they see it as an isolated career event, the focus of which is writing a resume and then hoping that the resume will generate some interviews.

In reality, job search is a holistic, big-picture process marked by a series of business meetings between you and networking contacts, and ultimately you and the hiring decision maker. The focus of these meetings is on achieving an outcome where both parties get their needs met. The employer wants value or return on investment, and you want a good *fit* where you can be radically rewarded and enthusiastically engaged in work that adds value to others. This win-win perspective gives you equal footing with employers and adds to your confidence and bargaining power.

So, celebrate! Over the past few chapters, you have made several achievements:

- Created an attainable goal backed by a focused (yet flexible) plan
- Intelligently targeted a position that takes into account your Master F.I.T. (functional strengths/gifts and fulfillment, industry and interests, things that matter, and personality type)
- Developed success stories and sound bites that focus on benefits (solutions or services) and value (return on investment and employer buying motivators)
- Taken steps to look and act the part with a cohesive image and compelling career brand

You've completed Phase I, the Analyze phase, of a job search, as well as much of Phase II, the Express phase (see chapter 5 for "Five Phases of a Job Transition"). The Express phase also includes writing your resume. Let's keep the momentum going and move on to chapter 8!

10 QUICK TIPS FOR COMMUNICATING YOUR CAREER BRAND

1. Job search is marketing. You are the product and the employer is the consumer. A clear and compelling career brand helps employers perceive the benefits of your product, giving you an advantage in the job market.

2. Successful career brands weave together three A's: Authentic image, Advantages, and Awareness. Project an image of your authentic self (the person God gifted you to be!), focus on the advantages the employer receives from you getting the job done, and make employers aware of those advantages. At the core of your brand should be Christ-like attributes.

3. Branding can be accomplished through verbal and visual means. Verbal branding includes your sound bites and success stories, whereas visual branding is accomplished through your actions, attitude, and attire.

4. Hone your product benefits into a Three-Point Marketing Message that conveys your unique strengths. This is a critical sound bite.

5. Create a Verbal Business Card to keep you focused, help networking contacts know how to help you, and explain your value to interviewers. Align your statement with employer buying motivators.

6. Mix and match your success stories and sound bites to create a comfortable yet compelling Mini-Bio. Consider using a tagline that helps people remember you in a unique and favorable light.

7. Practice. You must be able to deliver your sound bites naturally, without appearing as though you've memorized a script.

8. Visual branding means you must look the part. Ask for wardrobe advice from someone who is successful and has a good sense of style. If you're uncertain about how to dress for interviews or networking, err on the side of formality.

9. Visual branding also means you must act the part. Candidly evaluate your mind-set, beliefs, behaviors, and attitudes. Are these consistent with those of others in your field who have attained notable success?

10. Find a person or two who will respectfully and selflessly support you in your commitment to shaping and enhancing your ideal brand, as well as hold you accountable for having Christ-like attributes as the core of your brand.

MASTERFUL COACHING QUESTIONS

Envision life a year or two down the road. As you grow personally and develop your ideal image, what do you want your reputation to be? What do you anticipate the rewards to be? Be specific with respect to the positive impacts on your walk with the Lord, career, work relationships, personal relationships, self-esteem, finances, and so on.

_____

_____

_____

_____

Thinking back to the role model exercise earlier in this chapter, who can support you in achieving this goal?

_____

_____

In the next seven days, what small step can you take to get started toward your ideal image?

_____

_____

If you want to dig deeper on the topic of reputation/branding, read the book of Esther. What did Mordecai have a reputation for and how did he use this reputation in his career (see Esther 9:4, 20-23 and 10:2-3)?

_____

_____

Think about it! The King James Version of Philippians 2:7 describes Christ as making himself of "no reputation," taking on the form of a servant and being made in the likeness of man (Phil. 2:5-8). Get together with your accountability partner or career supporters and discuss this question: As followers of Christ, we know that He is our role model, so how do we make ourselves of "no reputation" and still thrive in today's business world?

_____

_____

_____

Pocket Prayer

Father, thank you for making me in Your image. As I work on furthering the brand and reputation that You want me to have, let it be, first and foremost, founded on You. May Christ-like characteristics be the bedrock of my brand—love, selflessness, servanthood, humility, perseverance, peace. Show me the areas that I need to work on and master as part of my personal brand. Produce those things in me that will make me of value to the work-world, and teach me how to communicate my value proposition with confidence yet humility. Thank you for finishing the good work You have begun in me. In Jesus' name, Amen.

CHAPTER 8

THE BLUEPRINT FOR A MASTERFUL RESUME

"Planning must be a deliberate prelude to writing."

—*E. B. White, author*

E. B. White is the coauthor of *The Elements of Style,* a "bible" for anyone who writes for a living or, for that matter, anyone who writes at all. White proposes that the first principle of composition is to "determine the shape of what is to come and pursue that shape." Just as an architect prepares blueprints before a contractor can build, you need an outline before you can write.

In this chapter, you'll decide on the format, or structure, of your resume, and then select the categories, or building blocks, that make up a masterful resume.

Résumé Magic, my first book that launched the *Magic* Series (also published by JIST), provides a comprehensive look at resume writing. At nearly 600 pages, it offers answers to virtually any resume question or quandary. Highlights from the book are included in the next few chapters.

The One Hard-and-Fast Rule for Resume Writing

Assemble a dozen hiring managers in a room and ask them their preferences for resumes, and you'll get a dozen different answers. Should it be one page or two? Should it be sent by snail mail or e-mail? Should older employment history be included if you have a work history of 20-plus years? You'll see many of the answers to these questions in a survey of employers' resume preferences in the next chapter, but the one item that is critically important, especially for Christians, is this:

> Don't lie on your resume.

Honesty is the best policy—it creates trust (2 Kings 12:15). In other words, don't mislead, don't stretch the truth, and don't take credit for things you didn't do. Business leaders much prefer you to tell the truth, not what you think they want to hear (see 1 Kings 22:16 for a similar story about the King of Israel wanting his prophet Micaiah to be honest with him and not just tickle his ears).

Be painstakingly accurate about resume details and double-check numbers related to your accomplishments. And on that subject, don't reveal financial details such as sales numbers or total market share if you've worked for a private company because this is confidential information.

You'll see the "don't lie" rule documented in the following sidebar, under items 3 and 25.

---

25 PET PEEVES AND COMMON RESUME MISTAKES NOTED BY SOME OF AMERICA'S TOP EMPLOYERS

Type of Offense	Comments from Staffing Professionals from Top U.S. Companies
Content	1. Leaving out dates
	2. No chronological listing of work
	3. Overstatement of responsibility
	4. Too much detail, usually around job descriptions
	5. Summary of work history by type instead of listing the exact company and job performed
	6. Baseless description of personal strengths
	7. Entitlement mentality ("I have my degree; I'm sharp; what can you do for me?")
Accomplishments	8. No accomplishments listed, only job duties
	9. Statements of accomplishments without a clear indication of where or when they were made

Type of Offense	Comments from Staffing Professionals from Top U.S. Companies
	10. Pumped up to look as if the candidate has qualifications that he or she does not possess
	11. Accomplishments separated from work history so that it's not clear what was done where
Visual	12. Fancy fonts
	13. Photo included
	14. Graphics
Grammar, Technical	15. Typos
	16. Misspellings
	17. Fluff wording
	18. Poor grammar
	19. Incomplete sentences
Organization	20. Disorganized
	21. Too long
	22. Two pages from beginners
	23. Poor organization
	24. Lack of clear direction, focus
	25. Covering up or lying about gaps in employment or lack of degree

Two Tried-and-True Winning Formats: Chronological and Functional

Ninety-nine percent of business resumes fall into one of two distinct genres: chronological or functional. (The other 1 percent can be lumped into a "creative" category, reserved for those artistic gurus who have been blessed with extra right-brain gray matter!)

The Chronological Format

Just as its name implies, the chronological format offers a chronology—a historical timeline—of your work experience. The chronological format wins "The People's Choice Award." Why? Plain and simple: Employers prefer it! In economic parlance, the buyer (your prospective employer)—who usually holds the upper hand in the supply-demand model—can better evaluate what the seller (you, the candidate) has to offer. Most hiring managers have an innate curiosity about what you've done and where you've done it. A logical, straightforward chronological format answers their questions.

A Chronological Format Worked for David

Because the chronological is the most common format, you're probably familiar with its look. Nonetheless, check out David Dillingham's resume for a *Before* (figure 8.1) and *After* (figure 8.2) of a standard chronological format. Compare how bullets are used in the *Before* and *After* resumes. This sales tool worked for David, landing him a job with a leading textbook publisher.

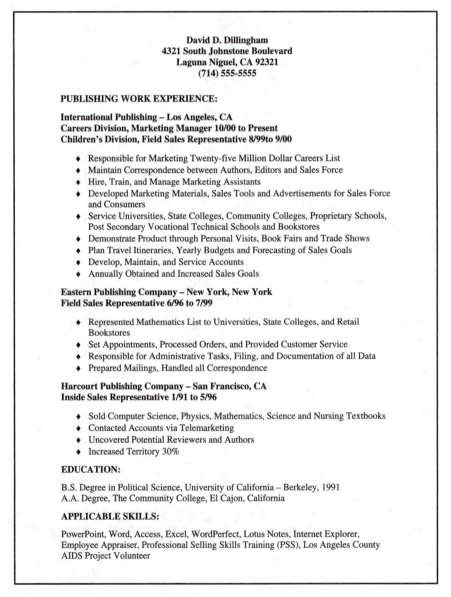

David D. Dillingham
4321 South Johnstone Boulevard
Laguna Niguel, CA 92321
(714) 555-5555

PUBLISHING WORK EXPERIENCE:

International Publishing – Los Angeles, CA
Careers Division, Marketing Manager 10/00 to Present
Children's Division, Field Sales Representative 8/99to 9/00

- ◆ Responsible for Marketing Twenty-five Million Dollar Careers List
- ◆ Maintain Correspondence between Authors, Editors and Sales Force
- ◆ Hire, Train, and Manage Marketing Assistants
- ◆ Developed Marketing Materials, Sales Tools and Advertisements for Sales Force and Consumers
- ◆ Service Universities, State Colleges, Community Colleges, Proprietary Schools, Post Secondary Vocational Technical Schools and Bookstores
- ◆ Demonstrate Product through Personal Visits, Book Fairs and Trade Shows
- ◆ Plan Travel Itineraries, Yearly Budgets and Forecasting of Sales Goals
- ◆ Develop, Maintain, and Service Accounts
- ◆ Annually Obtained and Increased Sales Goals

Eastern Publishing Company – New York, New York
Field Sales Representative 6/96 to 7/99

- ◆ Represented Mathematics List to Universities, State Colleges, and Retail Bookstores
- ◆ Set Appointments, Processed Orders, and Provided Customer Service
- ◆ Responsible for Administrative Tasks, Filing, and Documentation of all Data
- ◆ Prepared Mailings, Handled all Correspondence

Harcourt Publishing Company – San Francisco, CA
Inside Sales Representative 1/91 to 5/96

- ◆ Sold Computer Science, Physics, Mathematics, Science and Nursing Textbooks
- ◆ Contacted Accounts via Telemarketing
- ◆ Uncovered Potential Reviewers and Authors
- ◆ Increased Territory 30%

EDUCATION:

B.S. Degree in Political Science, University of California – Berkeley, 1991
A.A. Degree, The Community College, El Cajon, California

APPLICABLE SKILLS:

PowerPoint, Word, Access, Excel, WordPerfect, Lotus Notes, Internet Explorer, Employee Appraiser, Professional Selling Skills Training (PSS), Los Angeles County AIDS Project Volunteer

Figure 8.1: Before.

DAVID D. DILLINGHAM

4321 Johnstone Boulevard   (714) 555-5555
Laguna Niguel, CA 92321   ddd234@excite.com

SALES & MARKETING

Publishing Industry

SALES & MARKETING EXPERIENCE

MARKETING MANAGER—International Publishing, Los Angeles, CA   2000–Present

Manage marketing for $25 million careers list. Develop product strategies, marketing materials, sales tools, and advertisements for international sales force of 500. Hire, train, and manage marketing assistants. Forecast and manage operating budgets and sales goals. Personally sell to and service universities and retail booksellers. Promote product at trade shows and book fairs.

- Delivered 27% sales growth through development of innovative international marketing strategies.

- Doubled individual sales volume from $149,000 to $312,000, an unprecedented increase for territory.

- Led region of 10 reps in sales volume, achieving 22% above goal (well above company average of 8%).

- Initially challenged with turnaround of product line that had not been serviced in over a year; successfully converted key clients from primary competitor and captured new nationwide sales.

FIELD SALES REPRESENTATIVE—Eastern Publishing Company, New York, NY   1996–2000

Generated sales for Mathematics Division in seven western states and three Canadian provinces.

- Gained access to prestigious clients, such as Stanford University and UC Berkeley (previously "no see" accounts).

- Increased sales in territory that had a several-year history of stagnant sales.

INSIDE SALES REPRESENTATIVE—Harcourt Publishing Company, San Francisco, CA   1991–1996

Promoted 100+ item catalogue of computer science, physics, mathematics, science, and nursing textbooks to college bookstore market in California, Nevada, and Oregon.

- Increased territory sales 30% to rank #1 in division (with no prior industry knowledge).

- Researched and uncovered potential reviewers and new authors.

EDUCATION & TRAINING

Bachelor of Science, Political Science—University of California, Berkeley   1991
Professional Selling Skills Training (PSS)

COMPUTER SKILLS

MS Office (PowerPoint, Word, Excel, Access), WordPerfect, Lotus Notes, MSIE, Employee Appraiser

♦ ♦ ♦

Figure 8.2: After.

A Chronological Format for a Ministry Position

This chronological resume (figure 8.3), created for a director of worship, is presented in a two-column format. Endorsements are presented in the left margin and traditional content in the right.

JEREMY JAY

♫ ♫ ♫ ♫ ♫

1234 Paradise Lane
Los Angeles, CA 91234
jjay@gmail.com
Home: (213) 555-1212
Cell: (213) 555-1313

"Jeremy has been instrumental in helping me make a deeper commitment to the Lord."

—Elizabeth Bentley, Choir Member

"Jeremy would be a great asset to any ministry organization. His gifts for leading congregations into intimate worship are truly God-given, and he uses them in humility and quiet strength."

—Blaine Stevens, Senior Pastor, South Hills Community Church

"Jeremy skillfully created blended worship experiences that have bridged the generational gap and given our congregation an increased sense of unity and mission."

—Bill Smithers, Chairman of the Deacon Board, South Hills Community Church

DIRECTOR OF WORSHIP

Passionate, innovative, and committed worship leader experienced in designing services that lead people into the presence of our life-changing God!

EDUCATION

♫ **Master's Degree: Music Ministry**—Seattle Pacific University
♫ **Bachelor's Degree: Music History**—San Francisco Conservatory of Music

EXPERIENCE

Director of Worship and Creative Arts   2006–Present
South Hills Community Church, Los Angeles, CA

Direct intergenerational worship, integrating arts and music ministries. Lead worship for three Sunday-morning services (attendance of approx. 1,000) and two midweek services.

♫ Cast a Biblical vision for dynamic worship and introduced drama and praise dance into worship experiences.

♫ Developed two new teams of worship artists to meet the needs of a new contemporary Saturday-evening service—attendance has grown from a handful at startup to 300+ each week.

♫ Supported urban outreach teams with a series of live outdoor concerts the past two summers, with more than 200 commitments made to Christ.

♫ Facilitated new music and worship ideas for church's annual Resurrection Celebration and Christmas Candlelight programs.

♫ Initially brought on as Choir Director and promoted in 18 months after existing Director of Worship retired.

PRIOR EXPERIENCE

Music Minister (part-time)   2004–2006
Faith Hills, Agora Hills, CA

♫ Led worship services for new church plant, a satellite church of Faith Bible Church.

Music Instructor, Grades 7–12   2002–2006
Lighthouse Christian Schools, Irvine, CA

♫ Taught junior high and high school concert band and marching band.

MUSICAL SKILLS

♫ **Primary:** Piano/Keyboard and Voice
♫ **Secondary:** Guitar and Wind Instruments (Flute, Saxophone, Oboe)

RECORDINGS

♫ **Let All the Earth Rejoice, CD**
♫ **Living in the Promised Land, CD**

Figure 8.3: Chronological format for a director of worship.

The Functional Format

A functional resume relies on categorical, skills-based sections to demonstrate your qualifications for a particular job. Company names, employment dates, and position titles are either de-emphasized or intentionally omitted. If your professional pilgrimage hasn't been a straightforward climb up the corporate ladder, give serious consideration to a functional format.

A Functional Format Helped Grace Get a New Life

Grace needed a change. Fragile after a messy divorce, she opted to leave her teaching career and explore other career options to give her a change of pace. Her new resume, a strong example of a functional format, landed her an "incubator" position (recall the term from chapter 4) in the tourism industry that was fun and upbeat. Here are Grace's *Before* (figure 8.4) and *After* (figure 8.5) resumes.

 Travel Tip: To determine the best resume format for your situation, take the "Resume Format Quick Quiz" at www. ChristianCareerJourney.com/resume_magic.html. Weigh the pros and cons of each format when determining which to use.

Now that you've selected a format, let's move on to the categories for your resume.

GRACE COLTERMAN

One Riverplace Parkway
Selton, Alabama 42315
(423) 413-9887

OBJECTIVE	Teacher: Elementary Education (K–8)
EDUCATION	UNIVERSITY OF ALABAMA
	Degree: Bachelor of Arts, Public Relations / Journalism – 1987
	Honors: Dean's List; Greek Leadership Award;
	Outstanding College Students of America
CREDENTIAL	Multiple Subject Clear Credential – 1989

EXPERIENCE

Teaching Experience

Alton Unified School District, Alton, Alabama   9/92–Pres.
1st Grade Teacher
Plan and implement integrated curriculum in all subject areas. Utilize Project READ, a multisensory approach to reading with emphasis on phonology strategies. Applied Rebecca Sitton's Integrated Spelling & Writing program, focusing on daily writing across the curriculum. Taught core literature books using whole language approach and incorporating McCracken Reading ideas.

Mifflin Union High School, Mifflin, Alabama
3rd Grade Teacher   9/91–6/92
Applied current teaching techniques, including AIMS projects, manipulatives, writing process, and cooperative learning. Implemented the Total Reading Program, a multi-sensory phonetic reading program that emphasizes development of reading, language, and spelling skills. Developed and taught units on reptiles, Indians, and Mifflin County; integrated all curricula areas and culminated in group experiences with the entire 3rd grade. Taught segments of a Physical Education course in a pilot cooperative teaching program.

Kindergarten Teacher   9/89–6/91
Utilizing a thematic approach, created and taught lessons incorporating programs such as Math Their Way, Project AIMS, Come With Me Science, and Sunshine/Story Box with big book illustrations emphasizing whole language. Administered the Brigance testing format; gathered parent input to determine children's classroom readiness prior to new school year.

Student Teaching

Atherton School District, Atherton, Alabama
2nd Grade Teacher — Sterling Elementary School   3/89–5/89
4th Grade Teacher — McKinley Elementary School   1/89–3/89

RELATED ACTIVITIES

Alton Unified School District, Alton, Alabama
- Served on School Site Council.
- Coordinated school-wide Speech Festival and Peach Blossom Oral Interpretation and Speech Festival.
- Participated in Learning Club, a monthly group for 1st graders and their parents; program focuses on introducing math and reading activities to parents that can then be reinforced with students at home.

INTERESTS

Coaching (Cross-Country) • Public Speaking • Yearbook Publications

Figure 8.4: Before.

GRACE COLTERMAN

One Riverplace Parkway

Selton, Alabama 42315

gracec@juno.com

(423) 413-9887

GOAL

Customer support position where my strengths in communications, sales, and administration will be of value.

PROFESSIONAL EXPERIENCE

COMMUNICATIONS: *Public Relations, Advertising, Training, Staff Development*

* *Degree in Public Relations/Journalism:* Completed comprehensive training in public relations, including advanced course work in mass communications, newswriting, editing, advertising, media, and graphic arts.

* *Writing/Verbal Skills:* Excellent communication skills for effective customer communications, proposals, correspondence, flyers, newsletters, internal communications, and public speaking.

* *Staff Development:* Successfully coordinated and implemented monthly training programs—assessed learning needs, created curriculum, presented instruction, and secured nationally recognized guest speakers.

* *Background as Educator:* Able to provide client-centered interactive training sessions, emphasizing practical applications for customer education and/or staff development.

SALES: *Presentations, Negotiations, Customer Relations, Event Planning, Fund-Raising*

* *Persuasive Communicator:* Made formal presentations to boards and decision makers; sold new program ideas and secured approval for funding. Demonstrated ability to sell varied products as "floater" for upscale retailer; generated daily sales equal to that of experienced sales associates.

* *Customer Relations:* Selected by management as liaison and troubleshooter to resolve concerns with coworkers, external customers, and vendors.

* *Event Planning:* Organized well-received special events in work and community volunteer capacities. Planned events for up to 400. Initiated fund-raising projects to offset a $250,000 reduction in state funding.

ADMINISTRATION: *Program Management, Planning, Development, Budgeting, Supervision*

* *Management:* Held direct accountability for planning, staffing, facilities management, and coordination of educational program with 250 enrollees and 15 instructors. Hired, placed, and evaluated certificated instructors.

* *Program Development:* Created successful programs (business-school partnerships, volunteerism, community outreach), from concept development through implementation at multiple sites.

* *Planning:* Served on cross-functional team that conducted strategic planning, developed budgets in excess of $345,000, determined programming, and ensured compliance for school site serving 650+ students.

EMPLOYMENT HISTORY

Prior experience in education as a teacher and site administrator. Excellent record with former employers, Alton Unified School District (1992–Present) and Mifflin Union School District (1989–1992).

EDUCATION

DEGREE: *Bachelor of Arts in Public Relations/Journalism—University of Alabama (1987)*

References on Request

Figure 8.5: After.

What to Include on Your Resume—and What *Not* to Include

Your resume will begin to take shape as you choose categories that best showcase your experience. In this section, you'll select appropriate resume categories and consider whether to include references to your faith. You'll also learn the seven items to avoid in your resume. Relevance is the name of the game!

Categories to Include

Many people base their resumes on the three most common categories—Objective, Experience, and Education—while overlooking other categories that can help catapult their resumes to the top of the "must interview" list.

In creating your resume outline, consider selecting some (not all) of the following categories:

- **Contact Info/Dashboard Data:** At the least, you should include your name, an e-mail address, and your phone number.

- **Objective or Focus Statement:** It is not necessary to create a separate category heading with the term "Objective" or "Focus" if the type of position you are targeting is set off with centering and bolding and clearly communicated below your contact information.

- **Key Features, or Qualifications Summary:** This can also be titled Background & Accomplishments, Key Accomplishments, or Professional Profile.

- **Professional Experience:** This can also be titled Career History, Experience, Employment Background, or Professional History.

- **Skills:** This can also be titled Core Competencies, Expertise, Strengths, or Talents.

- **Education:** This section can include credentials, licenses, continuing education, and informal training.

- **Activities & Affiliations:** This section can include your involvement in professional associations, community work, volunteerism (including work at church), and so on.

- **Supporting material:** This may include publications, presentations, patents, awards and honors, bio bites, and endorsements.

Should You List Your Christianity on Your Resume?

If you're looking for jobs in ministry or parachurch organizations, then by all means, include information on your resume that speaks to your faith.

If you're targeting traditional opportunities (jobs in business, industry, academia, government, and so on), then you wouldn't normally list information that discloses your religious beliefs. However, I've worked with a number of job seekers who aren't concerned about listing items that hint of their Christianity. Their rationale is that they'd rather the employer know ahead of time of their faith, especially when they don't "hide" their Christianity in the workplace. Most of my clients have the attitude that if they lose an interview opportunity because an employer is put off by these resume items, so be it.

Listing faith-related items can sometimes work in your favor. When a hiring manager or supervisor who is a Christian notices these items, it can lead to developing rapport more quickly.

Travel Tip: Make sure you don't use your Christianity as an excuse for not working hard. Some Christians think that a Christian businessperson will hire them just because of their Christianity. No! You should be hired because you will deliver great value and a return on investment. Your Christianity should be a bonus and blessing to the employer, not the essence of your qualifications.

Here is an example of how you might list Christian activities and community involvement on a resume for a nonministry job.

COMMUNITY INVOLVEMENT

Past President, Fellowship of Christian Athletes, Los Angeles Chapter
Board of Directors, Christian Businessmen's Association, Los Angeles Chapter
Volunteer, Big Brothers of America, Los Angeles Chapter
Volunteer, Habitat for Humanity

As you'll learn in the chapters on interviewing, it is illegal for interviewers to ask about your religious preferences (this doesn't mean you can't speak about your faith, of course).

What Not to Include

There are a few sound bites that will put you at risk for discreet discrimination. Resist the temptation to include these seven items:

- **Date of birth:** Some companies automatically return resumes to candidates who have referenced their date of birth or age.

- **Marital status/children and personal data:** Height, weight, health status, ethnicity, and so on.
- **Photograph:** Don't do it, even if your physiognomy is suitable for the cover of a magazine—which brings me to the exception to this rule. Actors and models do use a photo, typically an 8-by-10 head shot, on the back of which is the resume—a listing of performances or shoots/products featured.
- **Letters of recommendation:** Save them for a timely follow-up contact.
- **Salary history/requirements:** If at all possible, save this hot potato for the interview process. Check out chapter 14 for tips on dealing with this important issue in cover letters.
- **"Date-stamping" the resume:** Don't place the date you prepared the resume on the document.
- **Reference list:** Save this one, too, for the interview or a follow-up contact. You might, however, conclude your resume by centering the words "References on request." No, you don't need to include these words. However, it is still a common practice to do so.

Now that you have your outline, let's develop some compelling content!

Putting It All Together

"Writing is easy. All you do is sit staring at a blank sheet of paper until the drops of blood form on your forehead."

—Gene Fowler, American writer

Don't let this humorous analysis cause you dismay. Even experienced writers can feel some fear and trepidation when facing the start of a new project. First, we'll review keywords and how important they are to the copywriting equation. After that, you'll begin to draft text for the various categories of your resume. By the end of the chapter, you will have a strong rough draft of your resume.

Keywords: Key to Compelling Copy

Every resume, regardless of whether it is in electronic or paper format, should contain keywords that signal employers that you have the skills, talents, and experience to match their job requirements.

Keywords are nouns/noun phrases that describe your title, knowledge base, skill set, impressive "name-brand" or Fortune 500 employers, prestigious universities attended, degrees, licensure, software experience, or affiliations, to name a few.

Travel Tip: The most common type of keyword that employers search for is a position title. To improve your "hit" ratio, use your industry or discipline's keywords along with logical synonyms. For instance, the keywords "materials manager" might be referred to as "supply chain manager," "logistics manager," or "purchasing manager" in another company. To cover your bases, consider leading off your resume summary (or objective) with a list of synonyms.

There are a number of resources for locating keywords:

- The target company's Web site. Tour the site and click its link to jobs. Note the keywords used in postings relevant to your search. Also skim through pages such as About Us or Press Releases for keywords and terms that can help you master the company's unique "corporate speak."

- Google.com, Yahoo.com, or your favorite search engine. At the search engine's home page, search for "career Web sites" or other keywords pertaining to your discipline, such as "'civil engineering' +jobs." If you get an avalanche of sites (they sometimes number in the hundreds of thousands or even millions), be prepared to refine your search by city or a subdiscipline.

- Your professional association. Read its newsletter (there may also be an online version), attend meetings and conferences regularly, and network outside those meetings with colleagues and mentors.

- Informational interviews with other industry contacts.

- Your company's job description of your position.

- Classified advertisements (a.k.a. help-wanted ads) in newspapers, periodicals, and Web sites.

- Recruiter job orders.

- Current "how to" resume books with sample resumes from your profession.

- The career or niche Web sites listed in chapter 12.

Travel Tip: Avoid the temptation of "planting" keywords that are not part of your experience just so that your resume will be found in an electronic search. Some sneaky job seekers have tried making their keyword text white so that the terms are found in computer searches but are not visible to the human eye.

The Objective or Focus Statement

In surveys of employers' resume preferences, a number of pet peeves turned up, two of which apply to the Objective:

- "Not defining the type of position you want."
- "Not researching the company to know what jobs are available."

If you don't know what positions are available, find out—call on your networking sources or contact someone within the organization, whether a human resources manager or department representative. Following are two alternatives for presenting your Focus statement.

Title Statement

You can quickly convey your job focus with a short noun phrase, known as a title statement, centered below the header of your resume. This technique is clean, gets across your point, and saves you one or two lines of space by eliminating the Objective category heading.

Traditional Objective

To write the copy for this category, break it down into three key pieces of information:

- The position you want
- The key skills that qualify you
- The benefit(s) or value to an employer

Table 8.1 gives examples of these three points.

Table 8.1: Components of the Objective Statement

Column 1	Column 1A	Column 2	Column 3
Target Position	Connective Tissue to Pull the Sentence Together	Key Skills That Qualify You for the Position	Benefit(s) or Value to the Employer
Marketing research position ➜	that will use my strengths in ➜	demographic research and analysis ➜	to target and maintain a dominant market share for your company.
Opportunity	in which my	sales support, customer service, problem-solving, and human relations skills	will grow and retain your customer base.

Column 1	Column 1A	Column 2	Column 3
Target Position	Connective Tissue to Pull the Sentence Together	Key Skills That Qualify You for the Position	Benefit(s) or Value to the Employer
Retail buyer	with impressive record of		contributing to gross margin improvement, comparable store sales, and product development.
Elementary teacher	with commitment to		creating a rich, multi-media learning environment through student-centered activities and integrated lessons with meaningful "real-world" applications.
Social services position	that will benefit from my		12-year record of creating award-winning social service programs, accessing grant money and "hidden" funding, and delivering essential services to medically underserved populations.

Take a moment now to use these examples as a springboard for your Objective statement.

The Qualifications Summary

The Qualifications section can be a synopsis of your resume—everything you write below the Qualifications will support what you've said in the summary. This order mandates that you stay focused and not meander. In crafting your Qualifications Summary, consider these ingredients in table 8.2, along with "Dana's" example. To help develop your Qualifications Summary, fill in information applicable to your background in the right-hand column. Don't be concerned if you can't come up with information for each category. And even if you do have material for each element, you might not use it all—remember that the title of this category ends with the word *summary*.

Table 8.2: Ingredients of the Qualifications Summary with Room for Your Information

Ingredients for Qualifications Summary	Example (Dana)	Your Information
1. Title/functional area	International sales support.	
2. Subcategories of functional area or core competencies	Export documentation, government relations.	
3. Industry	Manufacturer of surveillance technology.	
4. Number of years of experience	Seven.	
5. Expertise, strengths, specialization	Internal communications with credit, production, engineering, manufacturing, and shipping to improve on-time shipment of orders.	
6. "Combination" accomplishment or highlights of accomplishments	Led preliminary market research and coordinated opening of international sales office in Mexico City. Supported sales growth of 35%.	
7. Advanced degree, certification, licenses	N/A.	
8. Language skills, international business skills	Fluent in Spanish; serviced Central and South American customer base.	
9. Technical/computer skills	MS Office 97, Access; WordPerfect.	
10. Personal profile/ management style	Dedicated and loyal; five-year record of perfect attendance.	
11. Affiliations	N/A	
12. Impressive employers and schools with name recognition	N/A	

The sample information from Dana in table 8.2 yielded this Qualifications Summary:

Customer service professional with seven years of experience servicing international accounts in the United States and Latin America. Worked in tandem with marketing team to support a 35% increase in sales. Improved on-time shipment of orders through collaboration with credit, production, engineering, manufacturing, and shipping matrix. Well-versed in export documentation, international transport, and government export regulations. Fluent in Spanish language, culture, and business protocol.

After completing the preceding table, sit down at your computer and begin trying different combinations of your information. The length of the summary will be determined by your material. If you find the task of formulating a Qualifications Summary more difficult than you anticipated, take heart:

"What is written without effort is in general read without pleasure."

—*Samuel Johnson, English lexicographer, 1709–1784*

Professional Experience

To catalog your employment history, use the resume worksheet guides or templates found at www.ChristianCareerJourney.com/resume_magic.html. Your word-processing program might have a resume template that you prefer; if so, outline your employment history at your computer. Refer to the resume samples in figures 8.2 and 8.3 for how to list the company name, location, position title, and time period.

The next step is deciding how to distribute the weight among the positions, or how much copy you will write for each position. This step will save you time and help you avoid writing full descriptions for every position. Don't give each of your positions equal treatment in terms of length—your resume is not a socialist project! Instead, determine where your most relevant experience is and leverage the greatest weight on that position.

How Far Back?

The jury isn't unanimous on this question. You can detail the most recent 10 to 20 years in a traditional presentation (company name, dates of employment, title, position description, and accomplishments). The further back in the most recent 20 years you go, the less you need to say. For experience that is more than 20 years ago, use one of these summary techniques:

> Eight years of prior background in production environments, gaining hands-on experience as Expediter, Cardex Clerk, Production Scheduler, and Manufacturing Analyst.

Where to Find Material for Your Job Descriptions

Consider one or more of the sources listed earlier in this chapter ("Keywords: Key to Compelling Copy") to help develop copy for your job descriptions.

ONE PAGE OR TWO?

Resume length should be determined by several factors, including the number of years of experience you possess, your position level, and your industry (for instance, resumes for educators are typically longer than resumes for sales professionals). Use this general rule of thumb for deciding on length:

- One page for new graduates or people with 5 to 10 years of experience.

- Two pages for management-level candidates and those with more than 10 years of experience.

- Two to three pages for "C"-level executives (such as chief executive officer, chief operating officer, or chief financial officer).

Skills

If you have chosen a functional format to present your experience, present the bulk of your talents and experience in this section. If you're using a chronological format or one of its cousins, skip this section. The development of a skills-based resume could warrant an entire chapter, if not an entire book. The basics are presented in a three-step plan:

1. **Focus on three to five skill areas—these will become your subheadings under the Skills category.** Choose disciplines or occupational areas for your subheadings rather than personal skills. Note the difference between occupational skills and personal skills in the following table. Occupational headings carry more weight with employers—remember that most employers dislike functional resumes to begin with; to pull off this format, you'll need to make sure it's meaty.

Occupational Skills	Personal Skills
Event planning, fund-raising, customer service, marketing, sales, engineering, case management, project coordination, training, office management, inventory management, and so on.	Analytical skills, communication skills, problem-solving skills, organizational talents, attentiveness to detail, and so on.

2. **The selection of your subheadings will be driven by the types of positions you are targeting.** Choose for your subheadings words that can be broadly interpreted, compared to specific job titles. For instance, "Customer Service" as a subheading would be more widely understood by the general public and preferred over a company-specific title such as "Client Account Specialist."

3. **After you have selected your subheadings, develop two to five sentences that encapsulate your experience for each subheading.** To develop copy for your experience, refer to the ideas under "Where to Find Material for Your Job Descriptions." You will add specific accomplishments later (see chapter 9). Whenever possible, pair experience statements with evidence of where you gained the experience.

Education, Credentials, Licensure

Place the Education section near the top of the resume if it is one of your strongest selling points. This applies to recent high school or college graduates who have graduated within the past three or so years. CVs, regardless of how long ago your degrees were received, also lead off with education.

Affiliations

In most cases, a simple inventory of your affiliations, presented in order of importance, will suffice. When your involvement included election to an office or some other leadership position, mention the title either before or after the organization (be consistent with the placement of the titles). When you held an office but are no longer in that office, preface the title with "past." It is not necessary to include the date you joined each organization.

Supporting Material

Publications, presentations, patents, awards and honors, biographical bits, and endorsements are often impressive and should be included in your resume. See *Résumé Magic* for specifics on citations and formatting of these lists.

Chapter Wrap-Up

You've made it through the bulk of the composition process. Congratulations! Your text is "raw" at this point, but that's okay—you'll take care of tweaking later. Now it's time to add accomplishments, the real buying motivators for hiring managers that will set you apart from—and above—your competition.

10 QUICK TIPS FOR RESUME STRUCTURE AND KEYWORDS

1. **Commit to writing a first-class personal marketing document.** This is a prime opportunity to fine-tune your professional image and personal brand. Your resume should accurately reflect your strengths, experiences, personal brand, value proposition, and ability to contribute. Don't rush this process. Enlist help from a professional resume writer if needed.

2. **Build a brand that is in market demand.** This is the all-important link between your passions and the employer's productivity and profitability. A "branded" resume should convey a value proposition and demonstrate a fit with not only the skills required for the position but the company's organizational culture as well. It tells recruiters or hiring managers that you are a "fast match" instead of a "Jack of all trades." It answers the eternally critical question "Why hire you instead of someone else with similar skills?"

3. **Decide on the format, or structure, of your resume.** The most common formats are chronological and functional. Review samples for ideas on the "look and feel" you want for your resume. Make sure the format you choose complements your career circumstances. Aim for five or fewer category headings on a one-page resume to create a document that's clean-looking and inviting to read. Typical headings will be Summary or Skills, Experience, Education, and Affiliations or Community Involvement. In many cases, a section for supporting information, such as interests or biographical highlights, is appropriate.

4. **Focus on the employer's needs.** Avoid the temptation to be all things to all people in your resume. One-size-fits-all does not apply to resumes. Likewise, avoid the tendency to write about what you want out of the employment relationship. Instead, focus on what the employer needs. It's about them!

5. **Mirror job postings with relevant content.** Before writing, select several job postings that epitomize your job target. Highlight key responsibilities and results from these postings. Then, diligently weave each of these items into your resume so that it is focused. (Yes, this means that you may need to write several versions.) If you lack certain qualifications from the postings, strategize about how your experience is close to or parallels the requirements. When writing job descriptions, filter every sentence to ensure that it is relevant to your target.

6. **Lead with a sizzling summary to capture interest and control impressions.** A meaty, introductory qualifications section can help employers zero in on the three to five greatest strengths that communicate your brand. Be sure to include tangible, "green" accomplishments (proof that you can contribute to the bottom line) to help substantiate each of your strengths and create interest.

7. **Balance descriptions with substance.** Keep job descriptions to three to seven lines at most (any more than this will make the paragraph look "thick" and uninviting to read). Separate accomplishments from job descriptions to make them more noticeable.

8. **Weave keywords throughout.** Comb Internet postings, company newsletters, and current articles, as well as talking to people in your target industry for terms that will help your resume be unearthed after it is dumped into a resume database. Emphasize critical keywords by leading off a bullet or paragraph with the keyword. For example, if "public speaking" is important to your candidacy, instead of writing "Made presentations to medical, educational, and business leaders," write **"Public Speaking:** Made presentations to medical, educational, and business leaders—regularly earned 'exceeds expectations' on evaluations."

9. **Don't overlook geographic keywords.** If a recruiter is searching for someone in California's Silicon Valley and your home is in "Campbell" rather than "San Jose," add the appropriate terms. For instance, "Campbell, CA 95432—Silicon Valley/San Jose area."

10. **Substantiate personality traits.** Prove you have the traits you claim. Note how the phrase **"Customer-focused:** Selected as primary contact for key account" adds more credibility than simply "customer-focused" or, worse, "good people skills."

MASTERFUL COACHING QUESTIONS

When it comes to writing your resume, in what area, if any, are you tempted to fudge the truth? For instance, are you leery of dates that might imply job-hopping, a progression of titles that reflects a demotion, or the lack of a degree? (Remember that your resume is not an exhaustive autobiography. It may not be necessary to include a position from seven years ago that you held for only two months. Work with a professional resume writer if needed to strategize how to handle resume "sticky wickets" in an ethical and honest manner.)

_____

_____

(continued)

MASTERFUL COACHING QUESTIONS *(CONTINUED)*

When will you complete your resume draft?

_____

_____

What might prevent you from meeting this deadline?

_____

_____

_____

What action can you take to take overcome those potential distractions?

_____

_____

_____

You've no doubt gained some new industry insights or additional market intelligence from researching keywords. How will you use this information in your networking and interviewing?

_____

_____

_____

If you are getting stalled in the task of writing your resume, who or what resources can help? (You can find a list of writers with the industry's most prestigious resume-writing credential, Master Resume Writer, at www.CareerManagementAlliance.com/mrw-list.php.)

_____

_____

_____

Pocket Prayer

Father, You are a God of excellence and we have been made in Your image. Allow me to write my resume as if I were applying for a job with the Host of Heaven! I ask that You would shine through on my resume—that excellence and perfection would be hallmarks of my resume. May the gifts and strengths You have given me be communicated clearly. Help me portray my experience accurately—giving credit where credit is due yet not being timid about communicating the value I have brought to former employers. Let that be the theme of my career, Lord, bringing value to others—value that is wrapped up in Your presence and power. In Jesus' name, Amen.

CHAPTER 9

ACCOMPLISHMENTS: THE LINCHPIN OF A GREAT RESUME

*"As the Lord commanded Moses, so he numbered
[the Israelites] in the wilderness of Sinai."*

—*Num. 1:19 (NASB)*

Numbers are important to the Lord. The word "number" appears more than 150 times in the Bible, with one Old Testament book even earning the title of "Numbers." If God, who counts the very hairs on our head, pays attention to numbers, then so should we. Numbers make what is vague, clear. They help us to measure, compare, and evaluate. They speak volumes, especially to hiring managers.

Put yourself on the other side of the interviewing desk for a moment. Pretend you're a hiring manager in a technology company who is recruiting for a procurement/ business contracts manager. You've been presented with the following resume excerpts. Read them and decide who you would hire.

Candidate A:

> - Led and managed core technology programs that helped steer organization through challenging growth, transition, and turnaround scenarios.
> - Managed supplier business contracts valued from $100K to $1B.
> - Negotiated contracts, engaging and influencing key stakeholders while working closely with in-house counsel, engineering, and procurement team to mitigate contract risk.

Candidate B:

> - Proposed establishment of an internal sales department that resulted in a $10 million cost savings on $30 million in purchases over a 3-year time period. Defined, designed, and developed structure, objectives, and processes...deal was lauded as "brilliant" by management.
> - Initiated revision of 30-page software agreement into a 2-page document for use with Tier 4 suppliers. Realized savings of $500,000 in prior year, and cut months off time-to-market for new products.
> - As core team member, contributed to $1.6 million annual savings with transition of key strategic initiative from outsourcing to in-house system. Negotiated 10-month extension from application service provider, giving company more flexibility to prepare for in-house operations.

At first read, Candidate A sounds impressive. But Candidate B really conveys her value with the hard-core numbers she shares. Now, I'll give you the full story: Candidate A and Candidate B are the same people. This exercise clearly illustrates what a disadvantage you can put yourself at by not including accomplishments! Whether you're saving $500,000 for a major technology company or saving $50 in office supplies for a ministry, employers want to know why they should hire you over someone else. That information is best communicated with numbers-driven accomplishments.

What Employers Really Want in a Resume

In the preceding chapter, I promised a survey of employers' resume preferences, which is presented in the next sidebar. Note that not one survey question received a unanimous response—disappointing news for left-brain types who like to "find the rules and follow them." Take heart, however, because there was *one* survey item that generated nearly universal agreement among human resources executives surveyed:

> Verifiable accomplishments should always be included.

Assembling your accomplishments will be a relatively easy task based on the work you've already completed in chapter 6. There, you learned about the 10 Employer Buying Motivators and wrote SMART Stories™ that included bottom-line results. This chapter offers examples of resume language that relate to those buying motivators, as well as strategies for presenting your accomplishments. By the end of this chapter, your resume should be nearly final.

SURVEY: WHAT EMPLOYERS REALLY WANT IN A RESUME

What do employers want to see in a resume and cover letter? The following statistics reflect feedback from companies that responded to a survey sent to employers listed in the book *The 100 Best Companies to Work For* (Plume/Penguin Books).

Although not statistically significant, responses are generally consistent with and support accepted job search protocol. This information is intended as a guide for resume preparation; I encourage you to use common sense and good judgment in applying survey results to your situation.

1. Applicants with 15 to 30 years of experience should list only the last 10 to 15 years on their resumes.

   35% agree   65% disagree

2. If salary history is requested in a job announcement and an applicant does NOT include it, but is otherwise qualified, the applicant would still be called for an interview.

   85% agree   15% disagree

3. If a Bachelor's degree is requested in a job announcement and an applicant does not have a degree, but is otherwise qualified, the applicant would still be called for an interview.

   39% agree   61% disagree

(continued)

SURVEY: WHAT EMPLOYERS REALLY
WANT IN A RESUME *(CONTINUED)*

4. If an applicant has valid reasons for gaps between employers or job-hopping (for example, downsized, spouse relocated, career on hold to raise children), the applicant should briefly list these reasons on the resume.

    74% agree   26% disagree

5. When listing personal strengths on the resume, the applicant should also include a statement that shows evidence of the trait (for instance, the trait "committed" should be followed with a statement such as "frequently volunteered extended hours to meet critical project deadlines").

    72% agree   28% disagree

6. Thorough descriptions of past job responsibilities should always be included.

    48% agree   52% disagree

7. Verifiable accomplishments should always be included.

    88% agree   12% disagree

8. Military service and honors should always be included.

    79% agree   21% disagree

9. A separate list of references should also be included with the initial application materials.

    19% agree   81% disagree

10. A resume that is poorly organized or has typos will eliminate an otherwise qualified applicant.

    82% agree   18% disagree

11. Tasteful use of spot color or a small graphic related to the industry can enhance the applicant's resume.

    39% agree   61% disagree

12. A resume should always contain evidence that the applicant can make your company stronger (in other words, more competitive, more profitable, smoother functioning).

    75% agree   25% disagree

13. If an applicant started a new job in the past two months, but found the job was not what it was represented to be and is therefore looking for another position, the applicant should include this recent job on the resume.

    85% agree   15% disagree

14. Paper color should always be white or off-white.

    70% agree   30% disagree

15. The length of a resume should be
    1-page, never longer: 12% agree
    kept to 1 or 2 pages: 67% agree
    as long as needed to convey the applicant's qualifications: 21% agree

16. What are the most important elements you look for in an applicant?

    1. Directly related experience
    2. Accomplishments
    3. Evidence of leadership skills
    4. Communication skills (clear, concise)
    5. Work ethic (hard worker, loyal, good attitude)
    6. Education
    7. Initiative
    8. Team-orientation
    9. Good fit with the company
    10. Job stability

Words to Woo Employers

Words that woo employers are words that address the employer's question of "Why buy?" The following examples illustrate how accomplishments, or impact statements, tie in to the 10 Employer Buying Motivators:

- **Buying Motivator #1—Make Money:** Built sales for start-up company from zero to $6.5 million over a four-year period.

- **Buying Motivator #2—Save Money:** Reduced expenses from 150% of target to goal attainment in all major expense categories.

- **Buying Motivator #3—Save Time:** Reduced time requirements for month-end close of books from seven to two days.

- **Buying Motivator #4—Make Work Easier:** Anticipated HR issues associated with company's growing pains and put "expandable" systems in place that accommodated a 25% annual growth in staffing.

- **Buying Motivator #5—Solve a Specific Problem:** Suggested tie-line communication system that enabled employees to call Xerox locations nationwide from customer sites without long-distance charges; idea generated $8,000 savings in branch for first year alone.

- **Buying Motivator #6—Be More Competitive:** Managed post-acquisition strategy for divestiture of nonperforming assets and reinvestment in high-performance assets, in some cases generating as much as an eightfold increase in annual returns.

- **Buying Motivator #7—Build Relationships, Brand, and Image with Internal/External Customers, Vendors, and the Public:** Spearheaded concept for educational/public relations video and brochures that document the mining industry's success in reclamation of mined areas into viable wetlands, agricultural lands, and commercial uses.

- **Buying Motivator #8—Expand Business:** Collaborated on new product development, pricing, and rollout; all new products met or exceeded first-year distribution goals.

- **Buying Motivator #9—Attract New Customers:** Attracted top sales performers from competitors with established client lists, expanding active customer database by more than 200%.

- **Buying Motivator #10—Retain Existing Customers:** Boosted policy renewals from below average to top 5% in the country.

These sample impact statements should trigger the salivary glands of any profit-conscious manager. Important to note is that the examples cut across professional boundaries. Buying motivators are "seamless" when it comes to your profession—virtually all for-profit employers want someone who can help make money, save money, save time, solve problems, and so on. Although ministry organizations may not have "making money" as their number-one priority, they certainly need you to be able to save money, save time, solve problems, and so on. And because every organization needs money to operate, it doesn't hurt if you can also facilitate cash flow.

Strategies for Presenting Accomplishments

Following are several resume-writing trade secrets for presenting accomplishments. Each will strengthen your resume communication and confirm your commitment to the bottom line.

Numbers: The Universal Language

Numbers, unlike words, are universal, no matter what the reader's business idiom or corporate culture is. Note how the lack of numbers in this maintenance director's impact statement creates confusion about whether the statement is even an accomplishment:

BEFORE

> Implemented preventive maintenance program that improved downtime.

Thought-provoking! Did the maintenance program increase the amount of down-time? It's unlikely this is what the candidate intended to convey, but it could be interpreted in this manner.

AFTER

> Improved production 19% and reduced assembly-line down-time from 7 to .5 hours per week through implementation of preventive-maintenance program.

Specifying the production increase and the before-and-after numbers on downtime clears up any questions about "improving downtime."

Comparison—a Powerful Form of Communication

You've heard the saying "It's apples to oranges—you just can't compare the two." In communicating, we often use comparisons to help make our point. Careful use of comparisons can help convey that you can run faster, jump higher, and "leap tall buildings in a single bound" better than the next candidate. For instance, this impact statement tells only half the story:

BEFORE

> Improved branch ranking for sales volume to #1.

A comparison with some elaboration tells much more:

AFTER

> As branch's sole account executive, improved sales production 42% and increased branch ranking from #12 to #1 in a 15-branch region.

In this case, the addition of the words "As branch's sole account executive" gives the reader a much clearer picture of your role in this accomplishment. And when you tell your reader that there are 15 branches total, the increase from #12 becomes much more impressive because it shows that you turned around sales in a branch that was ranking near the bottom of the barrel.

Other comparisons you might make include the following:

Comparisons between competitors

> Improved sales production 42% and increased company's market share from #2 to #1.

Comparisons with the industry average

> Improved sales production 42%, well above national average of 8%.

Comparisons with the company average

> Improved sales production 42%, the largest annual sales increase in the company's 12-year history.

Comparisons with your predecessor in the position

> Improved sales production 42% in a territory that had experienced declining sales and negligent account service.

Proceed with caution when you compare yourself with a team member or predecessor, respected or otherwise. Such comparisons can be offensive, so it is best in these cases to stick with a comparison to industry averages, other branches, or competitors.

You'll also want to avoid sounding like the Lone Ranger in a business climate that venerates the consummate team player. At the same time, don't be afraid to list contributions that were accomplished as a team. When it comes to developing impact statements, candidates, especially female candidates, commonly make the mistake of entirely omitting an accomplishment if they weren't 100 percent responsible for it. If you are concerned about taking credit for something that was a team effort, there's a simple answer to your dilemma. Simply begin your impact statement with phrasing such as the following:

Contributed to…

Aided in…

Helped to…

Member of 7-person task force that…

Participated on ABC Committee that…

Supported a…

Departmental efforts led to…

Selected for national team that…

In resume writing, there's a fine line to walk between self-adulation and self-effacement. Too much of the former, and you'll look like a narcissist. Too much of the latter, and you'll look like a milquetoast. If you're unsure, err on the side of self-effacement, because humility is a cornerstone of Christ-likeness (not to mention the fact that reference checks that reveal your resume to be inflated will be grounds for discontinuing your candidacy). You can always elaborate on your contributions in an interview, and you will probably score even more points when your explanations reveal that you did more than the marquee information contained in the resume. Err too far in understating your contributions, however, and you won't get to the interview.

ROI—How Quickly Can You Deliver?

ROI is another effective tool to quantify your value to employers. The acronym stands for *return on investment* and is a term companies use to determine how quickly their investment in new equipment or advertising or an expansion will pay for itself. Concentrate on generating a return on your employer's investment in salary, benefits, training, office space, business cards, and all of the other hidden costs associated with hiring you.

The CAR Technique—Challenge, Action, and Result

CAR is a vehicle (pardon the pun) you use to highlight a specific Challenge you encountered, the Action you took, and the measurable Result from your action. This technique works especially well if you are transitioning from one industry to another because it focuses the reader's attention on your skills rather than on the industry in which you used the skills. Figure 9.1 shows how "Brad" used the CAR strategy in his resume (note that the word "solution" was substituted for "action").

PROFESSIONAL EXPERIENCE

Zelner Unlimited, Salt Lake City, Utah   2002-Present

Sales Manager

Challenge: Recruited to revitalize stagnant sales and reverse declining profit performance in Rocky Mountain states.

Solution: Design an intensive staff training campaign linking marketing, sales, customer service, and operations; capitalize on use of team leaders to empower and motivate sales team of 27; negotiate partnerships with add-on service providers to counter company's major disadvantage as a standalone facility.

Results: Drove gross sales up from 60% of quota to 121% of quota; quadrupled several sales members' production to in excess of $5 million; contributed 8% to bottom-line profits.

Parkland Properties, Inc., Denver, Colorado   1998-2002

Sales Manager

Challenge: Tasked with rebuilding field sales team with 3-year history of declining sales.

Solution: Utilize industry contacts to recruit experienced sales performers; groom existing sales team through exposure to top performers, product incentives, and individual coaching in presentation and closing techniques.

Results: In just four weeks, improved sales production 250% beyond prior year figures; rebuilt sales team from 3 to 10 who generated collective revenues of $4.6 million, a record for the company.

Hall Enterprises, Denver, Colorado   1989-1998

Territory Manager

Challenge: Rectify account relations in territory suffering from history of poor service.

Solution: Implement company-sponsored speaker series for accounts featuring topics of interest, improve visibility in territory through consistent call schedule and direct mail campaign, target and convert key accounts to exclusive contracts.

Results: Built sales from $440,000 to $1.2 million in two years; ultimately grew territory to $4.1 million in sales despite an 80% reduction in geographic area.

Virtual Memories, Denver, Colorado   1985-1989

General Manager

Challenge: Tasked with start-up operations including site selection, capital equipment purchases, and corporate office development.

Solution: Recruit and train sales and management team of 12; design integrated marketing, sales, and operations strategies.

Results: Built company from zero sales to more than $2 million in first year; grew sales to high of $10 million during tenure.

Figure 9.1: A sample Experience section that uses the CAR format.

Where to Find Material for Your Accomplishments

For many people, developing impact statements is the hardest part of writing a resume. Developing the responsibility portion of the resume is generally easier because there are more sources from which to choose (refer to chapter 8 for source ideas, such as company job descriptions or job announcements). On the other hand, sources for accomplishments or impact statements are sometimes more difficult to come by.

Performance Appraisals

One of the better places for unearthing accomplishments is from the files of your company's human resource department. Performance appraisals can provide a wealth of material; however, many job seekers haven't kept copies of performance appraisals and many more haven't even received written evaluations. If you do have access to your past performance appraisals, look for instances when you met or exceeded specific goals your supervisor set.

Your Career Management File

By far the best place to find information for impact statements is your own *career management file* (CMF). Every professional should have a growing CMF, so if you can't lay claim to one now, grab the nearest manila file folder or 9-by-12 envelope and label it "How I've Made a Difference." (You can also create a folder in your My Documents folder on your computer.) Your mission is to solve problems and help affect the bottom line. Just as a CEO needs meaningful data to measure progress, you, too, must gather data to document your contributions. Whether you're beginning a new position or remaining with your present employer, begin today to assemble data and track your progress on performance standards. Consider tossing the following items into your CMF:

- Notes from meetings with supervisors that state what is expected of you or how your performance will be measured.
- Notes (handwritten is okay) that substantiate that you met or exceeded what was expected of you.
- Notes (with detailed names, facts, figures, and so on) of what you consider to be your greatest contributions.
- Company printouts of information relevant to your profession (quarterly sales, productivity, expense controls, and so on). Remember to keep proprietary information extremely confidential.
- Job descriptions.
- Performance evaluations.

- Examples of work you've produced (such as a company brochure or new business form).
- Attaboys (or "attagirls") from the boss.
- Memos documenting your contribution to a team effort.
- Nice notes from customers.

From this raw material, you will compose powerful, substantiated, and impressive impact statements that will give you entrée to better jobs, outfit you with ammunition to win at the salary-negotiation table, and document the fact that you *are* making a difference in the health of the company and in other peoples' lives.

To reconstruct data for past employers, you might need to call on former supervisors or contacts within the company. Ask questions such as these:

- What were sales (or profits, production, cost issues, and so on) when I began with the company, and what were they when I left the company?
- Did I (or teams on which I worked) make specific contributions that affected sales (profits, production, cost issues, and so on)?
- What do you think is my greatest contribution to the company?
- What kinds of problems did I inherit?
- What were the challenges I was hired to meet?
- What numbers were in place when I started the job?

As you add to your CMF, you'll begin to see how critical this file is to the all-important task of developing accomplishments for your resume.

Impact-Mining: Probing Questions to Unearth Hidden Treasures

Impact-mining is a term for the interrogative process used to draw out a job seeker's accomplishments. At this time, review your SMART Stories from chapter 6 and transfer the results from those stories to the appropriate employment entry on your resume.

Sifting Through the Accomplishments You've Gathered

Now that you've completed your impact-mining, you should have several potential impact statements for each employer. Next, take your impact statements and rank them separately for every employer, indicating the most impressive as number one. The number of statements you will use for each employer depends on the length of your resume, the length of your career history, and the length of employment with each employer.

Finalizing Your Resume with Formatting, Editing, and Proofing

Next, it's time for the "punch list" (a construction term for the final touches). In resume writing, that means tweaking the format for visual appeal, editing, and proofing.

10 Tips to Format to Impress

How do you impress employers *before* they ever read your resume? Just like the advertising gurus do—with visual appeal. This next sidebar will help you with the task of tweaking the format of your resume for maximum visual appeal.

10 QUICK TIPS FOR RESUME FORMATTING

1. Create a visual pattern—be consistent in your use of tab sets, fonts, and line spacing from section to section.

2. Apply white space liberally—learn how to add line space between paragraphs using the Format, Paragraph, Spacing command in MS Word.

3. Limit the number of tab stops on the page—more than three will cause the resume to look too busy.

4. Use no more than two fonts on the page—one for your name and perhaps the category headings, and another for body text.

5. Use the same font and point size for every heading; use the same font and point size for all body text.

6. Use bullets that complement the body-text font—make sure the size of the bullet doesn't overpower or detract from the text.

7. Divide long paragraphs (more than six or seven lines) into two. Lead off each of the smaller paragraphs with a logical category title.

8. Avoid the "Leaning Tower of Pisa" effect of placing employment dates in the left margin surrounded by too much white space. Dates placed on the right margin allow you to shift body text toward the left and gain room for important content and keywords.

9. Balance the text between top and bottom margins so that there isn't excessive white space at the bottom of the page.

10. Print the resume, tack it on a wall, and step back five or six feet. Make sure it has some semblance of form and design.

10 Tips to Edit for Impact

Next comes editing. If you don't consider yourself to have above-average editing skills, enlist the services of an experienced resume writer or editor. This will be a worthwhile investment.

---

10 QUICK TIPS FOR RESUME EDITING

1. Address your audience. Every sentence should pass this relevancy test question: "Is my reader interested in this?"

2. Be accurate. Check and double-check all details, especially numbers.

3. Be brief. Carve out information that is repetitive or irrelevant.

4. Be clear. Ask two or three people to read your resume. Is anything confusing?

5. Avoid jargon that is too specific to your current company (specific names of reports, company-specific acronyms, and so on).

6. Deliver the goods up front. Start accomplishment statements with the results and then describe the method for achieving the results.

7. Start sentences with action verbs (directed, led, performed, collaborated with) or sometimes noun phrases (operations executive, team member, team leader, sales professional) instead of passive statements such as "Responsible for" or "Duties included."

8. Sidestep any potential negatives. It's easier to address these issues in person.

9. Avoid baseless personality attributes. Use personality pairing to combine your soft skills with tangible documentation of the skills.

10. Use "resume speak," which converts a quiet, conversational writing style into a punchy, quasi-advertising writing style.

---

10 Tips to Proofread for Perfection

When it comes to proofreading, follow the 10 tips in this next sidebar.

10 QUICK TIPS FOR RESUME PROOFREADING

1. Print the resume. (It's easier to spot typos on a piece of paper than it is on a computer screen.)

2. Read it slowly, one word at a time. Give special attention to these items:

   • Dates of employment

   • Phone numbers and e-mail addresses (pick up the phone and call the numbers you have listed; send an e-mail to the e-mail addresses listed)

   • Spelling of proper nouns (your name, employers, cities)

   • Headings (if one category heading is boldfaced and underlined, are all of them boldfaced and underlined? and have you duplicated a category heading?)

   • Consistency of formatting (if one employer entry is indented half an inch, are all indented half an inch?)

3. Mark any changes on the proof with a pen (use ink colors such as green or red to help changes stand out).

4. Read the resume backward, one word at a time. This process forces you to look at each word, rather than each sentence, in which case your brain can "fill in" information because it knows what the sentence is supposed to mean. Starting at the bottom of the resume, take a business card or similar size piece of paper and cover up all but the last word. Read that word. Is it spelled correctly? Uncover the next-to-last word. Is it spelled correctly? Repeat this process for every word on the page. Mark any changes on the proof with a pen.

5. Make the changes to the document on your computer.

6. Print it again.

7. Read it again.

8. Compare the proof version with pen marks to the new proof. Check off that each correction was made.

9. Let the resume sit overnight. Looking at it with fresh eyes can make all the difference.

10. Ask two other capable proofreaders to read it with a critical eye.

Chapter Wrap-Up

Congratulations! By following the recommendations in this and preceding chapters, you should have a compelling resume that is employer-focused, relevant, chock-full of accomplishments, visually appealing, and supportive of your career brand! This will certainly help position you above your competition. Keep in mind, however, that the resume is a critical job search tool, but not the magic potion for job offers. You'll get the most mileage out of your resume when you combine it with smart networking activities, which you'll learn about in part 3, "Executing Your Job Search."

10 Quick Tips for Writing Accomplishments and Finalizing Your Resume

1. Always include relevant accomplishments that link to employer buying motivators, such as helping the company make more money, save money, save time, make work easier, solve a specific problem, be more competitive, build relationships/image, expand business, attract new customers, or retain existing customers.

2. Work smart! Review the SMART Stories you developed in chapter 6 and recycle the Results as the basis for your accomplishments (pare down the wording for resume accomplishments into succinct statements). You can also use the Tie-in or Theme from the SMART Story to introduce the accomplishment with keywords; for instance, "**Technology Innovation:** Cut R & D time-to-market 20% using live meeting technology to improve communications among offices in Asia, Europe, and the U.S."

3. Include numbers, such as dollar amounts, percentages, and totals, to convey the full impact of the accomplishment.

4. Use comparisons to demonstrate how you stand out from others, such as comparisons between competing companies, comparisons with the industry average, comparisons with the company average, and comparisons with your predecessor in the position. (Use discretion with your descriptions, so as not to disparage individuals.)

5. If your accomplishment was the result of a team effort, avoid sounding egotistical. Use phrases such as "Contributed to..." or "Member of 7-person task force that..." to give credit where credit is due.

6. When formatting your resume, create visual appeal by applying white space liberally. Be consistent in using tab sets, fonts, and line spacing. Divide long paragraphs into two.

7. Balance the text of your resume between top and bottom margins and left and right margins. Too much white space on the left side of the page can waste precious room; place dates on the right to avoid this.

8. Put your critical-thinking skills to use as you edit your resume. Every sentence should be relevant, concise, accurate, and clear.

9. Write in a manner that creates momentum and excitement. When writing job descriptions, start with action verbs. When writing accomplishments, position numbers near the beginning of the sentence.

10. Proofread without rushing! Print the resume, read it slowly, mark any changes, and then make the changes at your computer. Print it again and check that all the changes you intended to make were made. Then read the resume completely through again. Let it sit overnight and read it again. Enlist the support of others in proofing the resume.

MASTERFUL COACHING QUESTIONS

Reality check! Some job seekers have tunnel vision when it comes to the resume. They view it as the silver bullet that will magically result in job offers and therefore spend untold hours tweaking and perfecting wording when they should be out networking and uncovering employer needs. On a scale of 1 to 10 (1 is low, 10 is high), how would you rate yourself on this tendency?

_____

Based on your preceding score, what, if any, new action do you need to take so that you don't get caught in the resume "tweaking" tunnel?

_____

_____

If you have completed your resume, how does it feel to have finished this important task?

_____

_____

If you have not completed your resume, how can you break the task into smaller steps?

_____

_____

How will you reward yourself when you finish?

_____

_____

Pocket Prayer

Father, You are the one who deserves credit for every accolade and every accomplishment on my resume, for Your Word tells me in Romans 11:36 that all things are from You, and through You, and to You. I covet Your anointing to do the good works that You have assigned for me. Continue to work through me, for I know I can do nothing apart from You. And, Lord, for every future "win" You allow me in my career, I will cast it at Your feet, giving You all the glory. In Jesus' name, Amen.

CHAPTER 10

E-RESUMES, COVER LETTERS, AND OTHER CAREER MARKETING DOCUMENTS

"Learning is not compulsory but neither is survival."

— *W. Edward Deming*

A few years ago, job seekers had to ask themselves, "Will I need an electronic resume in my search?" Today, the question is not "will I?" but "which kind?" Ignoring the trends in technology is a bit like turning your back on the ocean—eventually you'll get blindsided by a wave that can leave you sputtering. Take the time to learn the basics.

Electronic resumes (e-resumes) come in assorted flavors—each with a specific form and function—including these two key types:

- **ASCII text resumes:** Used when pasting a resume into an e-mail message or a Web site e-form/resume-builder.
- **E-portfolios and blogs:** Web-based career marketing documents, which provide you with a 24-7 marketing presence on the Internet.

You'll find the essentials of electronic resumes in this chapter, as well as a brief look at e-portfolios and blogs. Cover-letter strategy and cover-letter samples are also included, along with a review of miscellaneous career marketing documents.

Creating ASCII Plain-Text Resumes

Your goal in creating an ASCII resume is to strip your original resume document of all formatting so that it is readable by any computer. There are several ways to convert a file to ASCII and several opinions on which type of conversion (with line breaks or without line breaks) is best. It depends on whether you'll need the resume to be pasted into an e-mail or pasted into an e-form at a Web site. We'll cover two different sets of steps: one for converting a resume to ASCII for e-mailing and one for converting to ASCII for posting at Web sites. We'll look at each process separately. Directions are for Microsoft Word.

Converting to ASCII for E-mailing

1. **Change the margins.** With your word processing software open and the resume on-screen, highlight the entire document (Ctrl+A). Select File, Page Setup. Enter 1.0 (for one inch) in the box labeled Left. Enter 2.0 (two inches) in the box labeled Right. Click OK. This step shortens the length of the lines, which is important for controlling line breaks.

2. **Change the font.** Use a fixed-width font, such as Courier or Courier New. With the document still highlighted, change the font by selecting Format, Font. Scroll through the font selections in the drop-down box labeled Font or Font Face. Select Courier. In the drop-down box for Size, choose 12 (for 12-point type). Click OK. Use the Esc (Escape) key to unhighlight the document. The 12-point font places fewer characters on a line and helps prevent unattractive line wraps—aim for no more than 60 characters per line (a space counts as a character).

3. **Use Save As, choosing Text Only with Line Breaks.** Select File, Save As. In the Save As Type box, scroll down and select Text Only with Line Breaks.

4. **Rename and save the file.** In the File Name box, type a new name for the file, for example, *resume4emailing*. This will help you differentiate this resume from other versions of the resume you might create.

5. **Accept the warning.** You might see a pop-up box that says, "[Filename] may contain features that are not compatible with Text Only format. Do you want to save the document in this format?" Click Yes.

6. **Close the file.** Select File, Close to remove the file from the screen. After doing so, follow the steps described later in the section for cleaning up the conversion.

Converting to ASCII for Pasting into E-forms

1. **Use the Save As function.** With your word processing software open and the resume on-screen, select File, Save As.

2. **Choose Text Only.** Click the drop-down arrow in the Save As Type box; scroll down and select Text Only.

3. **Rename and save the file.** In the File Name box, type a new name for the file; for instance, *resume4eforms*. This will help you differentiate this resume from other versions of the resume.

4. **Accept the warning.** You might see a pop-up box that says, "[Filename] may contain features that are not compatible with Text Only format. Do you want to save the document in this format?" Click Yes.

5. **Close the file.** Select File, Close to remove the file from the screen. After doing so, follow the steps for quick cleanup of an ASCII conversion in the next section.

> **Travel Tip:** White space is your best ally in creating a visually appealing ASCII-text resume. Use the Enter key on your keyboard to add a line space between paragraphs. This will "open up" the look of the resume. Add a line space above and below important words or subheadings, such as job titles or "Accomplishments." Add line spaces between a bulleted list of sentences. Break long paragraphs into a series of shorter paragraphs. White space won't matter a bit to a search engine, but a real reader will appreciate the readability.

Quick Cleanup of an ASCII Conversion

1. **Use a text editor for cleanup.** Use a text-editor program to tidy up your resume for e-mail transmission. Windows operating systems contain a built-in text editor called Notepad. To start the program, click the Windows Start button; then select Programs, Accessories, Notepad. Open the file (for instance, *resume4emailing.txt*) that you saved earlier (select File, Open).

2. **Format the contact information.** If your header (name, address, telephone, e-mail) was originally formatted with anything other than centered text, you'll find that the header information is all jumbled. Reformat this data, placing everything on the left margin. Use a separate line for your name; street address; city, state, zip; each telephone number; e-mail address; and Web resume URL or blog (if applicable).

3. **Fix any glitches.** Review the document, repairing any bullets that went astray. All bullets should have converted to an asterisk (*), although sometimes they morph into a question mark. Other characters that might have converted incorrectly include ellipses, em dashes (—), or any letters with diacritical markings (such as accented letters).

4. **Add white space.** To improve readability, separate paragraphs with two line spaces. Always place two line spaces before category sections to set them off clearly.

5. **Set off category headings.** Format resume category headings (Qualifications, Education, Experience, and so on) in ALL CAPS. Consider accenting category headings by adding a series of tildes (~~~) or equal signs (===). Use the same treatment for each resume category. When choosing the character you'll use to set off category headings, select only from the characters seen on your keyboard (as opposed to any special symbols you can insert from your word processing program).

Note how the following category headings were set off with different keyboard characters, each of which is readable by all types of computer systems:

PROFESSIONAL EXPERIENCE
~~~~~~

PROFESSIONAL EXPERIENCE
....

Caution: You can add visual accents to an ASCII-text version by using standard keyboard characters, such as an asterisk (*), a plus sign (+), a hyphen (-), a tilde (~), or the lowercase letter *o*. Any of these characters will convert without distortion. Avoid special characters such as "smart quotes" ("curly quotes" as opposed to "straight quotes") or mathematical symbols such as the plus-or-minus sign. Although it's a standard keyboard character, the greater-than sign (>) can cause conversion confusion in an e-mail message, so avoid this character as a replacement for bullets.

6. **Delete unnecessary information.** If your original presentation resume is two pages, it should contain your name and possibly a page number or contact number at the top of page two. Remove this header information from page two of your ASCII version because it is unlikely that it will appear at the top of a page when printed from an e-mail message.

> **Caution:** When sending e-mail communications to prospective
> employers, don't let the informal nature of e-mail be your undoing.
> Despite the casualness associated with e-mail, you must still pay close
> attention to spell-checking and correctly punctuating messages. If you
> forego what you know to be good grammar, syntax, capitalization, or
> punctuation in an e-mail message, your reader might assume that you
> really don't know any better.

7. **Save your changes.** After cleaning up your ASCII resume, you will need to resave it to keep the changes. With the document still in the Notepad text editor, select File, Save. The file will remain on your Notepad screen.

8. **Do a test run.** To see what your ASCII version might look like to an e-mail recipient, test it by sending an e-mail message to yourself and to a friend who has a different e-mail program from yours.

After following the preceding conversion and cleanup formulas, you should have an e-ready resume that you can use over and over again for e-mailing and posting to e-forms.

Creating an E-portfolio

A comprehensive career-marketing tool, an e-portfolio is a Web site designed to showcase your talents, experience, and accomplishments. The advantage of an e-portfolio is that you are not limited to a one- or two-page resume, and the documents provide you additional marketing exposure because they reside 24-7 on the Internet. Some people use the terms *Web resume* and *e-portfolio* interchangeably. Others reserve *Web resume* for a Web-based presentation of a traditional print resume and *e-portfolio* for a Web-based presentation of a traditional print portfolio. We'll focus on the latter in this chapter.

What to Include in an E-portfolio

Pages in your e-portfolio might include a project history, leadership profile, biography, executive summary, branding statement, philosophy statement, press clippings, technical skills, course work or professional-development workshops and seminars, research work, volunteer or pro bono work, publications, patents, awards, charts and tables, work-related pictures, testimonials, and success stories. Each category is typically given a separate page and identified with tabs that are indexed and linked to the home page of your e-portfolio.

E-portfolios can also include streaming audio and video clips. For example, an audio file might contain your networking introduction and a few of your main career highlights. Video might include clips of presentations that you have given. If you need help with developing streaming audio and video, www.audiogenerator.com or www.audioblog.com can manage the process for you.

Within your e-portfolio, include your resume in several downloadable file formats, such as Word document, PDF, and ASCII plain-text formats. And, if you publish a blog, you will want to add a link to your blog as well (as long as the content is professional and not personal).

Resources for Custom-Designed E-portfolios

The following providers can create an impressive online presence for you:

- **www.brandego.com:** Founded by Kirsten Dixson, Brandego provides a comprehensive career-management solution that combines the best of personal branding, career e-portfolios, Web design, and direct marketing.
- **www.blueskyportfolios.com:** The creation of Phil and Louise Fletcher, Blue Sky Portfolios allows job seekers to take control of their online image and personal branding. The team designs, writes, and hosts online portfolios for job seekers across a wide range of industries.

You can also use a blog platform to build an e-portfolio yourself (check the resources in the following section on blogs).

Getting on the Blog Bandwagon

With thousands of new blogs launched every day, blogs have become mainstream online publishing tools. Just what is a blog? Short for Web log, a blog is a Web page of thoughts, ideas, and commentary reflecting the personality of the writer. Typically updated daily or at least weekly, a blog also allows for public interaction and comment on the blog author's postings.

Corporate recruiters and executive search firms are now using blogs as a prescreening tool. To stay on the radar screen and build a personal online brand, create a blog focused on your area of expertise. (At the very least, you can post to blogs of recruiters or high-profile contacts in your industry.)

What to Include in a Blog

A blog gives you a chance to demonstrate your skills and expertise in your field, build a community, and create an interactive forum. You can write about projects you are working on, industry events, ongoing research, current trends, new products, and evaluations. You can also include articles or papers you have written, a bio, project histories, a downloadable resume, an audio presentation, links to your Web site, your Web resume, or links to other relevant Web sites. The content can also include a blogroll, which is a list of links to your favorite blogs. This allows you and your readers to connect with others who share similar interests.

Creating a Blog

Creating a blog is fairly easy and does not require knowledge of complex coding. There are several services that will host your blog—some are free, whereas some charge a small licensing fee. Here are two free sites:

- www.blogger.com/start
- www.wordpress.com

For a small fee, you can create a blog hosted by either of these sites:

- www.typepad.com
- www.blogharbor.com

Each site has a wizard to step you through the setup process. If you would like to host your blog on your own server, you can purchase Web log publishing software from www.movabletype.org.

You will need to publish regular posts and respond to questions from people posting to your blog. The goal is to create an ongoing dialogue with your visitors. Posts require a journalistic writing style. Remember, this is being published on the Internet and anyone can access your blog, so think carefully before posting any personal information. Your online content may be available for many years to come!

Using RSS (Really Simple Syndication) Technology

If you create a blog or post to others' blogs, you'll need to proactively add information and review recent posts. However, if you prefer that blog posts be sent directly to your e-mail inbox, you can use RSS technology—this will help you track your favorite blogs and alert you when new posts are published. An RSS news aggregator can download information into your blog and is an easy way to produce content-rich information for your blog while reducing the amount of research and writing involved. You can find examples of RSS news aggregators at the following sites:

- **Google Reader:** www.google.com/reader
- **Bloglines:** www.bloglines.com
- **Feed Reader:** www.feedreader.com
- **FeedDemon:** www.feeddemon.com
- **Pluck:** www.pluck.com
- **NewsGator:** www.newsgator.com

You can also use Google's alerts (described in chapter 11 in the sidebar "Online News Alerts: Create Your Own News Channel" under Step 2) as a source of information for content.

Advanced bloggers syndicate their blog content using RSS, giving them an especially high profile. To keep up with the latest in blogging and new media, visit Robin Good's site:

> **Master New Media:** www.masternewmedia.org

Good regularly updates the page "Best Blog Directory and RSS Submission Sites," where you can submit your RSS feed to increase the exposure, visibility, and reach of your blog:

> **Best Blog Directory:** www.masternewmedia.org/rss/top55/

Marketing Your Blog

To market your blog on the Internet, list it with these blog search engines:

- **Technorati:** www.technorati.com
- **Google Blog Search:** http://blogsearch.google.com
- **Blog Search Engine:** www.blogsearchengine.com
- **Blogarama:** www.blogarama.com

Another way to market your blog is to post to other blogs and embed a link to your source/blog. In addition, cross-linking on your blogroll to other blogs will increase your blog's presence and ranking in the search engines. You can track your blog's traffic with the services at these sites:

- **Sitemeter:** www.sitemeter.com
- **Feedburner:** www.feedburner.com

MONITOR RECRUITER BLOGS

The Electronic Recruiter Exchange blog at www.ere.net/blogs/ will keep you up on trends used by recruiters and executive search firms.

Cover Letters and Other Correspondence

Although resumes are the mainstay of career marketing documents, there are many other pieces that can showcase your value. We'll look briefly at cover letters, interview follow-up letters, reference lists, brand bios, and more.

Cover Letters

Cover letters are critical to your search success. They are a measure of your intelligence, business savvy, and confidence, as well as your professional experience and skills. Approach writing them with respect and reverence.

In the old days, there were three straightforward parts to a cover letter:

- **The introduction:** Typically a perfunctory statement that mentioned the position you were applying for and how you learned of it.
- **The body:** One or two paragraphs that summarized your experience and career goals.
- **A final paragraph:** Often an invitation to review your resume and request that the screener call if interested.

Today, those three parts have taken on new functions:

- **The carrot:** An introduction that is fresh, interesting, and relevant.
- **The corroboration:** Content that shows an intelligent understanding of the employer's needs and confirms your ability to fill those needs.
- **The close:** A confident finish that might suggest a meeting or invite the reader to take further action.

These elements are illustrated in the sample cover letters and interview follow-up letter shown in figures 10.1 through 10.3.

NENG YANG
333 North Vassar
Los Angeles, CA 90240
(213) 222-3333
nyang@excite.com

[date]

Li Kun Xie, Placement Specialist
Inner-City School District
1234 S.W. 42nd Avenue
Los Angeles, CA 90242

Re: School Counselor, Southeast Asian At-Risk Populations

Dear Ms. Xie:

A school counselor made the difference in my life.

Although limited in my ability to read or write English when I graduated from high school, my minority counselor encouraged me to go to college. A native of Laos, I had been in the United States for only a few short years. The prospect of college was appealing but daunting—no one in my family had ever gone beyond high school. Since that time, I have sharpened my literacy skills and gone on to earn a Master of Arts in Educational Counseling and Student Services. Working with special needs and underrepresented populations, such as those your district serves, is my primary goal.

From the enclosed résumé, you will note experiences in both academic/student services and psychological counseling roles. I am also active in the Hmong community—my reputation as a workshop presenter has earned invitations to speak at community groups and school districts throughout California. Literacy, family systems, and higher education for the Southeast Asian community are typically my themes.

Your School Counselor position would make use of these rich academic, cultural, and personal experiences. Moreover, your students have the promise of both a trained academic counselor and successful role model who understands the culture and the challenges facing youth.

In advance, thank you for your consideration. I look forward to meeting with your interview panel.

Sincerely,

Neng Yang

Enclosure

Figure 10.1: Traditional cover letter.

Jason Senong
EXECUTIVE RECRUITERS INTERNATIONAL
12122 W. 49th Street, Suite 123
Los Angeles, CA 90012

Dear Mr. Senong:

Conversations with John Bradford and Douglas Sterling indicate that your firm is a key player in the ag chemical industry when it comes to executive placement.

As you may have heard, Interchem International was recently acquired by Major Conglomerate, Inc. My division appears to not fit with MCI's long-term vision for growth. Accordingly, the timing is right to explore new opportunities. Could one of your clients benefit from my track record in domestic and international sales?

- As VP, Sales & Marketing for Interchem International, I was challenged with strategy plans and program execution to build domestic sales for the company's bio-tech subsidiary, one of the world's largest producers of synthetic technical pheromones. Over my six-year tenure, we were successful in growing business from start-up to near $40 million in annual sales.

- For the past two years, I have been charged with opening new markets in Europe, Asia, the Eastern Bloc, and Latin America as VP, International Sales. Our team's successes are significant, with more than $12 million in new business credited to the revenue line.

Given the right opportunity, I can duplicate these accomplishments. I would imagine medium-to-large ag chemical manufacturers would be most interested in my skills. There are tremendous market opportunities for specialty ag biopesticides in the Far East. From my perspective, these opportunities lie dormant for lack of proper distribution channels--something my contacts could quickly remedy.

May we talk?

Sincerely,

James Bradford

Enclosure

Figure 10.2: Executive recruiter letter.

CHARLES CANDIDATE

555 N. 14ᵗʰ Street   Work: (415) 555-5555
San Francisco, CA 94111   charlescandidate@msn.com   Mobile: (415) 555-5556

[date]

Javier Gomez, V.P. Marketing
HI-TECH PARTNERS
55 Market Street
San Francisco, CA 94111

Subject: Promotional Market Manager

Dear Javier:

Thank you for the opportunity to interview for the Market Manager position. I appreciated your time and enjoyed talking with you about the position. The interview confirmed my initial positive thoughts of Hi-Tech Partners and the strategic course you have charted for the company.

As I understand it, your goal is to match the position with someone who can deliver these three key priorities:

- **Offer a strong track record**—With 10 years of experience at two respected Fortune companies, I have demonstrated a solid trajectory of advancement. Highlights with Sony include a #1 ranking among 150 sales managers nationwide, with 45% sales growth; for HP, again a #1 ranking among 24 market managers, based on nearly doubling sales volume over the prior year.

- **Be a visionary leader and change agent**—I am currently sharing a new and aggressive vision with my national account to triple sales. This is being accomplished by tapping the right people for the right position, leveraging team members' strengths, and restructuring elements of the sales team to focus on key deliverables.

- **Deliver results**—Generating record-setting results has been the hallmark of my career. My commitment to you in the first few months would be to understand fully the needs of the business, identify underdeveloped and untapped opportunities, and then create a strategic plan that addresses growth in both core business and new business development. This would be the blueprint for executing initiatives to align the sales team with their inherent strengths, implement sales training, develop licensed and branded promotional premiums, and emphasize conceptual selling to generate more business for your accounts.

Given these experiences and competencies, I'm confident the 50% growth you are targeting for the division is attainable. As my track record shows, I have always exceeded growth expectations and am certain I would do the same for Hi-Tech Partners.

I look forward to speaking with you again soon.

Sincerely,

Charles Candidate

Figure 10.3: Performance-based interview follow-up letter.

10 QUICK COVER-LETTER TIPS

1. Mention a referral source whenever possible, for example, "John Doe mentioned you were looking for new talent for your new procurement project."

2. After mentioning your referral source, mention a benefit: "My 10-year background as a procurement supervisor has enabled me to cut costs at least 20% without sacrificing quality."

3. Briefly summarize the breadth of your experience, whether number of years of experience, relevant titles you have held, or range of qualifications in a certain area.

4. Include accomplishments—always!

5. Set off accomplishments with bullets.

6. Don't restate verbatim information from the resume.

7. Avoid obligatory language, such as "Enclosed please find a copy of my resume." Instead, you might say, "You'll note on the enclosed resume a track record for…"

8. Avoid lofty language. Read the letter out loud—if you stumble over polysyllabic words that are unnatural to your way of speaking, rewrite with simpler language.

9. When pasting a letter into an e-mail, make the letter as short as possible and use bullets to set off accomplishments. Recruiters get tired of scrolling through lengthy e-mails.

10. If you're sending your resume as an e-mail attachment, combine the letter with the resume into the same document attachment. This saves the recruiter from opening and saving two attachments. In the text of the e-mail, mention, "For convenience, I have included a duplicate copy of this letter as part of my attached resume file."

References

How many references do you need and who should you use? These guidelines will be of help:

- **Recent graduates** should include a minimum of three references consisting of college instructors, as well as former and present employers who can attest to your ability to juggle a full course schedule and manage that part-time job with maturity and professionalism.

- **Professionals** typically supply five or more individuals who fall within the categories of former bosses, subordinates, peers, clients, and vendors.

- **Senior executives** usually use the "my life is an open book" approach and provide broad access to former bosses, subordinates, peers, clients, and vendors.

Note how the following example of a reference list (figure 10.4) adds a sentence or two after (or to the side of) each contact, describing the relationship to the reference and what was accomplished while working with the person.

Other Career Marketing Documents

You may find a need for additional career marketing documents in your search, including these variations:

- **Networking resume:** Use a one-page slimmed-down version of your multipage resume for outreach to network contacts. It doesn't tell the whole story—just enough of the highlights to give contacts an idea of who you are.

- **PowerPoint resume:** A PowerPoint presentation can be used during interviews to address an interview assignment or to share expanded details about key projects, initiatives, or accomplishments that relate to the specific needs of the hiring company.

- **Brand bio:** Typically one to two pages, this narrative can include categories such as value proposition, career synopsis, value-added competencies, and other information to capture distinguishing brand attributes.

- **Accomplishment summary:** Typically a one-page document, a summary sheet details a list of projects or accomplishments in a particular area.

- **Special report:** The special report is a short document that details research on an industry issue along with proposed solutions for the issue. This is a powerful way for you to position yourself as a solution rather than just a job seeker!

For a comprehensive look at how to create these documents, check out *Executive's Pocket Guide to ROI Resumes and Job Search* (JIST, 2006) by Louise Kursmark and Jan Melnik.

ELAINE WELLER

elaineweller@msn.com
222 East Fruitlands ◆ Concord, MA 01642
(978) 444-2222

REFERENCES

Individual	Relationship and Range of Knowledge
Preston Whitehead, District Manager ASTRA MERCK PHARMACEUTICALS 432 North Wilson Avenue Lexington, MA 01565 (978) 444-3333 email@msn.com	Immediate supervisor at Astra Merck. Will verify three-fold sales increases in new hypertensive, respiratory, and migraine products. Can speak to my tenacity in courting "no see" physicians and turning them into loyal, major accounts.
Purvis Ellingham, Product Manager ASTRA MERCK PHARMACEUTICALS 432 Route 2A New Brunswick, NJ 02345 (888) 212-2121 email@msn.com	While I was employed with Astra Merck, Mr. Ellingham selected me and two other key sales professionals to collaborate on launch strategies for a new antiherpetic product. Northeast region met target goals ahead of schedule and gained top market share by close of first-year sales.
Marlene Sterling, District Manager ABBOTT, DIAGNOSTICS DIVISION 432 North Wilson Avenue Lexington, MA 01565 (978) 444-3333 email@msn.com	Immediate supervisor at Abbott Diagnostics. Can confirm consistent #1 ranking in a district with eight sales representatives, in addition to record incremental increases over goal, market share, and prescriptions sold. Will also elaborate on my ability to orient and train new sales representatives.
W. D. Steinberg, M.D., Chief of Pediatrics CHILDREN'S HOSPITAL 2121 North Minarettes Waltham, MA 01442 (503) 222-1122 email@msn.com	Dr. Steinberg served on the committee that granted hospital formulary status for new IV antibiotic. Can document my presentation skills, understanding of systems/disease processes, and ability to interface with medical team and hospital administrators. Children's Hospital was key to phenomenal territory sales growth.
William Metters, Ph.D., Executive Director NORTHEASTERN MEDICAL SOCIETY 925 East Welton Boston, MA 01223 (503) 222-1111 email@msn.com	Chief executive of a 2,000-member physicians group. Dr. Metters can speak to my planning and public relations skills as he has observed me plan and publicize major educational events for NMS physicians that featured nationally recognized leaders in healthcare.
Candace Fourche, Executive Director AMERICAN HEART ASSOCIATION 1234 E. Bountiful Concord, MA 01452 (978) 444-3333 email@msn.com	Community leader. Solicited my assistance with several fund-raising events, the most significant of which was Heart's annual gala, a formal dinner-dance and auction that netted more than 35% over prior year. Ms. Fourche will confirm my event planning and media relations skills, as well as my ability to motivate a tireless volunteer corps.

◆ ◆ ◆

Figure 10.4: Sample reference list.

Chapter Wrap-Up

Phase II, Express, of the Five Phases of a Job Transition (see chapter 5) is all about packaging your strengths and bottom-line value in both verbal and written form. This chapter has armed you with the information to create a complete suite of written marketing documents. As you tap the hidden job market and cover your bases with traditional search strategies (covered in chapters 11 and 12), you will likely gain additional insider information about your target companies and industry. Don't hesitate to revise your resume to incorporate these new ideas. Doing so will ensure that your documents reflect the latest in industry trends and keywords.

10 QUICK TIPS FOR CREATING E-RESUMES, COVER LETTERS, AND OTHER CAREER MARKETING DOCUMENTS

1. Resist any temptation to simply copy and paste your formatted resume into e-forms or e-mail messages. Instead, take the time to convert your formatted resume into an ASCII plain-text resume for online submissions and e-mail delivery.

2. Choose Text Only with Line Breaks when creating an ASCII resume for e-mailing and Text Only when creating an ASCII resume that will be pasted into e-forms. Give each file a distinct name, such as resume4emailing.txt and resume4eforms.txt.

3. As the final step in the conversion process, tidy up your ASCII text resume using a text editor (such as Notepad). Things to watch for include jumbled contact information, glitches caused by bullets or non-ASCII characters from the original document (such as em dashes, ellipses, and diacritical marks), and any unnecessary information (such as header information from a second page). Add white space between categories and set off category headings with a series of tildes (~~~) or equal signs (===). Save the changes after cleaning up the resume.

4. Always do a test run to see what your ASCII version might look like when received by others. Send an e-mail message to yourself and to a friend who has a different e-mail program from yours.

5. Consider an e-portfolio to give employers a multidimensional picture of you. With this expandable online document, you can include items such as a project history, a leadership profile, a biography, an executive summary, a branding statement, a philosophy statement, press clippings, technical skills, course work or professional-development workshops and seminars, research work, volunteer or pro bono work, publications, patents, awards, charts and tables, work-related pictures, testimonials, and success stories.

6. Get on the blog bandwagon. Consider creating your own blog with easy-to-use services such as blogger.com, or, at the very least, post to appropriate blogs to build your online presence.

7. Create a template for your cover letters to save time, but customize every letter to the needs of the particular company you are applying to. Review the "10 Quick Cover-Letter Tips," earlier in this chapter.

8. Leverage your reference list! Instead of a straightforward list of names with contact information, add a sentence or two after (or to the side of) each contact, describing your relationship to the reference and what you accomplished while working with the person.

9. Consider other career marketing documents that might be helpful, such as a networking resume, a PowerPoint resume, a brand bio, an accomplishment summary, or a special report.

10. Remember that all your career marketing materials are fluid documents that you should update frequently to reflect current trends in your industry.

MASTERFUL COACHING QUESTIONS

Stretch request: Choose one of the career marketing documents described in this chapter that you have not used in the past and implement it within the next seven days. What benefit resulted from expanding your comfort zone?

_____

_____

_____

Pocket Prayer

Father, You are a God of progress—You are continually moving things toward the plans and purposes You have for us. Likewise, You desire that we continually move forward in our knowledge of You and in our work in Your kingdom. Thank you for the progress You have given me on my career journey thus far. I want to stop right now and name all of the ways that I have seen Your hand moving on my behalf. [Name those things.] As I prepare to execute a job search, go ahead of me. Prepare divine appointments that will allow me to claim the new territory You have for me—may it be a place where I can know You, grow in my faith, increase my capacity, and reflect Your glory and grace to others. In Jesus' name, Amen.

PART 3

EXECUTING YOUR JOB SEARCH

CHAPTER 11

TACKLING YOUR JOB SEARCH WITH NEW ECONOMY STRATEGIES

"There is a better way for everything. Find it."

— *Thomas Edison*

G od has new territory for you to claim in your career, but it won't be won without action on your part. After being delivered from the slavery of Egypt, the Israelites were promised Canaan, the land flowing with milk and honey, but they had to fight for every inch of it. The Old Testament book of Joshua tells the story of its conquest. Arthur W. Pink, author of *Gleanings in Joshua* (Moody Press, 1964), captures the essence of the story well:

> *"The book of Joshua not only exhibits the sovereign grace of God, His covenant-faithfulness, His mighty power put forth on behalf of His people, but it also reveals what was required from them in the discharge of their responsibility: formidable obstacles had to be surmounted, a protracted warfare had to be engaged in, fierce foes overcome, before they entered into the actual enjoyment of the land."*

Fortunately, your battles won't be bloody, but they will require strength and courage (Josh. 1:7), and a full measure of wisdom along the way.

Six Misconceptions and Mistakes Christians Can Avoid in Their Job Search

Before tackling your search, let me share some of the misconceptions and mistakes I've seen Christians make when it comes to conducting a job search.

1. Letting the Fight-or-Flight Syndrome Take Over

Misconception/Mistake: As human beings, we find that our normal response to pain or danger is to fight it or flee it. In job search, we often fight and resist rather than yield and submit. We think that focusing on the externals (getting the resume letter-perfect, memorizing flawless responses to interview questions, and so on) is more important than the internals (abiding in Christ's faithful presence, listening for God's direction, obeying what we hear).

Reality: Job search is a strategic trial that God uses to refine us. Malachi 3:3a states, "He will sit as a refiner and purifier of silver; he will purify the Levites and refine them like gold and silver."

You may have heard the story about a woman who, curious about this scripture, went to observe the work of a silversmith. As she watched him working with metal over the fire, she asked, "Why do you put it over the fire?" He replied, "So that all of the impurities melt off of it and it can become pure." She said, "That's interesting, but how do you know when it is done?" He stated, "I know that it is ready when I can see my reflection in the metal."

It may feel as though God is holding you in the fire during your search. And yet the fire will neither consume nor destroy you (Exod. 3:2). Take heart, fellow follower. God wants His beautiful reflection to shine in you as a result of your trial.

THE WAIT ZONE

"God, move in me, or move me!" You may have prayed a similar prayer if you're still waiting on the Lord to formally move you into a new role. As I've analyzed dozens of stories told by Christians in career transition, a familiar pattern emerged. It started with a sense of restlessness or boredom that prompted a period of exploring and seeking God for answers. This was followed by an increasing certainty that God, indeed, was leading toward something new. More often than not, however, the transition was gradual—it didn't happen overnight. That period of waiting is often a period of refining...a time when you're called to do your existing line of work (or your job search if you've already left your old job) sacrificially, with a good attitude, a commitment to excellence, and meticulous attention to detail, even though your heart isn't in it.

I experienced this myself when going through a recent job transition. One of the companies I owned at the time was very challenging because it required the use of my secondary gifts the majority of the time. My friends, seeing the toll the job was taking on me, prayed that God would release me from the position. Eventually, I came to a point of total submission and cried out to God, "Lord, if you want me to do this job until I retire, I will. And I'll do it with all the dedication and love I possibly can!" In less than a month, out of the blue, I received a call from a company interested in buying my company. It took six months to close the deal, but God did eventually move me on to wonderful new things (like having the honor of writing this book!).

If you're in the "wait zone," make the most of it. The Master still expects us to increase our talents (Matt. 25:14-30), even during these times. It may be a time of sacrificial obedience, but He has wonderful rewards in store for you.

2. Misinterpreting Messages or Expecting Epiphanies

Misconception/Mistake: God has either given or will give me a clear epiphany of where I'm supposed to work and won't allow me to waste time wandering around.

Reality: Have you ever thought you heard clearly from the Lord, only to discover you heard in error? Sometimes we hear from the Lord but misinterpret the message. Other times, we hear from the Lord but don't realize that God's leading is just step 1 in the process. In the meantime, we've gotten so hyper-focused on what we initially heard that we don't listen for the next step.

More often than not, the Lord doesn't come to us in a dream and tell us the name of our future employer. Instead, we need to work on a number of leads and see what sticks. Ecclesiastes 11:6 tells us, "Sow your seed in the morning, and at evening let not your hands be idle, for you do not know which will succeed, whether this or that, or whether both will do equally well."

3. Allowing Pride to Get in the Way

Misconception/Mistake: I've seen many Christians prolong their job search by insisting they "deserve" a job similar to or better than their last one. Likewise, pride can get in the way when you try to go it alone.

Reality: If Jesus had held out for a similar or better job than what He had in heaven, He would never have come to earth! Instead, He humbled Himself and took on the form of a servant (Phil. 2:7-8).

If you're holding out for what you think you deserve, you may miss the best of what God has for you. Don't be afraid to accept something that seems "beneath" you. Jesus did, and it led to great things for Him and all of mankind. 1 Peter 5:6 reminds us, "Humble yourselves, therefore, under God's mighty hand, that he may lift you up in due time."

And, as mentioned in several prior chapters, do not attempt job search in a vacuum. It is a team sport requiring the support of prayer partners, your spouse, a career coach, and/or a job search support group.

4. "Going for It" Without Paying Your Dues

Misconception/Mistake: Because I serve a big God, He can do big things for me, like move me into an important position with lots of influence or income.

Reality: He certainly can! But He typically gives big things in gradual increases.

God told the Israelites that He would drive out the occupants of the Promised Land so that they would have victory. Exodus 23:29-30 explains why He didn't drive everyone out all at once: "But I will not drive them out in a single year, because the land would become desolate and the wild animals too numerous for you. Little by little I will drive them out before you, until you have increased enough to take possession of the land."

Have you "increased enough" to take possession of your Promised Land? God wants us to be increasing—increasing in our knowledge of who He is, increasing in our obedience to His Word, increasing in our faith—so that we might enjoy the land He has set aside for us. The Promised Land for today's Christians comes one step at a time.

5. Equating Ease and Speed with Success

Misconception/Mistake: Because God loves me, He won't let the job search be difficult or long and drawn out.

Reality: God *does* love you. He knows what you can handle, and what you're not yet ready for. When the Israelites were saved from Egypt, God did not take them directly to the Promised Land. Exodus 13:17-18 explains: "When Pharaoh let the people go, God did not lead them on the road through the Philistine country, though that was shorter. For God said, 'If they face war, they might change their minds and return to Egypt.' So God led the people around by the desert road toward the Red Sea. The Israelites went up out of Egypt armed for battle."

Sometimes God delays your entry into the Promised Land of a new job because He knows there's a battle that you're not yet ready for. Further, taking the Israelites "by the desert road" allowed God to perform perhaps His most famous miracle—the parting of the Red Sea. If God is detouring or delaying you, it may be that He's done so because He is protecting you and has an amazing miracle awaiting you.

6. Insisting on Doing Job Search the "Old-Fashioned" Way

Misconception/Mistake: I keep hearing that I need to network to find a job, but I'm going to do it the way I've always done it.

In the good old days, you mailed your resume in response to a classified ad and had a reasonably good chance of being called in for an interview. There was basically one place to look for jobs (the newspaper), and job seekers dutifully but somewhat anonymously applied only to employers with "help wanted" signs posted.

Reality: Today, most people think the Internet has simply expedited and expanded this same process. You read the ads (now called postings) and e-mail your resume, and then expect to have a reasonably good chance of being called in for an interview. Wrong! The days of relying on openings are long gone. Employers sometimes receive thousands of resumes in response to their Internet postings, making you the proverbial needle in the haystack. You must get out of the haystack, uncover opportunities, and show how sharp you are face-to-face. Armed with solutions and a servant's heart, you will be just what they are looking for!

The rest of this chapter is devoted to helping you play today's job search game with skill and success.

Tap the Hidden Job Market with a Targeted Search

How many interviews do you want to have in your pipeline? More interviews mean more options. Too often, candidates pin all their hopes on just *one* interview, thinking their ship has come in, only to see it turn into a sunken dream. If you've experienced this scenario, you know it can really take the wind out of your sails. On the other hand, there is nothing more empowering than having options.

The Difference Between Openings and Opportunities

To increase your options, you must increase your *opportunities*. Notice the emphasis on *opportunities* instead of *openings*. There's a world of difference between the two, as table 11.1 explains. Understanding this will give you an edge in your networking and interviewing.

Table 11.1: Differences Between Job Openings and Job Opportunities

	Openings	Opportunities
Definition	An advertised position soliciting a predefined skill set to perform specific tasks	An *un*advertised position or situation where your skill set can contribute to company/ shareholder value

(continued)

Table 11.1: Differences Between Job Openings and Job Opportunities *(continued)*

	Openings	Opportunities
Job seeker positioning	In openings, the job seeker has a tendency to come as a "supplicant" on bended knee, positioned in a role to sell and convince others of his or her worth	With opportunities, the job seeker has the ability to come as a "value proposition," positioned as a business solution or service
How accessed	Comb through online postings and print want ads to apply; human resources then winnows applicants to make the volume of resumes manageable, eventually conducting a formal, structured interrogative interview process	Target companies and then read, research, and conduct "focused networking" with people who will lead you to conversations with decision makers; needs are uncovered and solutions offered through an informal, fluid inquiry/ discovery process
Materials needed	Traditional resume, cover letter	Knowledge of company/hiring manager needs and how your strengths can deliver a return on investment; targeted resume or "solution or service" letter; project proposal
Quantity	Limited and restricted to those companies in hiring mode	Potentially limitless and unrestricted, as the focus is about building long-term relationships while exploring opportunities and innovations that will benefit the company's bottom line
Competition	Typically stiff when advertised broadly	Minimal; you're often competing with only yourself
Who controls the process	Controlled by human resources; usually a predictable two- to eight-week process	Controlled by hiring manager and decision makers; less predictable process
Human resources	Actively soliciting and screening applicants	The human resources department is often unaware that you are even on the premises
Connections	You are typically anonymous and an unknown commodity	You build relationships that lead to your being trusted and gaining insider status because of recommendations by colleagues, employees, and/or friends

	Openings	Opportunities
What the employer looks for	Features (an ideal "wish list," such as number of years of experience, degree, skill set)	Benefits (solutions or services offered) that will make the company money or save the company money, making you a valuable asset that boosts the bottom line
Employer's preferred method of contact	Anonymous submission of electronic or paper resume	Often e-mail or telephone to start, and eventually face-to-face exploration of issues that ultimately may lead to an employment proposal
Effectiveness	Leads to jobs 5% to 8% of the time (Source: DBM, a global human resources consulting firm)	Leads to jobs 58% to 62% of the time (Source: DBM, a global human resources consulting firm)

If you need to pump up your pipeline—get more interviews lined up—the seven steps to a targeted/active search explained in this chapter will help you do just that! In a world where jobs are disappearing due to automation and globalization, it's especially important that you understand active, "new economy" job search skills. To do so, master the seven steps of a targeted search:

1. Identify companies.
2. Read.
3. Research.
4. Talk to people in the know through focused networking.
5. Network online.
6. Stay on the radar screen.
7. Augment with traditional job search methods.

Seven Steps to a Targeted Search

In a targeted search, the starting point is identifying companies you'd like to work for. You'll then read, research, and talk to people in order to learn about TOP (Trends, Opportunities, and Problems/Projects) issues in these organizations. All the while, you need to stay on decision makers' radar screens and position yourself as a solution or service (we'll cover how to do that later in this chapter).

Step 1: Identify Companies

A targeted search requires a list of companies in a specific geographic area (or areas). To generate a list of, say, 30 to 50 companies, start by specifying the industry, interest/specialization, and geography/location. Write your responses in the following box, along with your preference for geographic area/location.

Industry sector (from chapter 3, Master F.I.T.™): _____

Interest/specialization within industry (from chapter 3): _____

Geography/location: _____

To create a solid list of companies, tap into people, print resources, and the Internet.

TARGETING CHRISTIAN EMPLOYERS?

Many Christians would love to work for a Christian organization or in a secular organization for a boss who is a Christian. They assume there will be freedom to pray, speak of God, and operate from a Biblical perspective. Ron Rutherford, executive director of Intercristo (www.intercristo.com), which connects believers with work opportunities in both ministry and secular arenas, observes that sometimes Christians' motives for wanting to work at Christian organizations are not entirely pure. He notes, "Many think they may not have to work as hard…that the employer will accept their faults and foibles without requiring them to be diligent about improving themselves. But these are selfish reasons. Being a Christian in the workplace does not mean you can be slack. In fact, it's quite the opposite."

Regardless of where you work, God wants you to give 100 percent!

Finding Target Companies Through People

Start your sleuthing by asking work associates, recruiters, or friends what they consider to be leading organizations. Use queries such as these:

- "What resources would you suggest for finding a list of some of the best companies to work for?" or "Who do you know who might point me in the right direction?"
- "I'm looking at making a career move. In your circles, what companies have a reputation for being a great place to work?"
- "Who is the 'cream of the crop' when it comes to widget makers in [fill in your industry]?"

Beyond your networking contacts and friends, inquire within local employment-related organizations, such as the Department of Labor's "Find It! By Location" Web site, www.dol.gov/dol/location.htm.

Finding Target Companies Through Print Resources

Reference librarians can be a career hunter's best ally. As a general rule, they are some of the brightest behind-the-scenes people you'd hope to meet! Request that he or she point you to business resources, such as business directories and trade journals. Although you won't need a librarian's help to find the Yellow Pages, remember that this ubiquitous tool can also give you easy access to company names in certain company categories.

Finding Target Companies Through Internet Resources

As a caveat, be forewarned that data found on the Internet may not be centrally located or as neat and tidy as you'd prefer. If you can't find what you want online within an hour or two, resort to other resources. The following sites can be helpful:

- www.weddles.com/associations/index.cfm: **Peter Weddle,** author of several employment-related and Internet resources (www.weddles.com), lists a directory of associations at his content-rich site.

- **Google**'s www.google.com/Top/Business/: Search more than 50 industry categories.

- **Yahoo!**'s   http://dir.yahoo.com/Business_and_Economy/Directories/ Companies/: Search more than 60 industry categories.

- www.bcwinstitute.com: **Best Christian Workplaces Institute** conducts regular surveys of Christian organizations and publishes its results in association with *Christianity Today,* as well as on its Web site (see the sidebar titled "Looking for a Top-Notch Christian Employer?").

- http://money.cnn.com/magazines/fortune/bestcompanies/full_list/: You'll find *Fortune*'s 100 Best Companies to Work For as well as other best-company lists, including a full list of the Fortune 100 companies, companies best for minorities, fastest-growing companies, the top 50 employers for MBA graduates, and the companies with the most-admired leaders.

- http://jobsmart.org/hidden/bestcos.cfm: **JobSmart.org** lists more than a dozen "best" lists, including 100 Best Companies for Working Mothers, Top Entry-Level Employers for College Grads, 100 Best Places to Work in IT, 50 Best Companies for Latinas to Work for in the U.S., and more.

- www.craigslist.com: Originating in the San Francisco/Bay Area as one of the best regional sites on the Internet for jobs and lists of companies in hiring mode, **craigslist.com** has expanded its reach to cover several major metro areas throughout the U.S.

LOOKING FOR A TOP-NOTCH CHRISTIAN EMPLOYER?

"Christian workplaces should set the standard as the best, most effective places to work in the world," says Al Lopus, president and co-founder of Best Christian Workplaces Institute. To advance that vision, his organization conducts a valuable annual survey, "Best Christian Places to Work" (with results published annually in *Christianity Today*). A portion of the 2007 survey results (reprinted with permission from BCWI) are found here:

Large Organizations (500+ Employees)
- Indiana Wesleyan University, Marion, IN (www.indwes.edu)
- Point Loma Nazarene University, San Diego, CA (www.pointloma.edu/home.htm)
- Wycliffe Bible Translators, Orlando, FL (www.wycliffe.org)

Media (100–500 Employees)
- EMF Broadcasting, Rocklin, CA (www.klove.com)
- Harvest House Publishers, Eugene, OR (www.harvesthousepublishers.com)
- Tyndale House Publishers, Carol Stream, IL (www.tyndale.com)

Higher Education (Up to 500 Employees)
- Dallas Theological Seminary, Dallas, TX (www.dts.edu)
- Evangel University, Springfield, MO (www.evangel.edu)
- The Master's College, Santa Clarita, CA (www.masters.edu)
- The Master's Seminary, Santa Clarita, CA (www.tms.edu)
- Olivet Nazarene University, Bourbonnais, IL (www.olivet.edu)
- Phoenix Seminary, Scottsdale, AZ (www.phoenixseminary.edu)

To see the full list of organizations, visit Best Christian Workplaces Institute's Web site, www.bcwinstitute.com.

You can also find Christian employers in the list of "Christian Job Sites" in the next chapter or go to Google.com and search for "Christian-owned businesses."

SEARCH BY LOCATION

There are some handy sites for honing in on companies within a certain radius of your home (or any address):
- www.SimplyHired.com
- www.Indeed.com
- www.Jobster.com
- www.SuperPages.com

Purchase Mailing Lists

The following services can provide you with mailing lists sorted by industry code, employee number, sales volume, and more:

- **AccuData America:** www.accudata.com
- **D&B's ZapData:** www.zapdata.com (powered by Dun & Bradstreet)
- **InfoUSA:** www.infousa.com (this company authored *Direct Mail For Dummies* by Wiley Publishing)
- **Pro/File Research:** www.profileresearch.com (specializes in helping job seekers)
- **American City Business Journals:** www.bizjournals.com (purchase a *Book of Lists* containing key contact information for thousands of top local businesses, industries, and nonprofit organizations in more than 50 metropolitan areas)
- **First Mark Church Mailing Lists:** www.firstmark.com
- **American Church Lists:** www.americanchurchlists.com

Prioritize Your List of Companies

After accessing people, print resources, and Internet resources, you should have a healthy list of target companies to pursue. If the initial list is large and unwieldy, pare it down by focusing on any of these parameters that are important to you:

- Passion for company's mission, products, or services
- Relationships already established with individuals in the company or opportunity to work under a certain individual or with high-caliber co-workers
- Company's culture or reputation
- Size (employees or revenue) or in growth mode
- Number or variety of opportunities within company
- Commute time; potential for flextime
- Benefits or perks

The size of the organization might be a critical consideration. According to the U.S. Bureau of the Census, roughly 55 percent of the U.S. workforce is employed by small businesses with fewer than 100 employees—meaning that there are potentially twice as many companies available to you should you target small businesses. Choose a manageable number of companies on your list to start off your campaign.

Build Data on the Companies

As you identify and prioritize target companies, begin assembling data on them (one handful at a time so as not to overwhelm yourself). We'll cover how to gather this data in steps 2 through 5. Use the following worksheet for your profiling (also available at www.ChristianCareerJourney.com/journey.html). As you gather additional data on your target companies, create a file folder for each company or create folders in MS Windows where you can keep information organized.

COMPANY PROFILE WORKSHEET

Company: _____

Address, telephone, Web site: _____

Basic info (length of time in business, major milestones, key products/services, strengths of company, number of employees, annual sales/profit):

_____

_____

Company's competitors: _____

Company executives, HR contact, hiring manager, and his or her bio highlights:

_____

_____

TOP issues (Trends, Opportunities, Problems/Projects): _____

_____

Internal key contact #1 (name, title, telephone ext., e-mail address):	Contact info…important issues/keywords… strategy for approach…my relevant S.O.S. (Solution Or Service) response
_____	_____
_____	_____
_____	_____

Internal key contact #2 (name, title, telephone ext., e-mail address):	Contact info…important issues/keywords… strategy for approach…my relevant S.O.S. (Solution Or Service) response
_____	_____
_____	_____
_____	_____

Internal key contact #3
(name, title, telephone ext., e-mail address)

Contact info…important issues/keywords…
strategy for approach…my relevant S.O.S.
(Solution Or Service) response

_____

_____

_____

_____

_____

_____

_____

_____

External key contact #1
(name, title, telephone., e-mail address):

Contact info…important issues/keywords…
strategy for approach

_____

_____

_____

_____

_____

_____

External key contact #2
(name, title, telephone, e-mail address):

Contact info…important issues/keywords…
strategy for approach

_____

_____

_____

_____

_____

_____

External key contact #3
(name, title, telephone, e-mail address)

Contact info…important issues/keywords…
strategy for approach

_____

_____

_____

_____

_____

_____

Notes and questions you'd like answered about the company:

_____

_____

How I can add value to the company:

_____

_____

Step 2: Read

"A" Candidates—prospective employees who stand out from the crowd—read voraciously. If you're already in the habit of taking in daily news and industry news, congratulations. If you're one who pays scant attention to the headlines, quadruple your normal reading material while job searching and preparing for interviews. If you're not sure which publications or business books to read, ask successful networking contacts what they find most helpful. Or ask a member representative in your trade organization(s) for reading recommendations.

ONLINE NEWS ALERTS: CREATE YOUR OWN NEWS CHANNEL

Receive relevant articles automatically by signing up for News Alerts. The alerts arrive daily, clustered as links in an e-mail. To sign up, go to www.google.com/alerts and enter your industry and target companies as alerts. Set up as many alerts as you'd like. You'll be aware of breaking news for networking and interview preparation. And, when you want to show appreciation to networking contacts who have helped you, e-mailing or mailing an especially relevant article can be a thoughtful yet inexpensive way to do so.

Respond to what you read by keeping a log of

- Any news that will give you a clue about which companies are growing and hiring
- Names of people within or connected to the company (and, if applicable, what you liked about their contribution to the material you read)
- Problems that need solved or interesting innovations
- Trends and how they might benefit your target companies

Step 3: Research

"Research is a reflection of a candidate's work ethic and how well he or she will perform when in the job," notes Valerie Kennerson, Director of Global Staffing for Corning, Incorporated, a diversified technology company with 70 manufacturing locations and 20,000 employees worldwide. She goes on to explain, "When deciding between two well-qualified candidates, the scales typically tip in favor of the candidate who is a little more prepared, interested, and engaged."

To look prepared, interested, and engaged, gather information outlined in the Company Profile Worksheet listed earlier in this chapter. Here are a dozen resources to help you access that information:

- **People in the know** (discussed in step 4 of this chapter, later).
- **Business information sites:** Some sites provide basic business capsules at no charge, with extended news and market analytics for a fee:
  - Hoovers: www.hoovers.com, the first place to go when you're researching public companies
  - Bizjournals: www.bizjournals.com/search.html (use your target company or industry to conduct a keyword search)
  - Dunn and Bradstreet: www.dnb.com
- **Company Web site:** Read, of course, the careers section, which might give you an idea of the company's culture, affinity groups, succession planning, and advancement opportunities. In addition, review the site's press releases, about us, history, and investor relations pages, as well as its products/services pages. (Prior to a formal interview, you'll want to thoroughly exhaust the company's Web site.)
- **Company blog:** Read the company's blog to gain an understanding of the corporate culture, projects that employees are working on, upcoming job openings not yet posted, and the challenges employees face.
- **Company marketing material:** Call and ask for marketing or sales literature if none is available at the Web site.
- **News sources:** Google.com searches can turn up interesting support information about the company or its industry (note the sidebar under step 2, titled "Online News Alerts: Create Your Own News Channel"). Journals for your industry can also provide leads.
- **Libraries:** Ask your new friend the resource librarian to run a periodical search using the company name and your functional area (marketing, sales, and so on) as keywords.
- **Associations:** Search your professional association(s) for any references to your target company. It might be that an employee from the target company will be presenting at an upcoming conference, or you might find an article that is of relevance to your target company's TOP issues.
- **Career Web sites:** Several career sites offer company research, including www.vault.com, www.wetfeet.com, and http://company.monster.com.
- **Company annual report:** This is often available at the company's Web site or through the investor relations department. If you're questioned by investor relations when you request an annual report, mention that you are interested in investing in the company.
- **Publicly traded companies' 10-K (annual report) or 10-Q (quarterly report) filed with the Securities and Exchange Commission (SEC):** A two-day subscription for $9.95 is available at www.freeedgar.com. Similar to an annual report, the 10-K contains more detailed information about the company's business, finances, and management, and is loaded with contact names.

- **Analyst reports intended for the investment community:** Read warily; analysts (who are employed by banks and won't want to offend potential client companies—the very companies they are analyzing) might be tempted to issue a rosier outlook for the company than what it really deserves. Use Google to find analyst reports on your company, or check sites such as Zacks (www.zacks.com) or Thomson Financial (www.thomson.com/solutions/financial/).

HOW TO NAVIGATE AN ANNUAL REPORT

For an excellent guide on reading an annual report (or reading between the lines of an annual report), visit www.investorguide.com/igustockreport.html.

Step 4: Talk to People in the Know Through Focused Networking

Often, career networking guides recommend that you network with everyone from your barber to your Aunt Sally's sister's husband's cousin when looking for job leads. It's true that employment referrals can come to you through these venues, but it might be the exception to the rule.

The greatest payoff will come from fundamental business relationships—focused networking—with people *who are closely linked to decision makers at your target employers.*

10 QUICK TIPS FOR TALKING TO NEW PEOPLE

1. **Leverage your strengths.** If you are an excellent researcher, make this the centerpiece of your networking effort. If you are an excellent organizer, lay out a seven-step plan for approaching each contact. If you are an excellent writer, craft well-conceived letters to your contacts as the first step. If you are more introverted than extroverted, start with online networking or by approaching contacts that are of a like mind.

2. **Look at networking as a learning (professional development) experience.** This is a chance to increase your industry knowledge, not through classroom training but in real-world, face-to-face research. Count your hours in networking as continuing education units (CEUs).

3. **Focus on what you can bring to the other person.** For people who shy away from networking, this mind-set often brings an "aha!" moment. You have value—concentrate more on giving value to your networking contact than on what you'll receive.

4. **Listen.** Don't make this harder on yourself than it really is! Good networkers listen more than they talk—all you need is a comfortable opening question or statement to get the process started.

5. **Recognize that the recipient of your call might be happy to talk.** If you discovered that you have a strong preference for introversion (see chapter 3, step 6), you might not have a natural affinity for networking. On the other hand, the person you're about to contact might be extroverted, in which case he or she might thrive on talking and welcome your call.

6. **Act as though this was a business meeting.** Think back to a time when you had to meet a new business associate, which blossomed into a fond business relationship. Consider that the person you are about to contact might become a long-term and respected colleague.

7. **Commit to building long-term relationships.** A relationship nurtured over months and years will be stronger than one that is just a few days or weeks old. A contact you meet today might not lead you to your next job, but it might lead to your dream job in a year or two. After you have made new contacts, stay in touch periodically, even after you've landed a new job.

8. **Don't be afraid to ask.** After doing networking the right way—building rapport, and approaching the relationship as a giver and not just a taker—don't forget to ask for what you need. The worst someone can say is "no" or "I can't help you." Get beyond fears of embarrassment or rejection using God's truths.

9. **Maximize short-term relationships.** Be completely credible and authentic, never overstating your achievements.

10. **Write instead.** If you're having trouble mustering the courage to call someone, write a brief letter or send an e-mail.

Who Are Focused Networking Contacts?

Focused networking is a career management technique wherein you connect with people who have both a *relationship* with decision makers and a *knowledge* of the target company, as figure 11.1 shows.

Contacts in Quadrant 1 will be most fruitful. These are often people inside the company (colleagues of hiring managers, potential co-workers, suppliers of the company, advisors to the company, and so on). Contacts in Quadrant 2 (for instance, professional association contacts, industry writers, and so on) and Quadrant 3 (friends or professional associates of the decision maker) might lead you to contacts in Quadrant 1, whereas contacts in Quadrant 4 (your barber, your Aunt Sally's sister's husband's cousin, your friends at the gardening club) might yield little or no benefit. Spend your time in quadrants that will get you to Quadrant 1 contacts.

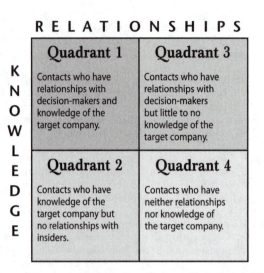

RELATIONSHIPS

	Quadrant 1	Quadrant 3
K **N** **O** **W**	Contacts who have relationships with decision-makers and knowledge of the target company.	Contacts who have relationships with decision-makers but little to no knowledge of the target company.
L **E**	Quadrant 2	Quadrant 4
D **G** **E**	Contacts who have knowledge of the target company but no relationships with insiders.	Contacts who have neither relationships nor knowledge of the target company.

Figure 11.1: Networking quadrants for a focused networking relationship.

Potential contacts, along with tips for approaching them, are shown in table 11.2. In general, when asking for help, remember the acronym REAP, which stands for

- **Resources:** What should you be reading?
- **Events:** What should you be attending?
- **Activities:** What should you be doing?
- **People:** Whom should you be talking to?

As contrary to your purposes as it might seem, do *not* ask your networking contacts for information about job openings. This often puts people in a position of having to say "no" to you, making them feel uncomfortable and less willing to help you in the future. On the other hand, contacts are often able to respond to requests for help regarding resources, events, activities, and people. Follow through and you will *reap* the benefit of uncovering new opportunities!

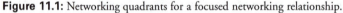

FIND E-MAIL ADDRESSES

Yahoo!'s Advanced People Search is an amazing tool for finding people, especially at larger organizations. Go to http://email.people.yahoo.com/py/psAdvSearch.py and fill out as much or as little information as you want (fewer data entries may yield better results). Enhance your search by choosing an organization name (your target company) and organization type.

Table 11.2: Tips for Approaching Focused Networking Contacts

Contact	Tips on Approaching
People inside target companies who are at your level	Speaking with people who might be future co-workers can be more effective than asking to speak to the CEO (if you're not going to report directly to the CEO). A conversation with the top sales rep for the company, an engineer who headed up a recent project, a project manager who knows people in different departments, and so on can reveal insider information. And, at some point, the hiring manager might ask this person what he or she thinks of you. Meeting with them before you meet with the hiring manager can serve you well.
	Personally e-mail or call with a warm referral, such as, *John, this is Susan. Jane Reddy suggested I connect with you. Is this a good time?* If not, ask when would be a good time to speak. If it is a good time, continue with: *I wonder if you could help me with some information. Jane mentioned you're in the production department at XYZ Co. I am a customer service rep and have some good skills, and am looking for opportunities in a company like yours. Jane thought you might be able to offer a good perspective on what it's really like to work at XYZ.*
	After listening and establishing rapport, ask more questions: *What would you say is the strength of the department?* Save this next question for later, as some people won't readily admit to problems. *Where could they use the greatest help?* Then test the waters with, *Who would you suggest I contact over in Customer Service? Joe Ramirez, you say? Great. What's the best way to approach him?* Remember to wrap up with, *You've been a great help. Is there something I might be able to do for you?*
People inside target companies who are in leadership or a position to hire	*This is Jane Doe. Garrett Bench at the Heart Association told me to give you a call. Have I caught you at a good time?…I'm an administrative professional with excellent technology skills and have seven years of experience providing admin support to marketing managers. Garrett mentioned the new marketing project you're working on, and it happens that that's just the type of work I'm looking to do more of. He also said you might be a bit short-handed in the admin department. If my skill set were clearly able to make your operation run more smoothly, would you be open to an exploratory conversation?*

(continued)

Table 11.2: Tips for Approaching Focused Networking Contacts *(continued)*

Contact	Tips on Approaching
Former employees of target companies	Some of the most truthful information you uncover may come from an employee who is no longer with the company. With no vested interest in politicking, former employees might be brutally honest about company culture, policy, key contacts, and the like. In addition to asking questions about TOP issues, ask, *What do you miss about working there?* and *What do you* not *miss about working there?* or *Would you recommend the company to a family member as a good place to work?* Finally, *Have you stayed in contact with any colleagues since you left the company?* If so, ask, *Who would you suggest I contact?*
Vendors or suppliers of your target companies	Call and ask, *Could I have the name of the individual who handles the XYZ account?* After you have the name, you can either speak directly to them or e-mail with this type of message: *I understand you work with the XYZ account and wondered if you could help me. I'm especially interested in their purchasing operations because of the innovative Web sourcing they're doing. Who would be the appropriate person to speak with about that?* After learning a bit more about the issue, you may want to ask to meet face to face with the person. Ultimately, ask, *Who would you recommend I contact at XYZ to learn more?* Ask permission to reference this person: *May I say that I spoke with you?*
Your present or past colleagues/co-workers	This sort of dialogue should help: *Joe, this is Susan. We worked together on the Billings project at Macmillan Company. I hope all is well in your world. Listen, I don't want to take up too much of your time—do you have just a few minutes?* Joe says yes. *Part of the reason for my call is to ask your advice. I'm researching some potential opportunities at Target Company A and Target Company B—they both have great reputations for their graphic design capabilities—and I'm wondering who you might suggest I speak with in their marketing or sales departments.* If Joe says no one comes to mind, follow with, *You don't know of anyone? Okay. How would you suggest I learn more about their graphic design department?* Joe mentions that Print-Co supplies some of their paper, and that Jane is the salesperson for the account. *Great.*

Contact	Tips on Approaching
	Anyone else come to mind who services them?...That's terrific. Thanks. This will give me a good start. Any tips on how I should approach Jane? Take notes. *Joe, you've been a great help. Let me make sure I've got the right e-mail address for you so I can keep you in the loop about my conversation with Jane.* This sentence gives you permission to follow up, should you need further advice.
	If Joe has no suggestions on how to learn more, ask: *May I ask you to keep an ear to the ground for me? I can e-mail you my resume if you'd like—feel free to forward it when appropriate. And, if I'm still looking a month from now, I'll touch base with you if that's okay.* Again, you've asked permission to follow up.
Your family, friends, neighbors, ex-neighbors, health-care professionals, members of groups (gym, political, sports, religious, hobbies), volunteer-mates, Christmas card list, and so on	Be specific. Don't say, *I'm looking for a job.* Instead, customize a specific request based on what you know about the contact (does the person golf, belong to an environmental club, jog with someone, or attend a certain group where insiders congregate?). For instance, *Joan, do you still work with the Habitat for Humanity group?* If so, *Well, at your next meeting, would you mind asking the other members if they know of anyone at these construction firms that I'm researching? Since my company downsized, I'm exploring some new opportunities and am interested in talking with someone who could tell me what it's really like to work there—it'd be especially great if I could get in touch with someone who handles the purchasing for their raw materials.*

Note that a few of the suggested scripts in table 11.2 might be interchangeable with your different networking contacts. In addition to the tips outlined in table 11.2, these general strategies for approaching contacts will be helpful:

- **Pave the way:** When contacting a decision maker at your target company, ask a peer to pave the way for you with a warm-up call. For instance, if John is your peer and Chris is someone you'd like to speak with, you approach John in this way: "John, I'm wondering if you could help connect me with Chris at XYZ Company. I think we'd both benefit from knowing one another...."

- **Relaxed settings:** Meet your new contact at an industry meeting, trade show, or social gathering. Face-to-face time at a conference, meeting, or event can be more relaxed than trying to eke out an appointment in a busy professional's daily schedule. You can either "accidentally" bump into the person at the event, or e-mail or call ahead of time. If you contact ahead of time, mention that you learned from Joe Blow (your mutual connection) that he or she will be at the event. Offer a sincere and customized compliment about the person or the company, and then state that you hope to have a chance to speak briefly and put a face with the name.

- **The buddy system:** Attend an event *with* your warm contact and have this person introduce you to new key contacts. If your warm contact has a telephone system with two incoming lines and a "confer" button, that person can be speaking to you on one line and put you on hold, dial the target contact and get permission to have you join the call, and then press the "confer" button on the phone and have all three people connected. In a similar vein, author Diane Darling in *The Networking Survival Guide* (McGraw-Hill) noted that although only 5 percent of cold calls end in a sale, a sale is made as much as 80 percent of the time if the person making the referral sits in on the sales call.

- **Request for a random act of kindness:** When contacting people for the first time, in addition to mentioning the person who referred you to them, mention that you are looking for help, resources, or advice. Choose your language carefully. Do not say, "I just wanted to pick your brain a little." Instead, try something like, "I was hoping you'd have a few minutes to point me in the right direction," or, "I understand you're knowledgeable in the area of _____ and I was hoping you could shed some light on something I'm exploring," or, "I'm hoping you have time for a quick random act of kindness. I'm looking for the name of the person who heads up the _____ [this might be a department or a project]."

- **Gatekeepers:** When encountering a gatekeeper or secretary to an executive, befriend this person and be honest about your intentions. State that you would like to speak with Ms. Jones (the executive) at the recommendation of a couple of colleagues (these warm contacts should be well known to the executive). Convey an understanding that the executive's schedule is quite busy and ask advice about the best way to approach him or her. The gatekeeper might direct you to e-mail, send a letter, or call at another time. Follow his or her advice, and then send a short e-mail back with a thank-you for the assistance. This person, too, should be a part of your network!

- **The S.O.S. response letter:** Write a letter that includes the name of your warm contact, conveys that you have done some research on the target company, and offers an S.O.S. (solutions or services) message, as the example in figure 11.2 illustrates.

Lionel Lillifax, Chief Financial Officer
Nano-spec
123 E. 54th
Philadelphia, PA 17555

Dear Mr. Lillifax:

Your company's success with nanotechnology is impressive. I have invested in your stock and spent time understanding why you are successful. I first learned of the company after purchasing a Babolat tennis racket last August and was intrigued by the use of the carbon nanotubes in the yoke of the racket. During my research, I studied your 10-K and had conversations with Marion Davenport and Michael Miller in your research and distribution departments. Both of them urged me to contact you (and may already have mentioned our conversations to you). Based on my research, I identified a few areas that might position your company for even greater profit.

First, I understand that your staff is stretched thin, as is often the case with startups. In a similar situation, I was able to cut overtime 30% by customizing existing technology to do things that the vendor claimed the program could *not* do — staff got the rest they needed and morale vastly improved. Although I'm an accounting professional, I believe my technology skills might relieve some of your immediate overtime issues.

Second, the accounting program you are currently using for R&D accounting will be cumbersome at best once your volume increases to the levels projected in the 10-K. You are likely already aware of this. There are two technology solutions that offer better scalability and tracking for the intricacies of expense, fixed-asset, inventory, and cost of goods sold. I selected one of these programs for my current company, which allowed for sophisticated data collection used in subsequent business planning and decision-making. The results helped to elevate and even out our monthly cash flow.

Finally, your long-term plans for acquisition growth are impressive. I assisted with due diligence on two M&A projects at Silicon Strategies. In one, I uncovered data that had been overlooked by prior auditors and analysts. This information shifted the strategy for negotiations and saved the company several million in acquisition costs. I believe my skills in this area would be an asset in your future acquisition initiatives.

I plan to attend the NSTI Nanotechnology Conference & Trade Show in San Francisco next month. I'm especially interested in Mr. Warren's presentation on the business perspective of nanotechnology from the venture-capital world. Your assistant, Sharon, mentioned that you will be attending. I'd enjoy getting together for a short visit at the conference. If you would like to call me, I can best be reached at 213-555-5432 between 8–9:30 a.m. EST (5–6:30 a.m. on the west coast) or after 8 p.m. EST. If I don't hear from you, I will contact you to coordinate a convenient time.

I'd enjoy getting together for a brief visit, as I believe it would be mutually beneficial to know one another. If you would like to call me, I can best be reached at 213-555-5432 between 8–9:30 a.m. EST (5–6:30 a.m. on the west coast) or after 8 p.m. EST. If I don't hear from you, I will contact you to further explore these ideas.

Best regards,

Kale Kolburn

Figure 11.2: An S.O.S. response letter.

For more ideas on crafting this sort of letter, pick up Jeffrey J. Fox's book *Don't Send a Resume: And Other Contrarian Rules to Help Land a Great Job* (Hyperion).

The Give-and-Take of Networking

Your goal in focused networking is to connect with others in a give-and-take relationship in which there is reciprocal benefit. Let's look at what you can give, as well as what you'll want to take away from your encounters.

THE GIVE

Before approaching anyone, consider what your "give" will be. Here are some ideas:

- An online or print article you found that would be of interest to your contact.
- An interesting fact you learned in your recent research (be cautious not to reveal insider secrets that competitors have shared with you).
- Industry knowledge you have that will be of value.
- Information about an upcoming event or valuable training.
- Information about a book or other helpful resource you encountered.
- The names of people in your sphere of influence whom the contact might benefit from knowing.
- A copy of a relevant article you wrote or a presentation you made.
- A prayer! If you are networking with another believer, ask how you can pray for him or her. If your networking contact is not a believer and the conversation unfolds in such a way that you sense the Spirit's leading, ask whether you can pray for him or her.

If you are uncertain about what you can give, ask your contact! For instance, "Based on what you know about me, is there anything that I might be able to help you with?"

THE TAKE—INSIDER INFO

What do you want to come away with from networking relationships? The goal of focused networking is *not* to find a job lead in every encounter. Instead, it is a process of becoming an INSIDER, an acronym that stands for *I*nformation, *N*ames, *S*upport, *I*deas, *D*ata, *E*nergy, and *R*elationships. Table 11.3 offers more information on these items.

Table 11.3: Finding the INSIDER Scoop in Networking

Item	Specifics
I = Information	Learn more about broad industry trends, opportunities, and issues, as well as companies that are growing or going through challenging times.
N = Names	Add new names to your network—find out what's of interest to these people and how you can help them.
S = Support	Garner supporters—people who will introduce you to others, endorse you, and be your champion.
I = Ideas	Come away with advice or spark new ideas and insights for your search—new strategies to access decision makers, new skills to learn, new companies to learn about, and new leads to follow.
D = Data	This is the nitty-gritty data that comes from due diligence on a target company—its financial picture, strategic plans, management team, TOP issues (trends, opportunities, problems/projects), and so on. Add this information to your Company Profile worksheet.
E = Energy	Build momentum by having encouraging encounters with others or taking proactive steps.
R = Relationships	Relationships—rapport and bonds—lead to referrals, endorsements, and the insider's edge.

Step 5: Network Online

Online networking offers an opportunity to connect with people beyond your immediate reach. Some of the more popular venues include blogs and online networking services such as LinkedIn.com.

Blogs

Savvy job seekers are now using blogs to network with corporate recruiters online. Microsoft's Senior Marketing Recruiter, Heather Hamilton, publishes a blog on Marketing and Finance at Microsoft (http://blogs.msdn.com/heatherleigh/archive/tags/Blogging/default.aspx). Hamilton was quoted in a *New York Times* article as saying, "I have great candidates in process that have resulted from blogging. Personally, I think blogging is going to change the way companies recruit."

To find corporate blogs, conduct a search using the blog search engines listed in chapter 10 under "Marketing Your Blog." Once you identify a target company's blog, determine who the author is and what position the author holds in the company. You can gain volumes of information about the company by reading the blog archives. If the blog is written by a corporate recruiter, you can learn more about upcoming openings before they are posted, ask questions about the opportunities, and position yourself as a candidate. When the position opens, you will have a better chance to land an interview because you have developed a network with important people in the company.

Before posting to a blog, be sure to read the archives and follow the posts for a while to get a sense of etiquette and the best strategy for approach.

LinkedIn and Other Online Networking Sites

Online networking sites, both business and social, allow you to contact others through a network of connections for the purpose of job search, business leads, and industry information. Most provide you with a profile page and allow you to post your bio. By far, the leader in the online business networking field is LinkedIn.com.

In just a few short years, LinkedIn's users have grown from 2 million to 12 million across the globe. Users link to one another, giving you access to other people's networks. The service allows members to post jobs and hire people within their network. It also offers a job search function so that you can search for jobs through your network and network with the person posting the position.

> **Travel Tip:** For tips on using LinkedIn, see Guy Kawasaki's helpful blog post: http://blog.linkedin.com/blog/2007/07/ten-ways-to-use.html.

ZoomInfo.com is another resource to consider for online networking. This site holds a database of nearly 40 million professionals that recruiters and others regularly search for profile information. Check the site to see whether you're listed. If so, update your profile so that it's accurate and reflective of your personal brand. If not, you can add your profile.

A new twist on online networking is Executive Locator (www.ExecutiveLocator.com), a partnership of the *Wall Street Journal*'s CareerJournal.com and Eliyon Technologies. You can identify potential contacts by company name, location, and a range of criteria. The fee for the service is $1 per contact, with a minimum purchase of 30 contacts. Each contact includes the individual's phone number, e-mail address, job title, and company address. The database contains the profiles of business people at 1.5 million companies.

Leading the list of social networking sites are these:

- **www.MySpace.com:** With an estimated 48 million users, MySpace is popular with Millennials. Despite some of the questionable content on this site, recruiters have tapped this hunting ground for positions requiring young talent.
- **www.Facebook.com:** Facebook is the second-most-popular social networking site.

Online networking sites designed for Christians include the following:

- www.FaithAtTheCross.com
- www.HisReach.com

Although there's value in online networking, the caution with these and other Web sites is to not lose track of time and neglect other important job search activities.

Step 6: Stay on the Radar Screen

"It's not what you know, it's who you know." When it comes to job search, that maxim might well be rewritten as "It's not who you know, it's who knows *you*!" Uncovering opportunities requires that you be seen and known by people with the power to hire. You can accomplish this through several tactics:

- **Write articles:** Write an article for a trade journal, an association newsletter, or an industry Web site.
- **Make a presentation at a conference or meeting:** Choose something timely to speak about, and find an audience. Local groups are often looking for speakers.
- **Attend** *and make your presence known at* **seminars, workshops, meetings, conferences, webinars, or teleseminars:** Going to an event, quiet as a church mouse, doesn't qualify as a radar-screen activity. Ask an intelligent question or offer an insightful comment so that the group notes your presence. (*Caution:* Be sure that your question or comment isn't grandstanding and truly offers value to others.)
- **Create an e-newsletter:** You thought e-newsletters were just from companies, right? There's no reason you can't create your own. Fill it with brief but interesting content, and send it to your network on a monthly basis.
- **Beef Up Your Online Presence:** Blogs and e-portfolios top the list (see chapter 10 for details on creating and marketing these tools).

ARE YOU DIGITALLY DISTINCT?

Use the online identity calculator at www.CareerDistinction.com/onlineid/ to calculate your online identity score.

- **Serve on an association committee that has visibility:** Serve on the program planning committee or hand out binders at the registration desk of a conference.
- **Volunteer:** Volunteer in a capacity that allows decision makers and potential teammates to interact with you and see your abilities in action.
- **Do project work:** Request an arrangement to do work on a short-term, contract basis for your target company. Your desire to prove your mettle will impress decision makers.

Step 7: Augment with Traditional Job Search Methods

To make sure you cover all the bases, include a few traditional/passive job search methods in your targeted/active strategy. An absolute must is to post your resume at the Web sites of your target companies. In addition, spend a *little* time (not a lot!) searching postings at major career sites and niche sites. Details on these and other traditional strategies are discussed in chapter 12.

Chapter Wrap-Up

A targeted/active approach can add more interviews to your job search pipeline because it opens you up to opportunities within the hidden job market. This new-economy search strategy will help you develop one of the skills most critical for career success in the 21st century: connecting with a web of fundamental business contacts. These connections are the infrastructure for accessing needed skills and resources while you're on the job, as well as the safety net for new opportunities when you go to access your next position. With the now-undeniable employment trend of spending just a few years at many employers (versus a lifetime with one employer), the targeted strategy and its emphasis on focused networking will serve you well throughout your career.

10 QUICK TIPS TO CONDUCT A TARGETED SEARCH AND TAP THE HIDDEN JOB MARKET

1. **God has new territory for you to claim in your career, but it won't be won without action on your part.** Allow God to refine you like silver during this time. Stay humble. Listen closely for His direction. Pay your dues. Equate obedience and faithfulness with true success. And, do job search the new-fashioned way.

2. **Get several interviews in the pipeline to increase your options.** Look for both opportunities and openings. An opportunity is an unadvertised situation or position where your skill set can contribute to company/shareholder value. An opening is an advertised position soliciting a predefined skill set to perform a specific task.

3. **Conduct a targeted, or "new economy," search—this allows you to uncover opportunities and openings.** In a targeted/active search, the starting point is companies—you identify specific companies you'd like to work for and target both opportunities and openings that align with your Magic F.I.T. Conversely, in a traditional/passive job search, the starting point is positions—you rely on advertised openings that align with your functional skills. Here, the openings might be available with any number of companies.

4. **Master the seven steps of a targeted search, the first of which is to identify target companies.** In step 1, tap into people, print resources, and the Internet to create a healthy list of companies you would like to work for. Several considerations might help you home in on specific companies, such as location/commute time, company size, reputation, opportunities available within the company, passion for the company's products/services, relationships with people in the company, company culture, benefits, and so on.

5. **Steps 2 and 3—read and research—go hand in hand.** Read your target company's Web site, industry/niche Web sites, company blogs, online news, trade journals, local/regional/national newspapers, analyst reports, industry white papers, popular business books, and so on. Keep a log of contact names that can lead you to decision makers in your target company. Uncover TOP issues (Trends, Opportunities, Problems/Projects) within your target companies. Find a way to offer a return-on-investment by adding value to the bottom line.

6. **In step 4, talk to people through focused networking—focused, meaning talking with people who have a relationship with hiring managers or knowledge of your target company.** The best approach is not necessarily to contact the hiring manager directly. Often, speaking first with people who are just one or two phone calls away from decision makers will "warm up" your candidacy, give you insider status, and greatly strengthen your standing once you get to the hiring manager.

(continued)

10 QUICK TIPS TO CONDUCT A TARGETED SEARCH AND TAP THE HIDDEN JOB MARKET *(CONTINUED)*

7. **Leverage your strengths in networking, especially when networking is not part of your immediate skill set.** For instance, if you are an excellent researcher, make this the centerpiece of your networking effort. If you are an excellent writer, craft well-conceived letters to your contacts as the first step. If you are more introverted than extroverted, start with online networking or by approaching contacts that are of a like mind.

8. **For step 5, take your networking online.** Join industry association e-lists; visit or participate in online chats, discussion boards, and blogs; and check out online networking Web sites.

9. **Step 6 requires that you stay on the radar screen.** It's not just who you know, it's who knows you! To be seen by the right people, write articles, make presentations, attend (and make your presence known at) meetings, send out a brief e-newsletter, publish a blog, serve on an association committee that has visibility, volunteer, or do project work.

10. **In step 7 of a targeted/active search, augment with traditional/passive search methods.** Cover your bases by posting a resume at your target companies' Web sites and searching for relevant postings at career portals and niche sites. But remember that these activities should be fill-in-the-cracks work, not the focus of your search!

MASTERFUL COACHING QUESTIONS

Of the six misconceptions and mistakes Christians might make in their job search, which items are you most prone to? What action will you take to avoid these misconceptions or mistakes?

_____

_____

Of the seven steps in a targeted/active search, which area is your strength?

_____

_____

How can you leverage that strength to make your job search easier?

_____

_____

Which of the seven steps is an area you'd like to build up? How will doing so enhance your job search...and your career over the long term?

_____

_____

What steps will you take to make that happen?

_____

_____

Who can help you with this?

_____

Before making contact with your network or target companies, pray for them as specifically as possible. Note what kind of difference this makes in your networking.

Pocket Prayer

O God, You are the creator of heaven and earth and have formed every living creature for Your purposes and Your pleasure. Thank you for forming me and walking with me every step of my journey. Like Abraham's servant in Genesis 24:42, I ask that You please "grant success to the journey on which I have come." Open my eyes to the companies or organizations where I can be of value and a blessing. Give me favor with the people I will speak with. For Your name's sake, fill me afresh and anew so that those I encounter would know that there is a living and loving God who desires to dwell within the heart of every human being. Show me how to connect with my networking contacts in a meaningful way. If there are opportunities for ministering to others while I network, open those doors. Thank you that nothing is a waste of time in Your economy, Lord, and so I know that every phone call, every meeting, and every e-mail can be used by You. Strengthen me to conduct my job search as if I were doing it for You, for I am most certainly Your servant first. In Jesus' name, Amen.

CHAPTER 12

COVERING YOUR BASES WITH TRADITIONAL SEARCH STRATEGIES

"Excellence is to do a common thing in an uncommon way."

—*Booker T. Washington*

For decades, job seekers have turned to traditional job search strategies to find new employment: responding to job announcements, sending resume mailings unsolicited to companies, and so on. Surprisingly, the success rate of these approaches is fairly low, often in the single-digit range. To improve their success, job seekers have turned more and more to networking, where approximately 60 percent or more of all new jobs are found. Chapter 11 introduced the concept of *focused networking*—a strategy to connect with people who have both a *relationship* with decision makers and *knowledge* of your target companies. Focused networking is at the heart of a targeted strategy and can yield the highest success rate when compared to other search strategies.

Why People Continue to Use Traditional Search Strategies

Many people continue to concentrate their efforts on traditional job search strategies instead of targeted search strategies. Why? Here are two key reasons, one stemming from job seekers and the other from employers:

- **Job seekers:** Most job seekers can learn fairly easily the steps of a traditional/passive search. However, many job seekers have not received solid training in how to engage in focused networking, making them uncertain about the process. And, for many job seekers, it's much easier to rest in the relative ease and anonymity of posting resumes or expecting an employment agency to do the legwork for you.

• **Employers:** The traditional system of soliciting and screening resumes is the mainstay of the corporate recruiting function. Fortune 500 companies report finding approximately 30 percent of their new hires in this traditional sourcing manner.

So it's apparent that the traditional system does work, *to some degree*—more so when the economy is booming and there is heavy competition for talent. However, relying *solely* on traditional search methods to get interviews is risky—the odds are not in your favor. Read on to learn which traditional strategies have the highest rate of return so that you can spend your time wisely.

The Seven Venues of a Traditional Search

The seven most common venues of a traditional search include the following:

1. Online searches
2. Resume posting
3. Resume distribution
4. Recruiters and agencies
5. Classified ads
6. Direct inquiry
7. Career events

Let's look briefly at each one.

Venue 1: Online Searches

The trend toward online recruiting continues to increase every year. Gerry Crispin and Mark Mehler, authors of *CareerXroads,* a reference guide to job and resume Web sites, recently released their annual *CareerXroads Source of Hires Study.* In it, they document where companies look for candidates when it comes time to fill positions. Here are the highlights:

• 33.9 percent of all open positions were filled by internal transfer and promotion, down from 38 percent the prior year (note that this sizable figure might be reason to accept a stepping-stone position in a larger company where there is a strong probability of being promoted).

• 66.1 percent of positions filled were from external hires, with this breakdown:

  • Referrals: 25.6 percent (95 percent of which came from employees)

  • Company Web sites: 20.7 percent

- Job boards: 12.3 percent
- Print media: 6.9 percent (these numbers, the highest in a decade, reflect a major comeback in publishers as a source of hiring)
- Direct sourcing: 6.4 percent
- Rehires ("boomerangs"): 5.2 percent
- Third-party agencies: 4.8 percent
- College: 3.8 percent
- Career fairs: 2.7 percent
- Temp-to-hire: 2.3 percent
- Search engine advertising: 2.0 percent
- Walk-ins: .5 percent
- All other: 7 percent

The importance of networking for referrals and applying at your target companies' Web sites was emphasized in the preceding chapter. When it comes to online searches, where should you apply? According to Crispin and Mehler's study, three sites account for the majority of hires from job boards:

- 35 percent from Monster.com
- 30 percent from CareerBuilder.com
- 29.5 percent from HotJobs.com
- 6.5 percent from all other job boards

It bears noting that smaller companies—those without the resources to underwrite sophisticated recruiting functions at their Web sites—may source a higher percentage of candidates from niche and career sites, as well as from referral networking.

Regardless of the size of your target company, prioritize your online searches (and subsequent resume posting) in this order:

1. Your target companies' Web sites (jobs/employment page, when available)
2. Major career Web sites, such as Monster.com, CareerBuilder.com, or HotJobs.com
3. Niche career sites

Company Web Sites

When you're targeting large companies, it's likely you'll be able to submit a resume directly at the company's Web site. Roughly 75 percent of Fortune 500 companies have a Careers button on their home pages.

Major Career Web Sites

The following major career sites are the heavy hitters when it comes to rich content and a significant collection of job listings. For some time, Monster and CareerBuilder have been jockeying for position as *the* premier career site. Yahoo!'s HotJobs.com also continues to stay in the game as a leader.

- www.Monster.com
- www.CareerBuilder.com
- www.HotJobs.Yahoo.com

Job Aggregators

Job aggregators capture and repost the listings of other job boards, giving you a convenient place to look for jobs. The leading aggregators include these:

- www.Indeed.com
- www.SimplyHired.com
- www.Jobster.com
- www.JobKaBob.com
- www.Oodle.com

Niche Job Sites

Niche job sites specialize in employment for a particular functional area or industry. One of the best resources I've found for a centralized collection of niche sites is John Sumser's interbiznet.com. The niche sites listed in this section are reprinted (with permission) from www.interbiznet.com/bugler/060412Specialedition.html. The lists are ordered by amount of traffic. (For updates, check the archives at www.interbiznet.com/interbizbugler/dailyindex.html.)

Review the following lists for sites appropriate to your functional or industry target. Search the sites on a weekly basis for relevant job postings. If the site has a job-alert feature, set up an account to receive e-mail notification of relevant positions.

TOP EXECUTIVE SITES

- www.TheLadders.com
- www.CareerJournal.com
- www.6FigureJobs.com
- www.ExecutivesOnTheWeb.com
- www.Exec-Appointments.com
- www.ExecuNet.com
- www.RiteSite.com
- www.MBA-exchange.com

- www.eKornFerry.com
- www.Heidrick.com
- www.ExecSearches.com
- www.SpencerStuart.com
- www.Netshare.com
- www.FutureStep.com
- www.BlueSteps.com
- www.ExecutivesOnly.com

- www.RussellReynolds.com
- www.EgonZehnder.com

INDUSTRY NICHE SITES

- www.Dice.com
- www.JobsInTheMoney.com
- www.CareerBank.com
- www.eFinancialCareers.com
- www.Hcareers.com
- www.ComputerJobs.com
- www.JobsInLogistics.com
- www.HealthCareSource.com
- www.BrokerHunter.com
- www.AllRetailJobs.com
- www.TelecomCareers.net
- www.AllNurses.com
- www.ComputerWork.com
- www.MarketingJobs.com
- www.EngCen.com
- www.eTeach.com
- http://Employer.JobScience.com
- www.SalesJobs.com
- www.DestinyGrp.com/Destiny
- www.TopLanguageJobs.co.uk
- www.HealthJobsUSA.com
- www.GreatInsuranceJobs.com
- www.TalentZoo.com
- www.BubbaJunk.com

- www.MBAJungle.com

- www.Medzilla.com
- www.TVJobs.com
- www.LeisureJobs.com
- www.MortgageBoard.net
- www.ClearanceJobs.com
- www.NurseTown.com
- www.SalesHeads.com
- www.NursingCenter.com
- www.MEPatWork.com
- www.Legalstaff.com
- www.Callcentercareers.com
- www.Lawjobs.com
- www.Jobs4HR
- www.CallCenterJobs.com
- www.HireBio.com
- www.TaxTalent.com
- www.EngineerJobs.com
- www.TAOnline.com
- www.AirlineCareer.com
- www.ConstructionJobs.com
- www.JustTechJobs.com
- www.TinyTechJobs.com
- www.Tech-Engine.com
- www.EngineeringJobs.Com

COLLEGE RECRUITING SITES

- www.CollegeGrad.com
- www.eRecruiting.com
- www.NACElink.com
- www.JobWeb.com
- www.CollegeRecruiter.com
- www.CollegeCentral.com

- www.Aftercollege.com
- www.CollegeJournal.com
- www.eCampusRecruiter.com
- www.CampusCareerCenter.com
- www.CollegeJobBoard.com
- www.CampusRN.com

(continued)

(continued)

- www.JobPostings.net
- www.HBCU-Careers.net

- www.AboutJobs.com
- www.EntryLevelJobs.net

DIVERSITY SITES

- www.LatPro.com
- www.HireDiversity.com
- www.IMDiversity.com

- www.DiversityCareers.com
- www.WorkplaceDiversity.com

Christian Job Sites

Thanks go to Kathy Bitschenauer, M.A., Career Change Coach, of New Pathways in Puyallup, Washington, for her research in compiling this helpful list of sites specific to Christian job search. (In instances where the name of the organization is not clear from the URL, it has been listed in parentheses following the link.)

GENERAL CHRISTIAN EMPLOYMENT SITES

- www.christianet.com/ christianjobs/
- www.crosssearch.com/ Business_and_Finance/ Jobs_and_Careers/
- www.christianjobs.com
- www.christianstaffing.org
- www.allchristianjobs.com
- www.christianopportunitiesonline.com

- www.christasites.com
- www.christiancareercenter.com
- www.123christianjobs.com/ christianbusinessdirectory/
- www.catholicjobs.com
- www.intercristo.com
- www.workministry.com

CHRISTIAN WORKPLACE MINISTRY SITES

- www.icwm.com (International Coalition of Workplace Ministries, click on "Directory")
- www.marketplaceleaders.org (Marketplace Leaders)
- www.faithintheworkplace.com (*Christianity Today*'s workplace site)
- www.releasing-kings.com (Christians in Marketplace Ministry)
- www.workplace-ministry.com (Workplace Ministry)

- www.cgcic.com/ christian-owned_businesses.htm (Common Ground Christian Internet Café)
- www.cibn.org (Christ-Influenced, Community-Impacting Business Network)
- www.fcci.org (Fellowship of Companies for Christ International)
- www.workmatters.org (WorkMatters)

- www.aclj.org (American Center for Law and Justice)
- www.ivmdl.org (InterVarsity's Ministry in Daily Life)
- www.christianworkingwoman. org (Christian Working Woman)
- www.marketplacenetwork.com (Marketplace Network)

- www.iccc.net (International Christian Chamber of Commerce)
- www.cmaonline.org (Christian Management Association)
- www.gcts.edu/ockenga/mockler (Mockler Center for Faith and Ethics in the Workplace)

CHRISTIAN INDUSTRY NICHE SITES

Church Ministry

- www.churchjobs.net
- www.churchcentral.com/jobs/
- www.churchjobsonline.com
- www.churchstaffing.com
- www.data-lists.com/ us-churches-database.htm
- www.hcmachaplains.org (Healthcare Chaplains Ministry Association)

- www.kingdomjobs.com
- www.nacpa.org (National Association of Church Personnel Administrators)
- www.ministryemployment.com
- www.vocationsplacement.org
- www.youthpastor.com/jobs/
- www.youthspecialties.com/jobs/

Education/University

- www.123christian.com
- www.ceai.org (Christian Educators Association International)
- www.christiancoachacademy.com
- www.christiancoachtraining.com
- www.christianschoolemployment.com/

- www.christianteachingjobs.com
- www.christianuniversityjobs. com/
- www.nics.org (Network of International Christian Schools)

Engineering

- www.calvin.edu/academic/ engineering/ces/ (Christian Engineering Society)

- www.emiusa.org (Engineering Ministries International)

(continued)

(continued)

Financial
- www.crown.org

Fine Arts
- www.cita.org/jobs/jobs.htm (Christians in Theater Arts)
- www.civa.org (Christians in Visual Arts)

House Parenting/Childcare
- www.christian.houseparent.net

Humanities
- www.calvin.edu/henry/ Christians_in_political_science/
- www.sbl-site.org/EIS/ default.aspx (Society of Biblical Literature)
- www.spu.edu/orgs/nacfla/ (North American Christian Foreign Language Association)

Legal
- www.clsnet.org (Christian Legal Society)

Librarian
- www.acl.org (Association of Christian Librarians)

Media
- www.americanrhetoric.com/rca/ (The Religious Communications Association)
- www.mediafellowship.org/ index2.htm
- www.salem.cc/ sitesOtherMedia.htm (Salem Communications)

Medical
- www.123christian.com/health/ hospitals.shtml (Christian Hospitals and Health Care Centers)
- www.biblebell.org/links/ medlinx.html (Links for Christian Healthcare Professionals)
- www.christianchiropractors.org
- www.cmdahome.org (Christian Medical & Dental Association)
- www.cvmusa.org/ NETCOMMUNITY/ Page.aspx?&pid=183 (Christian Veterinary Mission)
- www.hcfusa.com (Hospital Christian Fellowship)
- www.ncfi.org (Nurses Christian Fellowship International)

Realtors/Loan Officers

- http://americanchristians.org/ ChristianRealEstateBrokers.htm
- http://hismove.com (Christian Real Estate Network)

Sciences

- www.acmsonline.org (Association of Christian Mathematical Sciences)

Social Work

- www.caps.net (Christian Association for Psychological Studies)
- www.nacsw.org/index.shtml (North American Association of Christians in Social Work)

Venue 2: Resume Posting

Post your resume to *all* of the target companies you identified in chapter 11, along with major career sites and relevant niche sites. If there are relevant job postings at your target company's Web site, comb these ads carefully for keywords and load your resume with any terms that are applicable to your background. For tips on keywording your resume, see chapter 8. Include a cover letter that is tailored to the target company (see chapter 10 for cover letter samples).

Venue 3: Resume Distribution

Resume distribution refers to e-mailing recruiters en masse. With the click of a few buttons, your resume can be in the hands of hundreds of recruiters. Let me clarify that statement by saying your resume can be in the *e-mail bin* of hundreds of recruiters. Whether the recruiters choose to open the e-mail and add your resume to their applicant databases is quite another issue, especially when they are inundated with resumes from candidates.

The following services have a record for longevity and integrity in the resume-distribution market:

- **Resume Spider:** www.ResumeSpider.com
- **Resume Rabbit:** www.ResumeRabbit.com
- **Executive Agent:** www.ExecutiveAgent.com
- **Resume Machine:** www.ResumeMachine.com
- **Resume Zapper:** www.ResumeZapper.com
- **Resume Blaster:** www.ResumeBlaster.com

When using a resume-distribution service, remember to convert your resume before e-mailing. Steps for conversion and conversion cleanup are outlined in chapter 10.

Venue 4: Recruiters and Agencies

Clearly, the preferred strategy for job search is to hook up directly with hiring managers *or* people who can connect you with hiring managers. Don't overlook recruiters and employment agencies, because they often know which companies are hiring. At the same time, recognize that recruiters should not be the foundation of your search strategy, given the *CareerXroads Source of Hires Study* statistic that only 4.8 percent of hires come through this source. DBM, a global human resource consulting firm, lists slightly higher odds:

Only 10 percent of job seekers found new employment as a result of search firms or agencies.

When approaching recruiters, lessen your "unknown" factor in one of these ways:

- Ask a colleague who knows the recruiter to place a call for you to warm up the introduction.
- Mention the name of someone already in the recruiter's sphere—a former candidate the recruiter placed, a hiring manager in one of the recruiter's client companies, a professional association contact, and so on.
- Show the recruiter you've done some research on him or her—for instance, mention that you understand he or she frequently sources candidates for companies such as ABC Company and DEF Incorporated.
- Mention respectable projects that the recruiter will be familiar with, such as, "I recently worked on the conference planning committee for the regional meeting of the National Association of Purchasing Managers, and I understand you're a member."

Recruiter Resources

To access listings of recruiters, refer to these resources:

- **The Directory of Executive Recruiters (Kennedy Publications):** Also available online at www.RecruiterRedbook.com, with access to comprehensive data through a one-year subscription of $59.95.
- **Ken Cole's Recruiting & Search Report:** www.rsronline.com/.
- **Resume Distribution Services:** See "Venue 3: Resume Distribution," earlier in this chapter.
- **Riley Guide:** www.rileyguide.com/recruiters.html (this amazingly comprehensive site provides free and fee-based directories of recruiters).
- **Top Echelon:** www.topechelon.com.

Some of the larger recruiting firms include the following:

- **Heidrick & Struggles:** www.Heidrick.com
- **Spencer Stuart:** www.SpencerStuart.com

- **Russell Reynolds Associates:** www.RussellReynolds.com
- **Egon Zehnder International:** www.EgonZehnder.com
- **Korn/Ferry International:** www.KornFerry.com

Agency Resources

You can access a listing of employment agencies via these sites:

- **National Association of Personnel Services' Membership Directory:** www.napsweb.org/MemDir/index.cfm
- **Business.com:** www.business.com/directory/human_resources/ hiring_and_retention/recruiting_services/search_firms/

Some of the larger employment agencies with offices in major markets include the following:

- **Adecco:** www.adecco.com
- **Manpower:** www.manpower.com
- **Snelling & Snelling:** www.snelling.com
- **Kelly Services:** www.kellyservices.com

Travel Tip: Wondering how long your job search will last? As I was flying home from a business trip recently, I noticed a new addition to the seatback in front of me: a digital screen displaying the plane's progress as we traversed the United States. I loved seeing my progress! The screen displayed a map with the plane's location and showed how many more hours/minutes until arrival. Knowing there was an end in sight was comforting and helped me endure the cramped quarters.

Unfortunately, there's no digital display telling you how much time is left before you land your job. In fact, you don't even get to know where you're going to land! What you do know, however, is that God is at the controls.

Venue 5: Classified Ads

Despite the cost efficacy of posting positions online, some employers still advertise with good old-fashioned ink in newspapers and trade journals. Again, don't make this the mainstay of your search strategy. According to surveys by CareerXroads and human resources consulting firm DBM, the odds are slim:

> Only 3 percent to 7 percent of job seekers found new employment as a result of advertisements.

Review classified ads on Sundays and Wednesdays (or whatever day the paper typically has heavier employment advertising), and scour every issue of your industry's trade journals. Often, your local newspaper will carry its classified ads online. Newspaper Links (www.newspaperlinks.com) will help you find your local paper online. And, depending on your search, these national publications might be of help:

- *USA Today:* www.usatoday.com
- The *Wall Street Journal:* www.wsj.com

Venue 6: Direct Inquiry or Mailing

Odds with a direct approach or mailing are pretty slim. Surveys by global human resources consulting firm DBM and college career centers indicate the following:

> Approximately 3 percent of job seekers found employment as a result of a mailing or direct approach.

The odds appear to be better for six-figure professionals when it comes to direct mail. Some of the same resources mentioned under "Purchase Mailing Lists" in chapter 11 can provide you with company mailing information.

Venue 7: Career Events

Job fairs, or career fairs, are another venue to meet employers. Again, don't spend the lion's share of your time here, as job seekers report only single-digit success in landing a position via job fairs:

> Only 3 percent of job seekers found employment as a result of job fairs.

To find out where fairs are being held, do the following:

- Check your local newspaper. Announcements for job fairs are usually placed near the employment ads.
- Check with other in-the-know organizations, such as your professional association, alumni placement office, or local employment agencies.
- Call your target companies and ask which career fairs they recruit at.
- CareerBuilder.com hosts job fairs throughout the country. Listings can be found at www.CareerBuilder.com/Career_Fairs/.
- Google the words "job fair" or "career fair" and your geographic location, such as *job fair San Francisco* or *career fair San Francisco* for listings.

When attending these events, go with an agenda and use the networking techniques you learned in chapter 11.

Keeping the Momentum Going

As you implement strategies from the preceding chapter and this chapter, remember to use your calendar and set weekly and daily goals for yourself. Here are some considerations:

- Number of telephone contacts you'll make each week/day
- Number of face-to-face meetings you'll have with people each week/day
- Which target companies you'll research each week/day and what information you want to gather about them
- Follow-up you'll do on prior week's activities
- Companies that you'll submit resumes to; amount of time you'll spend each week/day to search for new jobs online
- Amount of time you'll spend practicing for interviews

Perseverance is the most important ingredient in your search. Calvin Coolidge said, "Nothing in this world can take the place of persistence. Talent will not; nothing is more common than unsuccessful men with talent. Genius will not; unrewarded genius is almost a proverb. Education will not; the world is full of educated derelicts. Persistence and determination alone are omnipotent." God alone is omnipotent, but He calls us to be perseverant in doing the right things, both in the spiritual realm and in the physical realm. 2 Thessalonians 3:4-5 offers encouragement: "We have confidence in the Lord that you are doing and will continue to do the things we command. May the Lord direct your hearts into God's love and Christ's perseverance."

Chapter Wrap-Up

Smart candidates make targeted search strategies the centerpiece of their campaign, and then use traditional search strategies to cover their bases. By all means, submit your resume to your target companies. Reinforce this strategy by including a customized cover letter that mentions a warm contact and conveys knowledge of the company's TOP (Trends, Opportunities, Problems/Projects) issues. Search for and apply to positions that are a good Master F.I.T.™ at target company Web sites, as well as at niche sites or major career sites. If the position you are targeting is frequently sourced by a recruiter, include recruiters in your strategy. Use other venues—direct-mail campaigns, job fairs, and so on—as a backup to your primary focus on targeted job searching.

10 QUICK TIPS TO COVER YOUR BASES WITH TRADITIONAL SEARCH STRATEGIES

1. Use traditional job search strategies sparingly—the odds are simply not in your favor. Spend the majority of your time on targeted search activities and use traditional strategies to cover your bases.

2. Conduct online searches in a strategic manner. First, search the Web sites of companies you've targeted for relevant postings. Second, search major career sites such as Monster.com and CareerBuilder.com. Third, search niche job sites—those that specialize in your functional area or industry.

3. Post your resume and a customized letter at each of your target companies' Web sites. Mention an insider contact in your letter, along with reference to the company's TOP issues and how you can be of value with regard to these issues.

4. When posting to sites that don't have the ability to receive an MS Word version of your resume, convert your resume to ASCII text to eliminate formatting glitches. If you're conducting a highly confidential search, don't post your resume online. To minimize the potential for identity theft, use a veiled e-mail address, such as mgmt-candidate@yahoo.com instead of johnsmith@cisco.com; omit address information (mentioning a regional area is okay); and use discretion regarding which telephone number you include on the resume.

5. Shop wisely for a resume-distribution service. Beware of those that boast the ability to e-mail your resume to thousands of recruiters. You don't want thousands. You want finely targeted numbers, specifically by functional/occupational area, industry, geography, or telephone area code. Quality is more important than quantity.

6. Determine whether recruiters or employment agencies are appropriate for your search and use them accordingly. Remember that the recruiter's first loyalty is to the client company and that he or she doesn't proactively market candidates to numerous employers. Agencies might take a more proactive role in helping applicants find employment.

7. Review classified ads in your local newspaper, national newspaper (if appropriate), and trade journals. When responding, find a warm contact to get the inside scoop on the company's needs. Follow up with a brief e-mail to the hiring manager with your resume, and submit your resume through proper channels with human resources, mentioning that you've already had a conversation with Ms. Hiring Manager.

8. Consider a direct-inquiry/direct-mail campaign. If your target position is a support-level or common position that is in high demand, cold-calling companies by telephone or in person might work. For other job targets, mail a "broadcast letter" that offers a quick thumbnail of your strengths and evidence of how you've contributed to solving problems that are common to your potential employer.

9. Find where career fairs are held by checking the classified section of your paper, inquiring with professional associations or local employment agencies, asking your target companies what career fairs they attend and recruit at, and looking online using the keywords "job fair" and your geographic location. Attend with an agenda. Know which companies you want to have conversations with, use your sound bites and SMART Stories™, and remember the mantra "It's all about them, not you!"

10. Keep momentum going by establishing weekly and daily goals. Remember to combine strategies in this chapter with a targeted/active approach in which you identify ideal companies, read, research, talk with people through focused networking, and stay on the radar screen of people who influence the hiring process.

MASTERFUL COACHING QUESTIONS

Which of the seven traditional job search areas do you need to stop doing or spend less time on?

_____

_____

What's the hidden payoff for spending time there? For instance, one of my job search clients recognized that she was spending too much time on attending job fairs because it felt "safer" and less intimidating than networking with connections to target companies.

_____

_____

_____

_____

On what activities will you refocus your time and energy?

_____

_____

_____

Who will help you stay accountable to this new focus?

_____

Pocket Prayer

Lord, You are a God of details. Nothing escapes Your notice, from the minute details of how to convert my resume into ASCII text to the best time of day to contact my target companies. Give me clarity of mind to be attentive to the details of my search. Lead me as I set weekly and daily goals for my search. Give me wisdom about how much time to spend on each of my activities. If I'm spending too much time on unproductive activities, forgive me and show me how to readjust. Help me to abide in You every minute of the day, not turning to the left or the right, but putting You front and center so that I, like Joshua, "may be successful" wherever I go (Josh. 1:7). In Jesus' name, Amen.

CHAPTER 13

THE FOUR *C*S OF INTERVIEWING: CONNECT, CLARIFY, COLLABORATE, AND CLOSE

"Most conversations are simply monologues delivered in the presence of a witness."

—*Margaret Miller*

"He who gives an answer before he hears, it is folly and shame to him."

—*Prov. 18:13 (NASB)*

hat might get in the way of your acing an interview? If you're like most people, one of these problems could trip you up:

- **Performance jitters:** They happen to everyone. Take a deep breath and make them work for you—they'll give you the endorphins you need to be "on." And, should you get out of the interview and think of something important you forgot to say, call the interviewer later or mention it in your follow-up thank-you letter (the one you'll send within 24 hours of your interview!).

  For performance jitters, hang on to this verse: "Do not be anxious about anything, but in everything, by prayer and petition, with thanksgiving, present your requests to God. And the peace of God, which transcends all understanding, will guard your hearts and your minds in Christ Jesus" (Phil. 4:6-7).

- **Anxiousness:** You may have a lot riding on this interview if you need to land a job soon. Or perhaps this is an interview for your dream job, and you don't want to blow it! God *will* provide for you.

  For anxiety, lean on these truths: "Peace I leave with you; my peace I give you. I do not give to you as the world gives. Do not let your hearts be troubled and do not be afraid" (John 14:27) and "'So then, don't be afraid. I will provide for you and your children.' And he reassured them and spoke kindly to them" (Gen. 50:21).

- **Pride:** You are more interested in impressing the interviewer than you are in learning about the needs of the company and how you can be of value.

  When pride may cause you to stumble, remember these verses: "Pride goes before destruction, a haughty spirit before a fall" (Prov. 16:18) and "God opposes the proud but gives grace to the humble" (James 4:6b).

- **Lack of Preparation:** You haven't spent enough time doing your homework. Or you spent a lot of time but didn't come up with as much as you'd like.

  If it was laziness that led you to not do your homework or perhaps poor prioritizing, confess this and move on. If you did the best you could and are asked a question in the interview that you can't answer, be honest (don't try to bluff your way through—see Psalm 12:3, "May the Lord cut off all flattering lips and every boastful tongue"). Tell the interviewer you did several hours of research but didn't come across that information, or ask a question that shifts the discussion from interrogative to collaborative.

- **Fatigue:** Are you burning the candle at both ends? There's no way you can be articulate and attentive in an interview if you're low on sleep, nutrition, exercise, or spiritual strength.

  If you're like me, you have a tendency to take care of other people before you tend to yourself. Remember the airline admonition to put your oxygen mask on before you help others!

Regardless of our problems, God always has a spiritual truth that will transform the situation. When grounded in His Word, you'll be able to manage any interview scenario.

> **Travel Tip:** Always pray before going into an interview, then let go of it and trust God for the outcome.

One important truth about interviewing is that you are to be Christ's servant in the workplace. Interviewing is about helping others (the employer) become more successful while also moving your career toward an ideal state (for example, gaining meaningful employment, adequate remuneration, responsibility, recognition). To better understand how that happens, this chapter focuses on a coaching framework that involves four *C*s. Your job will be to

1. *Connect* with the interviewer to enhance chemistry.
2. *Clarify* the primary "deliverables" of the job (what needs to be done).
3. *Collaborate* on how you would do the job.
4. *Close* in a respectful manner that indicates your desire for the position and commitment to the company.

> **Travel Tip:** Philippians 2:3 tells us, "Do nothing out of selfish ambition or vain conceit, but in humility consider others better than yourselves." That includes your interviewers! At the same time, you must possess a full measure of self-confidence—a confidence that is rooted in God's view of you as a gifted, purpose-filled human being whom He wants to use!

Phase 1: Connect with the Interviewer—How to Create the Right Chemistry

Recall from "Five Phases of a Job Transition" (U = Uncover Phase), in chapter 5, that you will be judged by your interviewers on three dimensions: Chemistry, Competency, and Compensation. This first dimension—Chemistry—is critical. You'll want to connect with the company's mission, its people, and its customers. You'll also want the interviewer to connect with you.

What does it mean to connect with someone? To get clear on this, think about someone in your work world with whom you connect well. When you speak to this person, what is present in the conversation? When you interact, how does this person behave? Chances are good that, in addition to having some things in common, the person you're thinking of respects you, supports you, and is a good listener and communicator. You can do the same in your interview.

To connect with interviewers, do the following:

- **Clear the 30-second hurdle with a positive halo effect.** You can predispose people to like you by praying ahead of time for your meeting. Ask God to give you favor with the interviewer, help you understand the interviewer's needs, and show you how to be of value. At the actual meeting, wear an engaging smile, shake hands firmly, dress appropriately, and make the person feel that you are absolutely delighted to meet them. You can also put on a halo by associating yourself with a trusted colleague or friend of the interviewer—this is where networking can really work for you!

- **Share something in common.** When entering an interviewer's office, notice your surroundings. It might be that you can make small talk about the interviewer's awards on the wall, interesting artwork, pictures of kids, plants, tidy desk, out-of-the-ordinary furniture, and so on. A terrific way to share something in common is to comment on the interviewer's background based on the company research you've done. Another bonding agent is laughter—share it whenever possible.

BE READY WITH OPENERS TO CONNECT WITH INTERVIEWERS

If meeting new people makes you nervous, practice an opener to help you feel more in control. One of these might suit you well:

- "It's so nice to meet you. Congratulations on your latest article. I loved your point about _____ [fill in the blank…using recycled materials, going to a flextime model, mastering the art of spiel, etc.]."

- "Nice to meet you." Then, if the interviewer's desk is cluttered with family photos, consider saying, "It looks like you've got a budding baseball star there!"

- "I'm pleased to meet you. I have to tell you that everyone I've met to this point has been nothing but first-class. Your assistant has been especially helpful."

- "Good to see you again. I'll be interested to catch up on what you've been doing since we last spoke."

- [And, if you have no clue about who the person is] "So glad to meet you. I've been looking forward to better understanding your organization and where I can be of value."

- **Respect them.** Acknowledge that interviewers likely have demanding schedules and difficult work. Respect them for the position of authority they have earned. You do not have to agree with them on everything. Seek to respect others first…it's the fastest way to earn respect in return.

- **Support them.** Make the interviewer's job easier by helping him or her find the right person for the position. You'd probably like it if *you* were that person, and you should do everything in your power to show that you are! If, however, you later discover that you're not, consider doing what one new grad did when he recognized he wasn't going to fit the needs of a particular department manager. He gave the manager the names of two classmates whom he thought would be ideal candidates. Talk about making a lasting impression!

- **Listen with laser accuracy.** It is impossible to connect with others if you don't listen well. Good listening is fueled by curiosity and compassion. Review the section on personality type from chapter 3—understanding that your inter-viewer may take in information or make decisions from a different perspective will help you tailor your message.

- **Communicate exceptionally.** Respond with relevance and an attitude of respect. Recognize that your interviewer's learning style, values, and personal-ity will impact your communication.

SHOULD YOU SHARE YOUR CHRISTIANITY DURING AN INTERVIEW?

"Joe" spent four months in a challenging job search during which he logged 8 to 10 hours a day doing research, making calls, and meeting with networking contacts (this was in addition to taking evening classes, staying involved at church, and hus-banding on the home front). At one point, there were five opportunities in which he was engaged in the interview process. Normally, he would be confused trying to figure out God's will, but through faith, prayer, and fellowship, he experienced a remarkable sense of peace. One of the five opportunities stood out because he initiated the phone call to the president of a division of a large organization. His purpose was to learn what it would be like to reenter a marketplace where he had managed a competitor's sales force years earlier. The president was interested in speaking further with Joe. They met and things clicked. Joe, who lived in California, was introduced via phone and e-mail to management in the Northeast and in Europe.

Leaving for the Northeast for an exploratory two-day interview for which he paid 70 percent of the expenses was, as Joe described it, "an act of faith!" He asked for prayers that God would make an opportunity to share his testimony while meeting with various people in the company. The interview went better than Joe had hoped. The primary interviewer eventually asked Joe what position he felt he was best suit-ed for. Joe's passion is coaching and mentoring leaders, so he described this type of role.

During lunch on the second day, Joe and his interviewer were making their way through the cafeteria line. The interviewer casually asked Joe what religion he prac-ticed, Protestant or Roman Catholic? Of course, in interviewing dos and don'ts, this is a don't—it's illegal to ask such a question. But Joe was happy to respond. He told him, "I have no affiliation to a denomination, only to the truth of the Bible."

Getting to their table, the conversation took an unexpected turn. Joe goes on to say, "I started sharing my testimony, especially my deliverance from Internet pornogra-phy, alcohol, and fear. While the interviewer saw Christianity as something that is practiced like a ritual, I explained to him the only way my deliverance could happen is through a power living inside of me—this power comes through a living relation-ship with Jesus Christ. I clarified that because I am Christian does not mean that I am perfect; rather, through this power and the Word of God I am in a constant self-correcting mode. I added that if he were to look around this lunchroom, he would think by looking at people from the outside that they are all fine; however, the truth is some are hurting with addictions, too."

(continued)

Lunch concluded with discussions on career pathing and other business topics, but Joe wondered to himself, "Why did I share such personal information with this man—more than I have shared with some friends—especially with such a promising opportunity ahead? Certainly, my career coach, Susan, did not advise me to reveal such potential vulnerabilities!"

Is it appropriate to share your testimony in an interview? Not usually. In Joe's case, it was definitely Spirit-prompted and, therefore, the right thing to do. Did Joe get a job offer from the company? Yes, a six-figure position with significant responsibility. Will it always work like that—share your testimony and get a job offer? No. The bottom line is that Joe was obedient and available to be used by God.

Phase 2: Clarify *What* Needs to Be Done

Now that you've learned the basics of connecting with your interviewer, you're ready to *clarify* the deliverables—ask lots of questions about *what* needs to be done. Before we proceed, though, let me make one point crystal clear. Out of respect for the interviewer, let him or her take the lead on clarifying whether you can do the job. You don't want to bulldoze your way in and start asking questions out of turn, so before we go further, let's talk about how you'll respond to the inevitable interview questions.

Answer Frequently Asked Questions and Industry-Specific Questions

Advertising executive William Bernbach said, "The truth isn't the truth until people believe you, and they can't believe you if they don't know what you're saying, and they can't know what you're saying if they don't listen to you, and they won't listen to you if you're not interesting, and you won't be interesting unless you say things imaginatively, originally, freshly." Let me clarify that truth is *not* dependent on someone believing you—God's Word is true and a lot of people don't believe it! But Bernbach does make a good point about being interesting, original, and fresh. You can be, by keeping these five *D*s in mind:

- **Discover** what the employer truly needs to have done (the deliverables).
- **Document** your knowledge, skills, and experience to capably do the job (talent/competencies).
- **Demonstrate** your ability to do the job with greater profitability or productivity for the company than other candidates (value).

- **Display** your ability to motivate yourself and/or others (energy and enthusiasm).
- **Describe** your ability to fit in with the company culture (chemistry).

For an example of how to answer frequently asked questions, with a helpful "before" and "after" response makeover, go to www.ChristianCareerJourney.com/J0163C.pdf. You'll also find a number of industry-specific questions with suggested response strategies at www.ChristianCareerJourney.com/ISQs-expanded.pdf.

Answer Behavioral Interview Questions

Past behavior is the best predictor of future performance. This is the premise for "behavioral interviewing," a system designed by interviewing gurus to determine whether you can, indeed, do the job at hand. As opposed to a series of disjointed, interrogative questions like you might find in a traditional interview, you will find that behavioral interview questions allow for a structured, logical conversational style. Behavioral questions frequently start with these phrases:

- Tell me/us about a time when you....
- Give me/us an example of a time when you....
- How have you handled _____ in the past...?
- When have you been in a situation where you had to...?

After you've answered the interviewer's anchor question, a series of probing questions might follow:

- What was your specific role? Who else was involved?
- How did you decide which task to do first?
- How did the outcome affect the company?
- What might you have done differently?
- How has that experience affected the way you would approach the situation today?

Train yourself to spot these behavioral interview questions, because interviewers will be looking for specific competencies that predict success. The most commonly sought competencies include analytical skills, communication skills, flexibility/adaptability, initiative, leadership skills, planning skills, problem-solving skills, team-work skills, technical skills, and time-management skills.

Ask Big-Picture Questions in the First Interview

Use open questions to gather information. Open questions start with what, how, and why. Some of your questions can also start with who, where, and when. In the first face-to-face interview, ask aerial-mode, big-picture questions to clarify what really needs to be done. Here are a dozen to get you started (do *not* ask all of these questions—choose just a few, or else the interviewers will feel as though they are at the Inquisition):

- What do you want to see accomplished in your team/department/company in the next three to six months? What would be the ideal outcome?
- How will you measure success?
- How will this position specifically support that goal?
- What do you see as the two or three most important tasks for this position in the immediate future?
- With the ideal person in the position, what can be accomplished?
- Who would you point to as a top performer in this position? What traits make them stand out? What specific actions make them so successful? (Interviewers may be hesitant to let the cat out of the bag and tell you specifically what qualities they are looking for; however, these questions can uncover them for you.)
- Who will this position work with internally? Externally? To whom would I report?
- Are you saying that the most important issues are _____ and _____?
- How soon do you want to make a decision?
- Do I understand correctly that when this position is filled, you'll be able to _____? (Fill in the blank: get started on the new launch, clean up the backlog, be freed up to do the work you need to do, catch up on your outstanding receivables, and so on.)

Do your best to get a head start on answers to these questions prior to walking into the interview (see "Step 3: Research," in chapter 11, for more details). Note that the questions on the preceding list center on *the position.* This next list will give you insights into *the company.* Again, learn as much as you can *before* your face-to-face meeting. Assuming that answers to the following questions aren't a matter of public record, you might want to ask the following:

- How long has the company been in business? Is it publicly or privately held? If privately held, by whom?
- What are the company's major milestones, key products/services, and strengths?
- How many employees are there? Where? Have there been recent layoffs? Are any planned?
- What does the organizational chart look like? Where does this position fit in?

Bring a notepad to the interview containing questions you want to ask, and use it to take notes. Beyond this purpose, a notepad can give you something to hold onto during the interview to ease any nervous tension.

Ask Deeper-Detail Questions in Second and Third Interviews

As you get further into the interview process, you'll have established the rapport, trust, and mutual interest to ask deeper, more probing questions. The more senior the position, the more questions you can and should ask. Whereas general questions are appropriate for the HR department, detail questions are more appropriate for managers.

Be cautious! If you ask deeper-detail questions too early in the process, you could come across as pushy or presumptuous. Save these types of questions for the second or third interviews:

- **Questions about the position:** "What would the ideal person in this job accomplish on a weekly basis?" "How is it that this position became open? May I ask, did the person leave or get promoted? What results were you most pleased with? What do you need done next? How many people have had this position over the past few years? What do you look for when considering someone for promotion?"

- **Questions about current and future challenges:** "What stands between where the project/situation is today and where you want to be?" "What have you already done or put in place to achieve those goals?" "What's gotten in the way in the past?" "What if that weren't an issue?" "What is the company's vision for the next 5 to 10 years?"

- **Questions about people:** "To whom would you report, who makes the final hiring decision, who will be your direct reports, whom will you service, who's in charge," and so on.

- **Questions about resources:** "What resources are in place to support this position/project?" And, for positions that would normally have access to financial information, "What information are you able to share about financial trends?"

- **Questions about strategy:** "What's your short-term and long-term strategy for this initiative/program?" Or, if you're being hired to help develop strategy: "What opportunities are available to us? How has strategy been developed in the past? How can that process be improved upon?"

- **Questions about systems and timeline:** "What systems are in place to measure success?" or "Tell me about the infrastructure and technology in place for this project. What's working well? What could be improved upon?" and "Do I understand correctly that you need to fill this position in the next 30 days?"

Listen for important issues and problems that need to be resolved—this is where the ultimate motivation to hire comes from. Move forward methodically with your questions. Don't jump into explaining how you can solve problems until you have asked enough questions and gathered the key information you need. Solving problems and documenting skills should be reserved for Phase 3, collaborating.

Phase 3: Collaborate on *How* to Do the Job

In the *collaborate* phase, your objectives are to

- Focus on *how* the deliverables established in Phase 2 *(clarify)* will be met.
- Offer evidence of meeting prior deliverables using SMART Stories™ and other documentary aids.
- Demonstrate tangibly how you'd do the job.
- Give the employer a glimpse of you doing the job.

To establish how the deliverables will be met, ask questions such as these:

- "What is currently working well?" and "What didn't work well?"
- "What did the prior incumbent do well?" and "What would you like to see more of?"
- "How would you prefer to see this handled?"
- "This is how I might approach that, based on my last position and training I recently attended…what have you found works best inside your company?"
- "I read recently in our trade journal how some companies in California had tried a new strategy for that issue…what are your thoughts on that?"
- "I really admired the way your team approached that situation. Will you be using the same strategy on the next project?"

THE SECRET TO BEING ABLE TO ASK ANY QUESTION

Mary Jansen Scroggins, former sales manager with giftware leader Applause and principal of Jansen & Associates, LLC, offers some sage advice for asking questions: **"You can ask anything if you ask permission."** For instance, preface your clarifying or collaborating questions with one of these permission-based questions:

- "May I ask more about that?"
- "When would be a good time to ask a question about your newest product?"
- "Would it be all right if I took a few minutes to explore that?"

To demonstrate tangibly how you'd do the job, consider using one of these methods:

- MS PowerPoint presentation addressing a typical challenge if this is something that would be applicable to the position
- Recent sample of work at your past employer (being careful to protect confidential information)

- Fictionalized case study
- Impromptu white-board brainstorm of steps you'd take to tackle a challenge
- Interaction with team members in an actual meeting

You've mastered the art of connecting, and learned the importance of clarifying and collaborating. Now it's time to understand and apply the art and science of closing.

Phase 4: Close with Professionalism—How to Wrap Up and Win

Closing should never be a manipulative, pressure-packed culmination of the interview. Because the employer holds the decision-making power, it would be inappropriate for you to be pushy or badger the employer into offering a position. More harm than good would come from such a strategy. It is, however, appropriate to

- Respectfully gain agreement from the employer that you have what they need. ("I've enjoyed our conversation. May I recap my understanding of what you need? We discussed customer retention as the key focus of the position, specifically improving the regularity of weekly e-mail updates and monthly follow-up, and well as creating and implementing a customer survey mechanism in the next three months. Are you satisfied that my demonstration of how I'd approach the survey will meet your needs?")

- Close any gaps between what the employer wants and what you can deliver. ("What would it take to assure you that I would be the best person for this position?" or "How could I improve my value even more?")

- Understand the company's interview process. ("How many steps are in your interview process?" or "What is the next step? When might we set that up?")

- Express your desire for the position—ask for the job! ("I know beyond a shadow of a doubt that this is the perfect position for me. There may be candidates who have heftier resumes than I do, but no one will give you more enthusiasm, commitment, and can-do attitude.")

A CHRISTIAN USES A GREAT CLOSE TO WIN A JOB WITH *O* MAGAZINE

Michelle Burford helps shape the voice of one of the most influential women in America, that of Oprah Winfrey. In the April 2004 issue of *Christianity Today*, Burford relays her story of applying for a job with *O* magazine. She was not what you'd call a front-runner candidate. Burford put it bluntly to her interviewer: "There are 100 people out there who have a better resume. But what you'll get with me is a real passion and a real understanding of what she [Oprah] would want to put out there. You won't find anyone who cares more." She was hired two days later, and played a significant role in one of the most successful magazine launches in history.

- Keep up the momentum and communication with the employer. (Consider using a "leave behind"—an item that you leave with the interviewers at the end of the interview, such as a fact sheet, a case study, before-and-after photos, a collection of testimonials, and so on. In addition, send a performance-based thank-you/follow-up note the same day.)

How to Determine Whether This Is the Right Position

It might be difficult for you to sound enthusiastic about a position if you're not sure that it's the right one for you. The checklist in table 13.1 outlines 10 areas that will help you determine whether the position is, indeed, a good match. In the column to the right, enter a number between 1 and 10 to indicate your satisfaction level. One equals "This is intolerable"; five equals "I can live with this"; and ten equals "This is a dream job!"

Table 13.1: Rate Your Fit with the Position (1–10)

Factor	Rating
FUNCTIONAL FIT:	
Is the position in sync with your gifts and favorite strengths? Will it allow you to use your honed skills, acquired knowledge, and wired-from-birth talents? Do you get to use these talents/ skills the majority of the time? For instance, if analytical tasks invigorate you, will you spend the majority of your time doing this? Or does the position also require that 50 percent of your time be spent doing tasks that aren't your favorite strengths or talents, such as making verbal presentations regarding the results of your analysis? Remember, work is less taxing physically and emotionally when you're doing something that fits with your gifts. (Rom. 12:6; 1 Cor. 12:7-12; Eph. 4:11-13; 1 Pet. 4:10; Ps. 139:13)	
INDUSTRY:	
Do you have an affinity for this industry? Is it aligned with a cause or higher purpose for you? Will you enjoy working with the products or services that the industry represents? Is this important to you? (Exod. 31:2-3; 1 Kings 7:14b; 1 Chron. 28:21; Prov. 22:29)	

Factor	Rating
INCOME:	

Is compensation within industry standards? Will you make
what you need to meet your financial obligations, tithe, and
save? If the offer is lower than you had hoped, do you sense
God's peace and promise to provide in other ways? Your financial
situation may influence your decision—in other words, if you are
presently unemployed, how long can you afford to wait?
(Phil. 4:19; Luke 3:14; Matt. 10:10; Heb. 13:5)

COMPANY AND CULTURE:	

Are employees treated fairly? Are team spirit and fair play evident?
Does the company do what it says it will do in its policies and
other communications? Are staff members viewed as the company's
greatest asset? What about company stability in terms of finances
and future…has there been a history of downsizing, mergers, or
acquisitions? Do trade-journal articles or conversations with
competitors or insiders reveal that the company may be in
financial trouble? Is the ambience and social structure in your
comfort zone? Is the company's mission statement aligned with
your values? If the company expects everyone to work 60-hour
workweeks, is this okay with you? Do you like the company's dress
code, stated or unstated? (Prov. 20:23)

ADVANCEMENT, GROWTH, AND GOALS:	

Will this position be a logical fit for your long-term plans? If this is
more of a bridge job than a dream job, will it allow you to still
have the time and energy you need to work on action steps
toward your dream job? If this is a position toward the end of your
career, will it allow you to create the legacy you want? If you're in
your early or mid-career, is this the right stepping-stone? Does the
company have a policy for promoting from within? Are professional
development and training programs offered? Will the company
reimburse you for training completed outside the company?
(Prov. 16:3,9)

LEVEL OF RESPONSIBILITY:	

Does the opportunity offer the responsibility you'd
like? Will the position give you what's important to
you, for instance, an intellectual challenge,
leadership opportunities, an impressive title, clout,
freedom, independence, the ability to influence change,
and so on? (Prov. 22:29; Isa. 56:4; Matt. 25:22-23)

(continued)

Table 13.1: Rate Your Fit with the Position (continued)

Factor	Rating
CAMARADERIE:	
Do you like the people you'll work for and with? If you prefer to be with like-minded people, will this be the case? Or, if you prefer to be surrounded by diversity and divergent opinions, will this be the case? Is the social atmosphere of the department or company in sync with what you want, such as honest communications, a sense of connectedness, trust, teamwork, interaction, autonomy, service, and so on? (1 Cor. 15:33)	
DIRECT SUPERVISOR:	
Does your immediate supervisor have a good reputation? Are employee turnover rates low? Does your supervisor-to-be appear to be committed to professional growth and development, as opposed to stuck in a rut and stagnant? What, if any, red flags or concerns might you have about personality conflicts or your boss's management style? (Isa. 2:22; Josh. 2:10-11; Ps. 14:2)	
LOCATION AND FACILITIES:	
Is the company's distance from your home acceptable? If the opportunity requires an excessive commute, is telecommuting or relocation a possibility? If no, are there measures you can put in place that will help salvage the commute time, such as taking a course that involves audiotapes? Beyond commute considerations, is the location safe? Will your work space be conducive to productivity and creativity? Does the company provide the equipment and support you need to do your job effectively? (Luke 14:28)	
PERSONAL/FAMILY:	
Will the position enhance or complement your personal/family commitments? Will the schedule or stress level prevent you from giving what you want to your spouse, children, or other important people in your life? (1 Tim. 3:5)	
Total Score:	

Sometimes the question of "Am I compromising or settling for less?" comes into play. A preponderance of low scores for the questions in table 13.1 will help you sort that out. You can also use this system to compare multiple employment offers. And remember that, in the 21st century, saying yes to a job offer is not a lifetime commitment. The more important question is, is God leading you in a direction such that this position appears right for now?

Measure Your Performance in a Post-Interview Analysis

After you finish an interview, do some post-interview analysis on your performance to help you learn and continue to get better with each interview. Ask yourself these questions:

- What went right?
- What would I change or do differently next time?
- What did I learn from the experience?

Further, consider rating yourself on a scale of 1 to 10 in various areas to measure how effective you were.

Item	Rating Scale									
I connected with the interviewer (dressed appropriately, arrived early, exuded professionalism, shared commonalities, used LASER listening, and so on).	1	2	3	4	5	6	7	8	9	10
I made the interview about *them* (the company's needs and how I could satisfy them), not me (what I want, need, or deserve).	1	2	3	4	5	6	7	8	9	10
I clarified both the deliverables of the job and how critical this position is to the interviewer/company.	1	2	3	4	5	6	7	8	9	10
I collaborated with the interviewer on how he or she would like the job done.	1	2	3	4	5	6	7	8	9	10
I offered a demonstration of how I would do the job; I gave the interviewer a sense of how I would perform in the position.	1	2	3	4	5	6	7	8	9	10
I offered *complete* SMART Stories for behavioral interview questions.	1	2	3	4	5	6	7	8	9	10
Every word out of my mouth was positive, pertinent, and precise.	1	2	3	4	5	6	7	8	9	10
I am a known commodity to the interviewer—people within the company or individuals who have strategic alliances with the company know me and recommended me to the interviewer.	1	2	3	4	5	6	7	8	9	10

(continued)

(continued)

Item	Rating Scale									
I closed the interview by gaining agreement, closing gaps, understanding the company's interviewing process, and expressing desire for the position.	1	2	3	4	5	6	7	8	9	10
I sent a performance-based thank-you/ follow-up letter within 24 hours.	1	2	3	4	5	6	7	8	9	10

Total Score: _____ out of 100

Chapter Wrap-Up

Throughout all phases of the four *C*s—Connect, Clarify, Collaborate, and Close—let your personality and natural enthusiasm shine through. *Employers love to hire people who love what they do (and are competent because of their passion!)*. Recognize that the more connection or rapport you gain with the interviewer, the more you'll be able to clarify and collaborate. The more you clarify and collaborate, the more natural it will be to close.

---

10 QUICK TIPS TO CONNECT, CLARIFY, COLLABORATE, AND CLOSE THE INTERVIEW

1. **Connect by remembering the interview mantra: "It's about them, not me."** Seek to respect others first…it's the fastest way to earn respect in return. Recognize that interviewers are people with challenges, deadlines, and stress—help them alleviate their stress by solving and serving. Offer your best case for why you are the right person for the job and able to support the company.

2. **Use the LISTEN acronym,** which stands for Laser your focus; Investigate and be curious; Silence your tongue—hold your judgment and open your mind; Take brief notes and take time to formulate your response; Elevate the other person; and Note the nonverbals, including your body language and that of your interviewer. It is impossible to connect with others if you don't listen well.

3. **RESPOND well,** meaning Remember your objective; Engage the interviewer; Share succinctly; Point to benefits; Offer proof; Never drone on; and Dedicate yourself to a win-win relationship. And pay attention to your delivery—tone, inflection, body language, attitude, and motive combine to make how you say it just as important as what you say.

4. **Connect with each of the various company contacts.** You may meet with the hiring manager, your boss's boss, a human resources representative, technical people, sales and marketing people, finance people, peers, subordinates, and key customers. Each of these individuals has a different agenda that you'll want to be aware of when formulating your responses.

5. **Clarify the employer's top two or three "deliverables."** Before asking clarifying questions of your own, answer the interviewer's questions. Use SMART Stories to confirm your competencies and tie in to their needs. After interviewers get a better sense of your qualifications, they'll be more open to answering your questions. Remember to time your questions so that it doesn't look like you're commandeering the interview.

6. **In your first face-to-face interview, ask big-picture questions.** "What do you want to see accomplished in your team/department/company in the next three to six months?" "How will you measure success?" "What are your long-range plans and how can this position support those plans?" Ideally, you should ask these types of questions of your networking contacts prior to the interview so that you can arrive prepared and ready to position yourself as a solution. As the interview progresses (either well into the first interview or in a second or subsequent interview), ask deeper-detail questions.

7. **After you're entirely clear on what needs to be done, collaborate!** Here, you'll focus on how the deliverables will be met. Discussion might include comments like these: "We had a similar situation at my last employer. The strategy we took involved _____, which worked out well. How would something like this work within your organizational structure?" Or "I saw a presentation at the last CMIN conference that addressed that very issue. I'm wondering whether we could explore how this might be tailored to your needs."

8. **To demonstrate how you would do the job, take action.** Consider giving an MS PowerPoint presentation to demonstrate your presentation skills, addressing a fictionalized case study to demonstrate your analytical skills, brainstorming marketing strategies to demonstrate your marketing skills, making a sales presentation to demonstrate your closing skills, and so on. Whatever you'll be doing on the job, show the employer how you can do it. The more the employer can visibly see you doing the work, the better.

9. **As the interview comes to a close, make it easy for the employer to say, "Yes, we want you!"** Start by gaining agreement that you have what it takes, such as "May I ask what you see as my greatest strengths for the position?" Or "Are you satisfied that I'd meet your needs in the position?" Close any gaps between what the employer wants and what you can deliver.

10. **Express desire for the position, and ask for the job!** Consider a "leave behind," such as a fact sheet relevant to the interviewers or a collection of testimonials. Keep the door open for future communications by asking, "What's the next step?" Ask permission to follow up. Send a performance-based thank-you/follow-up note **the same day** that you interview (see an example in chapter 10, figure 10.3). If the interview went really well, also consider a quick telephone call a few hours later in the day.

MASTERFUL COACHING QUESTIONS

What in your background will provide common ground with the interviewer, the company's mission, its people, and its customers?

_____

_____

_____

To clarify in the interview, what big-picture questions will you ask your interviewers? Prioritize the list. Review the list just prior to the interview to keep it fresh in your mind. How will you remind yourself to ask these during the interview?

_____

_____

_____

Are there any red flags you have about a position you're interviewing for?

_____

_____

_____

Review the collaborating questions in this chapter. What collaborating questions will you ask?

_____

_____

_____

How will you practice asking tie-in questions at the close of your SMART Stories to clarify and collaborate? Who can support you in this?

_____

_____

What specific action can you take to demonstrate to an interviewer your ability to do the job?

_____

_____

With regard to closing the interview, what gaps, if any, do you anticipate between what your skills are and what the employer wants done?

_____

_____

If you anticipate gaps, what actions would help close those gaps?

_____

_____

Refer to the factors in table 13.1. Which is most important to you? _____

What minimum score do you need for each of the factors before you'd consider taking the job? _____

What is the lowest total score you would accept? _____

Pocket Prayer

Gracious Lord, thank you for the interviews that You have prepared for me. I ask that You would go ahead of me and prepare the way. Give me favor with my interviewers. Allow me to see their needs, and how I can be of value and service to them. As Aaron spoke for Moses, Lord, I pray You would speak for me—take my tongue and let it speak words that best capture my experiences and convey my ability to contribute to this organization. Give me discernment to understand where the interviewers are coming from. Help me uncover things that might be important for my protection. If You want me to reveal my relationship with You during this interview, make that clear to me and open the door for it to happen. And if the timing isn't right during the interview, then Father I pray that they would know I am Your follower simply because of the way I act. May my brand be about excellence, love, and servant leadership. Give me a job where I can be a light for You while bringing value to those I work for. I rejoice to serve a God who does exceedingly above all that we ask or think. In Jesus' name, Amen.

CHAPTER 14

SALARY NEGOTIATIONS: TRUTHS AND TIPS FOR CHRISTIANS IN THE MARKETPLACE

"You may labor to be rich for God, though not for the flesh and sin."

—Rev. Richard Baxter, English clergyman, 1615–1691

"In the business world, everyone is paid in two coins: cash and experience. Take the experience first; the cash will come later."

—Harold S. Geneen, Accountant, Industrialist, and CEO

Salary negotiations. The thought causes most people to cringe. To a large degree, salary dictates our lifestyle. We typically enter negotiations hoping to make as much as or more than we did in our last position. Money is often a touchy topic because there's a lot riding on it.

Perhaps you've experienced a prolonged period of unemployment and funds are exhausted. Perhaps you're committed to getting out of debt and need some extra income. Perhaps the future is arriving more quickly than anticipated and you need to beef up your child's college fund or your retirement account. Perhaps you want to increase your support to missions or other causes. Perhaps it's all of the above! Regardless of your situation, God has much to say about money, as there are hundreds of references to this topic throughout the Old and New Testaments.

In this chapter we examine salary negotiations from first to last steps and give you ideas, strategies, and language you can use to negotiate a compensation package that rewards you fairly for your contributions. Before we do that, let's look at salary from a Biblical perspective.

Seven Situations That Cause Christians to Stumble over Salary

From personal experience and in my work as a coach, I have noted the following themes when it comes to the sensitive subject of salary:

1. **Lack of trust:** Much of the fear and anxiety that creeps into our lives around money is rooted in a lack of trust that God can and will provide for us. We tend to think of our Provider as little whereas He is so big! ("I was young and now I am old, yet I have never seen the righteous forsaken or their children begging bread" Ps. 37:25.)

2. **Withholding from God what is "ours":** We clutch what we think is ours (money, relationships, possessions, time, reputation), instead of realizing that everything belongs to God ("The earth is the Lord's, and everything in it, the world, and all who live in it" Ps. 24:1; "For every living soul belongs to me" Ezek. 18:4a).

3. **Seduction:** Our society and the media encourage us to buy into the lie that what we have is not enough. We think we need the newest techno gadget or brand-name shoes or late-model car to be happy. ("For the love of money is a root of all kinds of evil. Some people, eager for money, have wandered from the faith and pierced themselves with many griefs" 1 Tim. 6:10, and "Those who cling to worthless idols forfeit the grace that could be theirs" Jon. 2:8.)

4. **Identity:** We equate our identity with how much we make instead of how much Christ loves us. When Christ is our identity, everything else pales. ("What is more, I consider everything a loss compared to the surpassing greatness of knowing Christ Jesus my Lord, for whose sake I have lost all things. I consider them rubbish, that I may gain Christ" Phil. 3:8, and "Set your minds on things above, not on earthly things" Col. 3:2.)

5. **Pride:** We want to impress others. Outward appearances—the car we drive, clothes we wear, home we live in—pressure us to "keep up with the Joneses" instead of live for God. ("For all that is in the world, the lust of the flesh and the lust of the eyes and the boastful pride of life, is not from the Father, but is from the world" 1 John 2:16 [NASB].)

6. **Priorities:** We prioritize making money over creating relationships with people. ("And now I will show you the most excellent way…. If I give all I possess to the poor and surrender my body to the flames, but have not love, I gain nothing" 1 Cor. 12:31–1 Cor. 13:3.)

7. **Debt:** We have mismanaged our money and are now under pressure to land a high salary to pay off debt. We've not been disciplined in spending less than we earn. Proverbs 15:27a says, "A greedy man brings trouble to his family," and 15:32, "He who ignores discipline despises himself, but whoever heeds correction gains understanding."

If any of these situations rings true for you, confess where you're at to God and rest in His forgiveness (He will gladly give you strategies to overcome obstacles or dig out of debt). Then choose to live by God's truths. When doing so, we receive what Christians and most of the world are all striving for: to be filled with love, joy, peace, patience, kindness, goodness, faithfulness, gentleness, and self-control. 1 Timothy 6:17 reminds us to put our hope in God, "who richly provides us with everything for our enjoyment."

Five Truths to Take to the Salary Negotiation Table

As you approach salary negotiations, remember these spiritual truths:

1. God is your provider, *not* your employer. The Lord has promised to provide for your needs (and will give wisdom to discern between needs and wants). ("And my God will meet all your needs according to his glorious riches in Christ Jesus" Phil. 4:19.)

2. Christ died to free you from the slavery of always longing for more, more, more. And whomever the Son sets free is free indeed. (Keep your lives free from the love of money and be content with what you have, because God has said, "Never will I leave you; never will I forsake you" Heb. 13:5.)

3. If you've wandered from Him (and who hasn't!), God may be using your financial circumstances to lovingly get your attention so that you will repent of sin. When you do, He will immediately forgive and help you to walk blamelessly before Him. ("No good thing does He withhold from those whose walk is blameless." Ps. 84:11)

4. He is happy to give you more when you responsibly use what you have. ("His master replied, 'Well done, good and faithful servant! You have been faithful with a few things; I will put you in charge of many things. Come and share your master's happiness!'" Matt. 25:23.)

5. You are worthy of receiving your wages. ("…the worker deserves his wages" Luke 10:7.)

God's truths will enable you to approach salary negotiations without letting fear or pride get in the way.

> **Travel Tip:** If you find yourself between jobs, you understandably cut back on expenses. You think twice about buying incidentals, cancel the weekend getaway, and stop tithing. After all, God understands your situation, right? Yes, He understands, but by not giving, you are making two statements: (1) You are not willing to trust God to help with your financial obligations, and (2) You think your way is better than God's.
>
> The truth is that He set up the system so that we will trust Him and He can bless us for trusting Him. Don't stop tithing, even if you're living on unemployment checks or drowning in debt. Tithing is external evidence of your submission to God. Jesus acknowledged the widow's mites and will acknowledge your sacrifice as well (Mal. 3:8-12).

Preparing for the Salary Dance

The most important step you can take toward negotiating a fair salary is knowing and communicating your value. It's not about how much you need, but about how much your employer needs you! Pause and read that last sentence again, out loud. It is not your employer's problem that you need a certain amount to live on.

To effectively negotiate compensation that is competitive and fair, you must first understand your value, learn about the value of the position, and base your negotiation on the value you can deliver to the organization. Be prepared to negotiate salary from day one of your job search! Learn how to deal with these requests so that you don't harm your future negotiating position, box yourself into a lower salary, or eliminate yourself from consideration right at the start.

Research Comparable Salaries

First you must lay the groundwork by putting together some hard numbers about average compensation for someone with your skills, qualifications, years of experience, industry focus, and geographic location. It's unlikely that you will be able to identify a precise salary for the exact job you are considering, but the more information you have, the more confident you'll feel about negotiating your salary based on "fair market value."

Salary Tools and Surveys

The Internet abounds with tools and resources that will give you detailed information about salary ranges for specific professions in specific geographic areas. Additional resources are available in print publications, both books and periodicals, that you can find at your local library. Your reference librarian can help you find the most precise and most comprehensive sources for your particular field and level. Here are a few to get you started:

- **JobSmart.org Gateway** (www.jobsmart.org): This Web site is a gateway to hundreds of salary surveys available on the Internet.
- **Salary tools:** The following sites are a good place to start; you can easily find many more by entering the word "salary" into your favorite search engine.

  www.careerbuilder.com
  www.monster.com
  www.salary.com
  www.salaryexpert.com
  www.wageweb.com
  www.erieri.com (Economic Research Institute)

- **Professional associations:** If you are a member of one or more professional associations, contact them directly to ask about salary surveys.
- **U.S. Department of Labor,** *Occupational Outlook Handbook:* This resource is a treasure trove of career information including salary ranges. Explore www.bls.gov/oco/ to find data for your profession.
- **Federal government salary tables:** If you are interested in a job with the federal government, you can review salary ranges for every grade and profession at this site: www.opm.gov/oca/07tables/index.asp.
- **The Riley Guide to Employment Opportunities and Job Resources on the Internet:** See www.rileyguide.com/salary.html for a comprehensive resource list for salary information.

Internet Postings and Want Ads

During your job search, as you review online job postings or print classified ads, you will find that many include salary information that you can add to the data you are collecting.

Network Contacts and Recruiters

Include questions about salary as part of your networking interviews:

- "Tell me, what is an average salary for someone with my experience at your company? What would a top performer earn?"
- "How does your company determine its salary ranges?"
- "What does your company pay for Java programmers with five years of experience?"
- "I've been at the same company so long, I'm out of touch with salary ranges. Can you help me out with some general information about your company?"

Be sure to talk to people who work at large companies. Most large organizations have fixed salary ranges based on job grade, which are often published in an employee handbook. Recruiters are also an excellent source of information. During contacts with them, ask for a "market check" on your salary expectations.

Put It All Together

Relying on multiple sources means that you will have a wide range of data that, together, should give you a fairly accurate picture of the "going rate" for your profession. Table 14.1 shows a sample of comparative salary data developed by a Web designer.

Table 14.1: Research on Comparative Salary Data

Source	Low Range	Median	Upper Range
Salary tool: workindex.com/salary/ (national averages)	$46,027	$54,704	$58,315
Salary tool: www.salary.com (national averages)	$45,662	$54,269	$57,853
Salary tool: www.salaryexpert.com (New York/statewide average)	$37,383	$47,798	$56,517
Salary survey: American Institute of Graphic Artists	$40,000	$48,000	$56,700
Print ad: Flash Designer/Graphic Artist *(Kansas City Star)*	$32,000		$40,000
Online ad: Production Artist (New York)	$57,000		$66,000
Network contact: president, Kansas City Ad Club	$40,000	$45,000	$50,000
Network contact: Acme Corporation, job grade 8	$45,000	$47,500	$50,000
Average	$42,965	$49,544	$54,423

Keep in mind that these figures do not include benefits or performance bonuses, which can drive up your compensation significantly. Now it's your turn. Follow the "Masterful Coaching Tips" at the end of this chapter to research your own comparative salary data.

Develop Your Salary Targets

Now that you know what the "going rate" is for people in your profession, you can begin to develop your target salary ranges for your next position. Compare your data to your current or most recent salary, taking into consideration the number of years of experience you have, your level of expertise, and the current job market for people in your profession. As you develop your salary targets, don't forget about projected bonuses or long-term benefits that you might be losing if you leave your current job.

After analyzing all of your findings, develop your target compensation in three ranges:

- **Your "reality" number:** The lowest salary you will accept; the bottom line you need to pay bills comfortably and work toward your long-term financial goals.
- **Your "comfort" number:** An amount you can accept and feel that you are being adequately compensated for your value; a reasonable and realistic goal.
- **Your "dream" number:** Your ideal salary and/or the level of compensation commanded by top performers in your target positions.

The higher your value to the employer, the more likely you will be able to achieve your "dream" number. What can you do to move yourself up the value chain?

Use the "Masterful Coaching Tips" worksheet at the end of this chapter to identify your own reality, comfort, and dream numbers. Armed with this information, you are prepared to negotiate your salary based on fair market value.

How to Deflect Salary Questions Until the Offer

At what point should you share your requirements and start the salary dance? In a nutshell, the time to discuss salary is *after* a firm job offer has been made. Before you receive an offer, you have no negotiating power, and you are more likely to harm than help yourself with a too-early discussion of salary. Think of it this way: Hiring is like shopping. The employer will first peruse a large number of candidates, "try on" a few via interviews, and then make a selection. At that point, the employer has switched from "shopper" to "buyer," and this switch gives a powerful boost to your ability to negotiate.

To preserve your negotiating power, learn to deflect questions about salary until you have received an offer. Here are some strategies.

In Cover Letters

There are several ways you can handle the salary question in your cover letters:

- **Ignore.** In all likelihood, making no mention of salary now will not harm your chances of being selected for an interview.
- **Defer.** "I will be happy to discuss salary considerations during an interview."
- **Address without revealing anything.** "My salary requirements are open; I am more interested in the challenges and opportunities of this position and expect that your company pays a competitive salary." This response might be seen as evasive, but it does indicate that you read the ad and are at least responding to the company's request.

- **Share a range.** "Based on my understanding of the fair market value of this position, I anticipate a salary in the $85,000 to $95,000 range." Or, "My current compensation is in the high forties, and I anticipate this would increase 10 to 15 percent in a new position." The only problem with this response is that the employer now knows what you expect and can initiate negotiations at that level…or below.

RECRUITERS: THE EXCEPTION TO THE RULE

Because recruiters are seeking candidates who fit their client company's specifications to a T, they need to know whether your salary expectations are in line with what the company is offering. Most recruiters won't continue conversations if you aren't forthcoming about your current salary and expectations.

During Telephone or In-Person Interviews

Here are a few suggestions for turning the salary question around without appearing difficult, stubborn, uncooperative, or manipulative. Remember that how you say this will be as important as what you say. Strive for politeness and objective curiosity.

- "Salary is important, but it's not my first consideration. I am more interested in finding the right position, where I can make a real contribution. I'm very interested in what you've told me so far; can we continue that discussion?"

- "I've always been compensated fairly based on my contributions; I anticipate this would be the case at Widget Products, too. Can you tell me more about your current challenges? So far I'm excited about the position, and I'd like to learn more."

- "To tell you the truth, I don't have enough information about this position yet to be able to determine a meaningful salary. Can you tell me more about the scope of the position and your performance expectations?"

You get the idea. Address the question but stay focused on what's really important—whether you are a good fit for the position and the company. And, in case you feel compelled to provide an answer, prepare and practice a statement that includes salary ranges, rather than hard numbers, and is based on your research:

- "I understand that fair market value for this position is in the $80,000 to $95,000 range. Is that what you expect?"

- "I've always been paid competitively based on my contributions to the company. Most recently I've earned in the low seventies, and I would expect a 15 to 20 percent increase for this challenging role."

NEVER STATE A RANGE BELOW YOUR REALITY NUMBER

When stating ranges, never mention a figure that is below your reality number. Keep in mind that while you are focusing on the upper end of your range, the employer hears and homes in on the lower number you recite. It's likely you'll receive an offer that is closer to the lower end of your range than the higher.

When an Offer Is Made

Congratulations! You've accomplished your goal in the interview process and earned a job offer. The employer has switched from "shopper" to "buyer," and the salary dance has fully begun. Prepare diligently for all possibilities, and you'll be able to negotiate with confidence and ease.

The Employer's First Move

The first move might come as a question from the employer: "So, what will it take to bring you on board?" or "We'd like to make you an offer. What salary range were you thinking of?"

Your First Move

Be careful! In your relief at getting the offer, it's tempting to jump right in and share your research and your target ranges. But it's better to keep your cool and remember the strategies for deflecting salary discussions that you practiced earlier in the process. For the most beneficial outcome, you must "deflect" one more time so that the employer, and not you, is the first to associate a salary number with your job offer. These responses will help:

- "Thank you! I'm excited about the opportunity! Based on the value I can bring to meet the challenges we discussed, what do you think is fair compensation for this position?"
- "I'm glad we agree that I have the right mix of skills and experience to really make an impact in this position. In what salary range do you see me?"
- "Thank you. I appreciate your confidence in me. We've discussed some significant challenges, and I'm looking forward to tackling them. What figure did you have in mind?"

Next comes your first real move in the salary dance. When the employer comes back with a number or a range, your initial response is critically important.

The Moment of Silence

In every case, whatever the number, whether high or low, your first response should be to repeat the number, thoughtfully and nonjudgmentally. Then stop talking. This is called the Moment of Silence. Bite your tongue, and let the employer make the next move.

REPEAT THE TOP END OF THE RANGE

When the employer states a range, your repetition of the number should be the top end of the range. Let's say the employer answers, "Well, our range for this position is $47,000 to $52,000." Your thoughtful response: "Fifty-two thousand dollars...." Your goal is to plant the top end of the range in your listener's mind, rather than the minimum amount offered.

During the silence, you'll be calculating silently to compare the number to your reality, comfort, and dream numbers. During this Moment of Silence, you will need to determine whether this is a reality, comfort, or dream number so that you can make your next move with confidence.

Be Sure You Are Clear About the Parameters of the Job

At this point in your discussions you should have an excellent understanding of the position scope, challenges, and performance expectations. But before you start to negotiate your compensation, it is essential to clear up any questions that remain about the job description, reporting relationships, start date, and your employment status.

INDEPENDENT CONTRACTOR OR EMPLOYEE?

Many employers are hiring workers as independent contractors instead of employees. The distinction has important tax and employment benefits consequences. Those who should be classified as employees but aren't may lose out on Workers' Compensation, unemployment benefits, and, in many cases, group insurance (including life and health) and retirement benefits. In general, if the business provides training in required procedures and you receive extensive instructions on how work is to be done, this suggests that you may be an employee. For more information, visit the IRS Web site at www.irs.gov/faqs/faq-kw54.html.

All of these factors can have a significant impact on your compensation and working conditions and therefore will affect the way you react to the salary that has been offered.

Agree on Base Salary Before Benefits or Bonuses

You might also be wondering about benefits, performance bonuses, and perks that you will be entitled to or that you can negotiate. Although these must be factored into your decision, at this point you need to come to an agreement on base compensation (salary) for a clearly defined position. Then you can tackle the additional issues one by one as you work your way through the negotiation. Keep in mind that if you accept a lower salary now, it will affect your compensation going forward with the company, because most salary increases are given as a percentage of current salary.

What to Say When the Offer Is Just Right

You've done your research into fair market rates for this kind of position, and you have a full understanding of the job scope and expectations. The interviewer offers you a salary that is in the comfort or dream range and is eminently fair given the parameters of the position. It's a great company to work for, and the job will advance your long-term career goals. There's absolutely no reason you can't accept on the spot.

> *That sounds terrific, Ms. Williams. My research tells me that that is a very fair market value for this position. I appreciate your confidence in me and am excited about delivering the results we've discussed.*

Next, you'll move on to discussion of your complete compensation package, including bonuses, benefits, and perks…and here you can certainly negotiate, even if you haven't negotiated the base salary figure.

To Counter-Offer, or Not to Counter-Offer?

News flash! Counter-offers are *not* compulsory. Some companies lay their "best and final" offer on the table when they offer you the job. Because you've done your homework, you will know when an offer is good. In some circumstances, when the job market is very tight—the demand for your expertise is low and the supply of candidates is high—you will have little if any negotiating power. Don't be overconfident or greedy; if the offer is attractive and meets your needs and expectations, take it!

How to Initiate a Counter-Offer

When the employer has not laid his best offer on the table (or his best offer isn't matching up to your reality number), you'll have some work to do.

What to Say When the Offer Is Too Low

Here's how to reply when the offer is below your reality number and/or below what you consider to be fair compensation for the position.

Express appreciation for the offer:

> *Mr. Martinez, I'm flattered that you think I'm the right person for the job, and I'm excited about meeting these challenges.*

Clarify job parameters:

> *Let me be sure we both have the same understanding about the position. This would be a full-time, exempt position as Warehouse Manager for your Columbus facility. I would be reporting to the Operations Director and be responsible for a staff of 10 hourly employees. I would be expected to manage the implementation of new bar-coding software in the first six months and lead some vigorous cost-cutting programs to achieve at least 10 percent cost savings in the first year.*

Be sure you have accurately summarized the position. Wait for the interviewer's assent and clear up any differences before you proceed.

> *Do I have that straight?*

Make a persuasive case for a higher salary, based on the *value* you can bring to the position. Mention the employer's *most pressing problem,* as uncovered during the interview process, and your ability to solve it.

> *As we discussed, I have the right skill set to make an immediate impact in this position, and I am confident of my ability to deliver 10 percent cost savings or even more in the first year, based on my track record with Acme Corp. And, as you know, I've led successful software implementations of this type twice, and I project a smooth process completed in four to six months. Based on my contributions, and what I understand to be fair market value for this type of position, a salary in the X to Y range would be more appropriate. What can you do in that range?*

> **Travel Tip:** God expects you to increase the "talents" He has given you (Matt. 25:14-28), and He expects you to steward the increase for His kingdom. The following quote, though written in the somewhat stifled prose of 15th-century English, admonishes us to earn as much as possible for the purposes of furthering God's work:

> *"You are bound to improve all your master's talents, but then your end must be that you may be the better provided to do God service and may do the more good with what you have. If God show you a way in which you may lawfully get more than in another way (without wrong to your soul, or to any other), if you refuse this...you refuse to be God's steward...you may labor to be rich for God, though not for the flesh and sin."* –Rev. Richard Baxter (English clergyman, 1615–1691)

Other Ways You Can Initiate a Counter-Offer

Here are some other options for language to use when responding to an offer that is too low. Avoid being confrontational, acting insulted, or being scornful. Use a curious, genuine tone:

- "I've talked to peers in the industry and researched salaries on several well-respected Web sites, and to be honest, I expected an offer in the *X* to *Y* range, based on fair market value. What flexibility do you have?"
- "Quite frankly, I'm disappointed. Is there any room to negotiate?"
- "I have some concerns; can you help me?"

Three Possible Responses from the Employer

Now it's the employer's move. He has three options, and your next step will depend on what he does.

1. Employer Stands Pat

I'm sorry, but that is what we've budgeted, and we consider it to be a very fair salary for the position.

Don't give up yet! Perhaps you can negotiate performance bonuses that will bring the amount up to your reality or comfort level. Maybe the benefits are terrific or you can negotiate some additional perks. Unless the number is totally out of the question, I recommend that you table the base salary discussion and continue negotiating other aspects of your compensation.

OK, I understand your position. I do feel confident of my ability to achieve these goals for the company, so maybe we can build in some performance bonuses that will make us both happy. And what is the benefit package like? It might be I've overlooked something in my calculations.

2. Employer Ups the Offer a Bit but It's Still Below Your Expectations

Well, I guess we could go to X.

Follow the pattern of your initial response—be polite and enthusiastic, reiterate key challenges, and express your confidence in achieving results for the company.

> *I appreciate your flexibility. You know, we talked about the problems you're having with personnel and team issues in the warehouse. I know that is affecting your productivity. I have a very consistent history of building strong teams in environments just like this, and I have full confidence in my ability to do the same here at Acme Widgeters. I've calculated that a 5 percent productivity boost would improve your bottom line by $100,000 in the first year alone. Based on this kind of contribution, don't you agree that a salary in the X to Y range is fair?*

You can continue in this vein as long as the employer is receptive. It's always helpful to tie specific dollar benefits to your contributions; this will help the employer see that hiring you will deliver more value than cost to the company.

When you are satisfied that you have negotiated base pay that is appropriate for your value and meets your expectations, accept enthusiastically and move on to phase two, where you negotiate details of your total compensation package, including performance bonuses, benefits, and perks.

3. Employer Counter-Offers an Attractive Salary That Is in Line with What You Can Deliver to the Company

You don't have to negotiate further; you can move on to discussing your total compensation package, including performance bonuses, benefits, and perks.

> *That sounds terrific. I appreciate your flexibility and feel confident in my ability to deliver the results we've discussed.*

LARGER TAKE-HOME PAY ON A SMALLER SALARY

"Mary" felt sure that God was leading her to move from a high-paying job with the state to a lesser-paying position with a local church. Her biggest concern was that the church job was going to require a drop in salary, but she obediently accepted the position. After receiving her first paycheck, she was pleasantly surprised to learn that she was actually making just a tad more than she had at the state because the church took out far fewer deductions!

Negotiating Additional Elements of Your Compensation Package

After base salary is settled, you can discuss and negotiate additional components of compensation. Company benefits might or might not be negotiable, but your package can also include performance bonuses and additional perquisites (commonly known as "perks") that offer more room for creativity and flexibility.

You want to be absolutely clear about all the parameters of your compensation package, such as bonuses, raises, overtime, benefits, health insurance, stock options, 401(k) or other retirement plans, profit-sharing plans, performance evaluations, vacation policy, sick days, tuition reimbursement, and so on.

Get the Offer in Writing and Think It Over

A formal written offer is standard operating procedure at most companies. Within typically two to five days, you will receive a package of materials that includes a description of the job and detailed information on salary, benefits, bonuses, and total compensation. Carefully review the material to be sure it reflects everything you discussed. There may be items you'll want to negotiate further. Write down any questions you have and make notes about further requests or changes. Then contact the hiring manager and set up a time to discuss the package in person. Don't ask for a meeting to talk about "compensation"; instead, ask to get together to answer a few final questions to help you in making your decision.

If you haven't already done so, use table 13.1, "How to Determine Whether This Is the Right Position," in the preceding chapter, to help you evaluate the offer or compare this offer to another offer.

> **Travel Tip:** Take some time to pray about the offer you've received. Ask the Lord to reveal anything to you that you might be forgetting. It's easy to overlook details when you're excited about the prospects of new employment!

When you've made the decision to accept a job offer, confirm it in writing as soon as possible, and always within the time you promised. Your professional, positive, enthusiastic acceptance will set the right tone as you start your new position.

Chapter Wrap-Up

Hiring costs money, and companies want a return on that investment. They are not looking for seat warmers, cubicle fillers, or office decorations; they want people who will add value to the company and improve its bottom line. Be confident of your value and assured in your negotiations. Such an attitude will enable you to dance across the high wire with ease and arrive safely at your career destination.

10 QUICK TIPS FOR SALARY NEGOTIATIONS

1. **Communicate your value during interviews and through salary negotiations.** Enter negotiations as a confident optimist—if you expect more, you'll be more likely to get more.

2. **Memorize responses to deflect salary discussions until the employer has shifted from "shopper" to "buyer."**

3. **Be prepared.** Learn the fair market value for your talents by researching the low, median, and high range for similar positions.

4. **Identify your reality, comfort, and dream number salary range.**

5. **Base your salary requests on what you bring to the company and what you will achieve—not on what you need, want, or deserve.**

6. **First, agree on base compensation. Then, explore and negotiate bonuses, benefits, and perks.** Know what "throwaways" you can concede. When you are willing to give something away, it makes you look flexible.

7. **Frame any counter-offer requests in employer-centered language instead of you-centered language.** Express your requests without anxiety, anger, or attitude, but in a manner that is positive, poised, and professional.

8. **Get the offer in writing.** If you can't, draft and submit your own letter outlining your understanding of the position. Evaluate offers on multiple planes—salary, job duties, future potential, location, commute, schedule, company culture, and so on.

9. **When there's uncertainty, pray.** If the salary is lower than your reality number, ask God for discernment. It may be that God is leading you to walk away, or He may impress on you that He will provide for the gap in some other way.

10. **Don't cut off other options until you have actually started work.** Wait to share the good news with your network until you are actually on board. And remain courteous and professional...don't forget that you will be working with the people with whom you are now negotiating.

MASTERFUL COACHING TIPS

When Researching Salary

Using table 14.1 near the beginning of this chapter as a guide, develop your own comparative salary data.

My Research on Comparative Salary Data

Source	Low Range	Median	Upper Range
Salary tool: workindex.com/ salary/ (national averages)	$	$	$
Salary tool: www.salary.com (national averages)	$	$	$
Salary tool: www.salaryexpert.com (New York/statewide average)	$	$	$
Salary survey: professional association or other source	$	$	$
Print ad/source:	$	$	$
Online ad:	$	$	$
Network contact	$	$	$
Network contact	$	$	$
Average	$	$	$

When Developing Your Salary Target

Develop your own salary range of reality, comfort, and dream numbers.

	Current Salary	Reality Number	Comfort Number	Dream Number
Base				
Bonus				
Commissions				
Projected raise				
Stock options not yet vested				
Benefit/retirement plans not yet vested				
Other				
Total				

(continued)

MASTERFUL COACHING TIPS *(CONTINUED)*

In reviewing the "Seven Situations that Cause Christians to Stumble over Salary," at the beginning of this chapter, which are you most prone to? Ask God's forgiveness. Psalm 103:12 reminds us of how complete God's forgiveness is: "as far as the east is from the west, so far has he removed our transgressions from us." Write your commitment to not let this temptation cause you to stumble again.

_____

_____

Reread the "Five Truths to Take to the Salary Negotiation Table," near the beginning of this chapter. Which of these speaks to you the most at this time in your life? Choose one of the verses associated with these truths and memorize it. Write it out here:

_____

_____

Pocket Prayer (in Preparation for Salary Negotiations)

Father, in Psalm 50:10 You remind me that every animal of the forest is Yours, and the cattle on a thousand hills. You are the creator of all, and the owner of all, including me—all that I am and all that I have. Lord, I recommitment to You my "treasures"—the things that You have entrusted to me—abilities, talents, money, time, property, relationships…everything! Let me use them all for You. If I have fallen short in the area of tithing, forgive me and help me get back on track. Make me a faithful steward. And when it comes time to negotiate salary, I trust You to bring what I need, for You have promised to meet all my needs according to Your riches in Christ Jesus. Let my interviewers see Your presence and peace in me, not greed or an attitude of "going for more" at the detriment of others. Thank you for being with me every step of the way. In Jesus' name, Amen.

Pocket Prayer (for Salary Negotiations)

Father, I rejoice that nothing You intend for me can be snatched from Your hands, and so I ask that You would loose on earth what has been loosed in heaven and bind on earth what has been bound in heaven. Bring these negotiations to Your perfect conclusion…give me wisdom to know when to assert and when to be silent. I praise You that the Holy Spirit is my counselor and that You won't leave or forsake me as I meet with all the individuals involved in this process. Allow me to be a beautiful reflection of You, as I work with diligence and excellence. I rejoice that I will cast down every accolade and treasure won during this earthly race at Your feet, for Your glory. In Jesus' name, Amen.

CHAPTER 15

YOUR NEW JOB DESCRIPTION: 10 CAREER COMMANDMENTS

"It is the Lord Christ you are serving."

—*Col. 3:24b*

Whether you have already landed a new position or are confidently headed in the right direction, allow me to offer a "permanent" job description that you can carry with you regardless of where your career travels take you.

As a kingdom worker, whether in ministry or the business marketplace, your job description as God's child includes these "career commandments":

1. **Love:** "Teacher, which is the greatest commandment in the Law?" Jesus replied: "'Love the Lord your God with all your heart and with all your soul and with all your mind.' This is the first and greatest commandment. And the second is like it: 'Love your neighbor as yourself.'…" (Matt. 22:36-39)

   In the context of careers, neighbors include bosses, co-workers, colleagues, clients, customers, students, patients, and so on. Love can be expressed in the workplace by simply caring about other people and wanting what is best for them. It doesn't mean being a doormat. Love is keeping your eyes off yourself and considering the feelings of those around you as you treat them the way you want to be treated.

2. **Serve:** "…whoever wants to become great among you must be your servant, and whoever wants to be first must be your slave—just as the Son of Man did not come to be served, but to serve…." (Matt. 20:26-28)

Promotion and advancement require a servant's heart. Whether in the mail room or in the boardroom, service means seeing what needs to be done and taking the initiative to do it. It means cooperating with others and contributing value to your network. This, too, is part of the Golden Rule.

3. **Be Glad:** "Rejoice in the Lord always. I will say it again: Rejoice!" (Phil. 4:4)

   Always means always. Even the most challenging days and difficult people don't need to interfere with the joy you have knowing the Lord is with you each step of the way.

4. **Walk in Submission and Humility:** "Submit yourselves for the Lord's sake to every authority instituted among men…" (1 Pet. 2:13); "He has showed you, O man, what is good. And what does the Lord require of you? To act justly and to love mercy and to walk humbly with your God." (Mic. 6:8)

   Submission and humility will keep you from getting stuck in pride, position, and politics.

5. **Trust:** "Trust in the Lord with all your heart and lean not on your own understanding; in all your ways acknowledge him, and he will make your paths straight." (Prov. 3:5-6)

   Trust in all ways, at all times. We can't always trust people to do what they say they will do, but we can always depend on the Lord.

6. **Obey:** "…to obey is better than sacrifice…." (1 Sam. 15:22)

   To obey means to follow God's policy and procedure manual—the Bible. It also means sticking to company protocol, honoring company policy, and following instructions (as long as they are not in conflict with your Christian values and the law).

7. **Increase:** "The man who had received the five talents brought the other five. 'Master,' he said, 'you entrusted me with five talents. See, I have gained five more.' His master replied, 'Well done, good and faithful servant! You have been faithful with a few things; I will put you in charge of many things. Come and share your master's happiness!'…" (Matt. 25:20-21)

   God entrusts us with gifts, abilities, experiences, and opportunities. He expects us to do something with them—to get out and take some calculated risks in order to produce an increase for His kingdom. Be thankful for all He has given you to perform well and enjoy the benefits that come your way because of them, never forgetting to thank God and credit Him for the success.

8. **Persevere:** "Do not neglect your gift…. Be diligent in these matters; give yourself wholly to them, so that everyone may see your progress. Watch your life and doctrine closely. Persevere in them, because if you do, you will save both yourself and your hearers." (1 Tim. 4:14-16)

   Claiming territory in the Promised Land requires effort. Be tenacious through the challenges and don't give up.

9. **Believe:** "And without faith it is impossible to please God, because anyone who comes to him must believe that he exists and that he rewards those who earnestly seek him." (Heb. 11:6)

   Stay true to your faith, no matter what is going on around you.

10. **Witness:** "But you will receive power when the Holy Spirit comes on you; and you will be my witnesses in Jerusalem, and in all Judea and Samaria, and to the ends of the earth." (Acts 1:8)

    St. Francis said to "preach always and sometimes use words." In the world of work, we are to witness always, and sometimes use words. God has people on your spiritual job description who need to know of His love and power to save. They will see His love through you.

You can be assured that even if you aren't entirely faithful in fulfilling each "commandment" in your job description, God will be faithful in carrying out His (2 Tim. 2:13). And what is His job description? John 21:25 tells us that the whole world would not have room for the books that could be written about all that Jesus did. In the meantime, we have His holy Word, *full of promises* about all that He has done, is doing, and will continue to do, for He is the same yesterday, today, and forever (Heb. 13:8).

God has graciously chosen and gifted *you* to partner in His work on earth. May heaven one day greet us with, "Well done, good and faithful servant," and may we, in unity, cast every success at the feet of Him who has been faithful and has brought it to pass.

Pocket Prayer

Father, I lift my brothers and sisters who are reading this book before Your throne of grace. You have loved them with an everlasting love, wept over them when they strayed, and welcomed them with open arms when they turned from their willful ways. Lord, they are on a journey—a journey that will end in the unspeakable glory of Your presence. Bless them and keep them, make Your face shine on them, and be gracious to them. Lift up Your face to them and give them peace. Let them soar on wings like eagles, run and not grow weary, and walk and not be faint. Fill them with courage and strength as they claim the new territory that You have carved out for them. Thank you for bringing them into a good place, a land flowing with milk and honey, rich and sweet. May You nourish and satisfy them in every way. As You send them out into the world of work, anoint them for Your purposes. Give them favor. Protect them by the power of Your name. Thank you that nothing can snatch them from Your hand. Give them success, as they turn neither to the left nor to the right, but as they fix their eyes on Jesus, the author and finisher of their faith. In Christ's name, Amen.

CHRISTIAN CAREER AND LEADERSHIP COACHES

The following Certified Career Management Coaches (CCMC) from Career Coach Academy (www.CareerCoachAcademy.com) and Certified Leadership & Talent Management Coaches (CLTMC) from Leadership Coach Academy (www.LeadershipCoachAcademy.com) also call Jesus their Lord and Savior. They provide fee-based coaching services for individuals wanting to incorporate a Biblical perspective into their career and life-work.

M. Jean Austin, M.S., CCMC
Grafton, Wisconsin
E-mail: Jean.Austin@cuw.edu

Kim Batson, CLTMC, CCMC, CPBS, CJST, CTC
Career Management Coaching.com
Seattle, Washington
E-mail: Kim@careermanagementcoaching.com
www.careermanagementcoaching.com

Nancy Branton, M.A., CCM, ACC, CCMC, JCTC, CPBS, COIS, CLTMC, CLC, CCC
People Potential Group, Inc.
Minneapolis/St. Paul, Minnesota
Phone: (651) 459-0528
E-mail: nancy@peoplepotentialgroup.com
www.PeoplePotentialGroup.com

Diane Hudson Burns, CPCC, CLTMC, CPRW, FJSTC
Career Marketing Techniques
Boise, Idaho
E-mail: dianecprw@aol.com
www.polishedresumes.com

Bill Cullins, CCMC
Bartlesville, Oklahoma
Phone: (918) 333-4519
E-mail: billjo67@cableone.net

Tina Fay, CCMC
Cincinnati, Ohio
Phone: (513) 761-8832
E-mail: ccs1@fuse.net
www.conciseclericalsvcs.com

Robyn Feldberg, CCMC, VAL
Abundant Success Career Services
Frisco, Texas
Phone: (866) WIN-AJOB
  (866-946-2562) (toll-free)
E-mail: AbundantSuccessCoach@gmail.com
www.AbundantSuccessCareerServices.com

Terri Ferrara, CCMC, CLTMC
Summit View Career Coaching
Traverse City, Michigan
Phone: (231) 938-0766
E-mail: terri@summitviewcareercoaching.com
www.SummitViewCareerCoaching.com

Al Garcia, ACC, CCMC, CLC
Oak Lawn, Illinois
Creative Coaching Concepts Inc.
Phone: (708) 499-5006
E-mail: al@creativecoachingconcepts.com
www.creativecoachingconcepts.com

Michele J. Haffner, JCTC, CPRW
Advanced Resume Services
Glendale, Wisconsin
Phone: (414) 247-1677
E-mail: michele@michelehaffner.com
michele@resumeservices.com

Karen Hagans, CCMC
KMB Career Quest
Medina, Ohio
E-mail: karen@kmbcareerquest.com

**Makini Theresa Harvey, CPRW, JCTC, CEIP,
CCMC**
Career Abundance, LLC
Menlo Park, California
Phone: (650) 630-7610
E-mail: makini@careerabundance.com

David A. Howe, M.S., CLTMC, CLC
Life Dreams Coaching
Durand, Michigan/Elkhart, Indiana
E-mail: david@lifedreamscoaching.com
www.LifeDreamsCoaching.com

Evelyn W. Kaufman, CCMC, CLC
Journey to Fullness
LaGrange, Kentucky
Phone: (502) 845-6345
E-mail: coach@journey2fullness.com
www.journey2fullness.com

**Cindy Kraft, CPBS, CCMC, CCM, JCTC,
CPRW**
Valrico, Florida
Phone: (813) 655-0658
E-mail: cindy@cfo-coach.com
www.cfo-coach.com

Eric Laughlin, MS, CCMC, CLTMC
Pittsburgh, Pennsylvania
E-mail: e.Laughlin@verizon.net

Lorie Lebert, CCMC, IJCTC, CPRW
The LORIEL Group/Résumés For Results
Brighton, Michigan
Phone: (800) 870-9059 (toll-free)
E-mail: Lorie@DoMyResume.com
www.CoachingROI.com; www.ResumeROI.com

Lacy J. Nelson, M.Ed., CMP, CLTMC
Lacy J. Nelson, M.Ed., Career and Life Coach
Nashville, Tennessee
E-mail: lncoach@mac.com

Gregg Pawlowski, CCMC
BreakThru Coaching & Consulting
Sugar Hill, Georgia
Phone: (678) 478-2000
E-mail: gregg@breakthrucac.com
www.BreakThruCAC.com

Stephanie Peacocke, MA, CCMC, CPRW
SRP Consulting
Gig Harbor, Washington
E-mail: stephanie@srpcareertransitions.com
www.srpcareertransitions.com

Karen H. Prevatt, ACC, CCMC
Living Tall, Inc.
Savannah, Georgia
Phone: (912) 897-5815
E-mail: karen@livingtall.com
www.livingtallministries.org

Tanya M. Smith, PHR, MBA, CCMC
Be Intention Career Coaching
Dallas, Texas
Phone: (214) 929-0693
E-mail: tanya@beintention.com
www.beintention.com

Sharon Stenger, CLTMC
FreshStart Resources
Rocklin, California
Phone: (916) 625-4213
E-mail: Sharon@FreshStart-Resources.com
www.FreshStart-Christian-LifeCoach.com

Ellie Vargo, CCMC, CPRW, CFRWC
Noteworthy Résumé Services
St. Louis, Missouri
Phone: (866) 965-9326 (toll-free);
  (314) 965-9362 (local)
E-mail: ev@noteworthyresume.com
www.noteworthyresume.com

Felicia H. Vaughn, M.Ed., CCMC
Dallas, Texas
Phone: (972) 998-0860
E-mail: fvaughn@hotmail.com

Kathy Warwick, CCMC, CPBS, NCRW
Confident Careers LLC
E-mail: kwarwick@aconfidentcareer.com
www.aconfidentcareer.com

Melissa Williams, LPC, CCMC
London, United Kingdom/Los Angeles, California
E-mail: Melissa.D.Williams@hotmail.com
www.lifepurposecoachingcenters.com

Marie Yager, MA, CLTMC
Yager Coaching Solutions
Bowling Green, Kentucky
Phone: (270) 779-8337
E-mail: marieyager@bellsouth.net

INDEX

A

ability versus availability, 8–13
Abram, calling of, 21
accepting
    God's promises, 24
    salary offer, 289, 293
accomplishment summaries, 204
accomplishments, 178–184
Advantages (in career brand), 133
affiliations in resumes, 169
agencies (employment), 252–253
alternative job search plans, 101
ambassador for God, 7–8
annual reports, reading, 226
answering questions, 264–265
anxiousness in interviews, 260
Artistic skill area, 40
ASCII text resumes, 191–195
asking questions, 265–268
assessing job search factors, 94–96
Authentic Image (in career brand), 133
availability versus ability, 8–13
Awareness (in career brand), 133

B

behavioral interviews, 119–123, 265
belief. *See also* faith
    in capabilities, 59
    incorrect beliefs, 25
benefits
    to employers. *See* value
    features versus, 114–115
    negotiating, 289, 293
big-picture questions, asking, 265–266
blessings of God on work, 12
blogs, 191
    creating, 196–198
    online networking, 235–236
books
    for entrepreneurs, 87
    finding target companies, 219
    researching career options, 67
brand. *See* career brand
brand bios, 204
bridge jobs, 64
budget for job searches, 102
burning bush, Moses and, 23
buying motivators of employers. *See* Employer
    Buying Motivators

C

calculated risks versus red flags, 71
calendars, tracking progress, 90
calling
    Biblical examples of, 21–22
    categories of, 19–21
    hearing God in, 22–27
    questions about, 17–18
    tips for, 27–28
Canaan, conquest of, 211
capabilities, belief in, 59
capacity, increasing, 6–7
CAR technique in resumes, 181–182
career
    as ambassadorship for God, 7–8
    confirmation of decision, 22
    increasing capacity and influence in, 6–7
    job versus, 6
    questions about calling, 17–18
    role in life journey, 4–5
    seasons in, 64–65
    as service to God, 13–14
    spiritual growth in, 5–6
career assessment for Master F.I.T. model, 49–51
career brand
    benefits of, 132
    Christian attributes in, 132
    elements of, 133
    tips for, 148
    verbal branding, 134–142
    visual branding, 142–147
"career commandments", 297–299
career decision, 70, 74–75, 77–78
career fairs, 254–255
Career Liftoff Interest Inventory, 39–41
career management file (CMF), 183–184
career marketing documents, 204–205, 207
career needs in Master F.I.T. model, 42
chemistry in interviews, 261–264
Christian attributes in career brand, 132
Christian employers, 218, 220
Christian job sites, 248–251
Christian online networking sites, 237
Christian references in resumes, 160–161
Christianity, sharing during interview, 263–264
chronological resume format, 153–156
clarification phase in interviews, 264–267
classified ads, 253–254
closing interviews, 269–270
clothing in visual branding, 143, 147

CMF (career management file), 183–184
collaboration phase in interviews, 268–269
college recruiting sites, 247–248
comfort number (salary), 285
compensation package, negotiating, 289, 293
connection in interviews, 261–264
contacts for focused networking, 227–234
Conventional skill area, 41
converting resume to ASCII format, 192–195
core skill areas, described, 39–41
correction to spiritual course, 12–13
counter-offers, 289–292
cover letters, 198–203, 285–286
credentials in resumes, 169

D

debt and salary, 281
deflecting salary questions, 285–287
delays in job search, 98–99
direct mailing, 254
diversity sites, 248
dream number (salary), 285

E

ease, success equated with, 214
editing resumes, 186
educational history in resumes, 169
e-forms, converting resume for, 192–193
e-mail addresses, finding, 228
e-mailing
    converting resume to ASCII for, 192
    resume to recruiters, 251
employees versus independent contractors, 288
Employer Buying Motivators, 112–113, 138,
    177–178
employers
    Christian employers, 218, 220
    response to counter-offers, 291–292
    resume preferences of, 175–177
    traditional search, reasons for using, 244
    value to, 112–115, 129
employment agencies, 252–253
employment history in resumes, 167–168
energy (in personality type), 46–47
enhancing identity in Master F.I.T. model, 45
Enterprising skill area, 41
entrepreneurs, tips for, 84–87
epiphanies, expecting, 213
e-portfolios, 191, 195–196
e-resumes (electronic resumes)
    ASCII text resumes, 192–195
    blogs, 196–198
    e-portfolios, creating, 195–196
    tips for, 206–207
    types of, 191
    whitespace in, 193
exaltation of God, 23–24
external F.I.T., 36
extroversion, 46–47

F

failures in success stories, 116
faith. *See also* belief
    as career commandment, 299
    strengthening, job search as, 5–6
    unexercised faith, 25
    waiting versus, 74
faithful servant parable, 7
fear, as obstacle to job search, 105
features versus benefits, 114–115
fight-or-flight syndrome, 212–213
finances as obstacle to job search, 106–107
F.I.T. *See* Master F.I.T. model
fit for position, rating, 270–272
flexible work schedule, negotiating, 96
focus statement, 75–77, 163–165
focused networking, 226–235, 243
follower of Christ, calling to be, 19–20
formatting resumes, 185
forms. *See* e-forms
freedom in truth, 57
frequently asked questions, answering, 264–265
fulfillment in Master F.I.T. model, 43–44
function in Master F.I.T. model, 38–41
functional resume format, 157–159
functional skills and length of job search, 97–98
future, preparation for, 10–11

G

gatekeepers, 232
gifts, usage of as career commandment, 298
give-and-take in focused networking, 234–235
goals
    importance of, 255
    SMART goals, 90–101
God
    accepting promises of, 24
    ambassador for, 7–8
    blessings on work, 12
    brainstorming with, 59
    definition of success, 83–84
    exaltation of, 23–24
    hearing, 22–27
    hunger for, 23
    ignoring, 26
    interest in marketplace, 3
    misinterpreting message of, 213
    ordinary people, use of, 8
    perspective on reputation, 131–132
    practicing presence of, 35
    purpose versus passions, 9–10
    purposes for work, 4–8, 14–16
    redirection from, 8–9
    refinement by, 212–213
    response to, 24–25
    service to, 13–14
    will of. *See* will of God
    withholding from, 280

Golden Rule, 112–113
GPTP (Golden Personality Type Profiler), 46
group brainstorming exercise, 61–63
growth. *See* spiritual growth

H

H.E.A.R. (Hear, Exalt, Accept, Respond), 23–25
hearing God, 22–27
honesty in resumes, 152–153
humility, 213–214, 298
hunger for God, 23

I

identity
    enhancing in Master F.I.T. model, 45
    as obstacle to job search, 107
    salary and, 280
ignoring God, signs of, 26
image in visual branding, 142–143
impact-mining, 184
impact statements. *See* accomplishments
incorrect beliefs, 25
increasing capacity and influence, 6–7
independent contractors versus employees, 288
industry experience and length of job search,
    97–98
industry in Master F.I.T. model, 42
industry niche sites, 247
industry-specific questions, answering, 264–265
influence, increasing, 6–7
informational interviews, researching career
    options, 67–69
INSIDER (Information, Names, Support, Ideas,
    Data, Energy, Relationships), 234–235
interests in Master F.I.T. model, 42
internal F.I.T., 36
interviews
    behavioral interviews, 119–123
    clarifying the position, 264–267
    closing, 269–270
    coaching framework for, 261
    collaborating on how job would be done,
        268–269
    connecting with interviewers, 261–264
    follow-up letters, 202
    importance of multiple, 215
    openers for, 262
    post-interview analysis, 273–274
    problems in, 259–260
    researching career options, 67–69
    salary expectations and, 286–287
    sharing testimony during, 263–264
    tips for, 274–275
introversion, 46–48
Investigative skill area, 40
isolation, as obstacle to job search, 107–108
Israelites' journey, 5

J

Jesus' parables, 7
job aggregators, 246
job boards, list of, 246
job change as correction to spiritual course, 12–13
job description in God's view, 297–299
job fairs, 254–255
job opportunities versus job openings, 215–217
job search. *See also* targeted search; traditional
    search
    length of, 97–98, 253
    as marketing, 133
    misconceptions in, 212–215
    as spiritual growth opportunity, 5–6
job search factors
    assessing, 94–96
    delayed by God, 98–99
    God's will in, 92–93
    list of, 93–94
job search goals, importance of, 255
job search plans
    alternative plans, 101
    breaking down, 87–88
    obstacles to, 104–108
    resources and budget for, 102
    SMART goals, 90–101
    support team, 102–104
    tips for, 108–109
    tracking progress, 90
job transitions, phases of, 88–90
job trials, researching career options, 69
Joshua, conquest of Canaan, 211

K–L

keywords in resumes, 162–163
lack of preparation in interviews, 260
Lazarus's death, 5
licensure in resumes, 169
life journey, 4–5
love as career commandment, 297

M

mailing lists, purchasing, 221
manifestation gifts, 39
marketing. *See also* career brand
    blogs, 198
    career marketing documents, 204–205,
        207
    job search as, 133
    Three-Point Marketing Message, 134–137
marketplace, God's interest in, 3
Master F.I.T. model
    career assessments for, 49–51
    focus statements and, 76
    fulfillment in, 43–44
    function in, 38–41
    identity, enhancing, 45

industry/interests, 42
personality type in, 45–48
preparation for brainstorming, 57–58
prioritizing items in, 58–59
salary in, 48–49
"Things That Matter", 42
tips for, 51–52
MBA students and personality types, 47
Mini-Bio, 134, 139–142
ministry gifts, 39
misconceptions in job search, 212–215
misinterpreting God's message, 213
mistakes in resumes, 152–153
modesty, 143
moment of silence in salary negotiations, 288
Moses, 21, 23
motivational gifts, 38–39
multiple interviews, importance of, 215
mundane work as preparation for future, 10–11
Myers-Briggs Type Indicator (MBTI), 45

N

negotiating
flexible work schedule, 96
salary. *See* salary negotiations
networking. *See also* targeted search
focused networking, 226–235, 243
importance of, 214–215
online networking, 235–237
salary information from, 283
networking resumes, 204
news alerts, 224
newspaper ads, 253–254
numbers in resumes, 173–174, 178–179

O

obedience
availability versus ability, 8–13
as career commandment, 298
trials despite, 11
objective statement in resumes, 163–165
obstacles
to hearing God, 25
to job search plans, 104–108
offers, 287–292
ongoing calling, 20–21
online networking, 235–237
online resources. *See* Web sites
online searches, 244–251
openers for interviews, 262
opportunities (job) versus job openings, 215–217
ordinary people, God's use of, 8
orientation (in personality type), 46–47

P

parables of Jesus, 7
passions versus God's purpose, 9–10
Paul's calling, 19, 21

pay rates. *See* salary negotiations
performance appraisals, 183
performance jitters in interviews, 259
perseverance, 55–56, 255
as calling, 20–21
as career commandment, 298
personal visioning exercise, 59–61
personality type, 45–48
planning, Biblical role of, 34–35. *See also* job
search plans
Pocket Prayers
abiding in God, 26
calling, 31
career brand, 150
career journey, 299
career marketing documents, 207
finalizing resume, 189
God's purposes for work, 16
hearing God, 25
helping unbelief, 59
interviews, 277
job search plans, 110
Master F.I.T. model, 53
researching career options, 80
resume structure, 172
salary negotiations, 296
success stories, 130
support team, 103
targeted search, 241
traditional search, 258
Web site for, 15
portfolios. *See* e-portfolios
post-interview analysis, 273–274
posting resumes, 251
PowerPoint resumes, 204
practicing God's presence, 35
prayer before interviews, 260. *See also* Pocket
Prayers
preparation
for future positions, 10–11
lack of, in interviews, 260
for salary negotiations, 282–285, 296
pride
humility versus, 213–214
in interviews, 260
salary and, 280
priorities and salary, 280
prioritizing
items in targeted company list, 221
Master F.I.T. model items, 58–59
priority calling, 19–20
professional associations, researching career
options, 66–67
professional experience in resumes, 167–168
profiling target companies, 221–223
Promised Land, 33–34, 214
proofreading resumes, 186–187
purpose in Master F.I.T. model, 43–44

Q

qualifications summary in resumes, 165–167
questions
    about calling, 17–18
    about salary, deflecting, 285–287
    answering and asking, 264–268

R

ranking accomplishments, 184
rating
    fit with position, 270–272
    performance, post-interview analysis,
        273–274
    SMART stories, 127–128
reading, importance of, 224
Realistic skill area, 40
reality number (salary), 285, 287
REAP (Resources, Events, Activities, People), 228
recruiter blogs, monitoring, 198
recruiters, 252–253
    e-mailing resume to, 251
    salary expectations, 283, 286
red flags versus calculated risks, 71
redirection from God, 8–9
references, 203–205
refinement by God, 212–213
rejoicing as career commandment, 298
reputation, God's perspective on, 131–132
researching
    career options, 65–69, 78–80
    companies, 224–226
    salary, 282–283
resources for job searches, 102
response to God, 24–25
resumes. *See also* e-resumes
    accomplishments in, 178–184
    affiliations in, 169
    categories to include, 160
    Christian references in, 160–161
    chronological format, 153–156
    editing tips for, 186
    educational history in, 169
    e-mailing to recruiters, 251
    Employer Buying Motivators in, 177–178
    employer preferences for, 175–177
    formatting tips for, 185
    functional format, 157–159
    honesty in, 152–153
    keywords in, 162–163
    length of, 168
    mistakes in, 152–153
    networking resumes, 204
    numbers in, 173–174, 178–179
    objective statement in, 163–165
    posting, 251
    PowerPoint resumes, 204
    professional experience in, 167–168
    proofreading tips for, 186–187
    qualifications summary in, 165–167
    skills in, 168–169
    supporting material in, 169
    Three-Point Marketing Message and, 136
    tips, 170–171, 188–189
    what not to include, 161–162
ROI (return on investment), 113, 181
role models, 142–146
RSS (Really Simple Syndication) technology,
    197–198

S

salary
    in Master F.I.T. model, 48–49
    researching, 282–283
    stumbling blocks with, 280–281
    target range, developing, 284–285
salary negotiations, 279–280
    accepting offer, 289
    after job offer, 287–289
    compensation package, 293
    counter-offer, 289–292
    deflecting questions, 285–287
    preparation for, 282–285
    receiving offer in writing, 293
    spiritual truths in, 281–282
    tips for, 294
sales profession and introversion, 48
Saul. *See* Paul
seasons in career, 64–65
secondary calling, 20
seduction and salary, 280
self-confidence in interviews, 261
self-employment, tips for, 84–87
service as career commandment, 297–298
service to God, career as, 13–14
sin, unconfessed, 25
skills
    core skill areas, 39–41
    in resumes, 168–169
small business ownership, tips for, 84–87
SMART goals, 90–101
SMART stories, 119–128. *See also* success stories
    Three-Point Marketing Message and, 135
social networking sites, 237
Social skill area, 41
S.O.S. (Solutions Or Services), 115
S.O.S. response letter, 232–233
sound bites, 134–142
special characters, avoiding in e-resumes, 194
spiritual course, correction to, 12–13
spiritual gifts, 38–39
spiritual growth, job search as, 5–6
spiritual truths in salary negotiations, 281–282
stories. *See* SMART stories; success stories
submission as career commandment, 298

success
    ease and speed equated with, 214
    God's definition of, 83–84
success stories, 115–118. *See also* SMART stories
support team, 58–59, 102–104
supporting material in resumes, 169
surrendering to God's will, 27

T

taglines, 141
take-home pay, 292
talents
    parable of, 7
    usage of as career commandment, 298
target salary range, developing, 284–285
targeted search
    focused networking in, 226–235, 243
    identifying companies, 218–223
    online networking, 235–237
    reading, importance of, 224
    remaining visible, 237–238
    researching companies, 224–226
    steps of, 217
    tips for, 239–240
    traditional search methods in, 238
team. *See* support team
telephone conferencing, 62
testimony
    as career commandment, 299
    sharing during interview, 263–264
"Things That Matter" in Master F.I.T. model, 42
Three-Point Marketing Message, 134–137
"tingle factor", 43
tithing, 282
title statement in resumes, 164
traditional search methods, 238, 251–257
trials despite obedience, 11
trust
    as career commandment, 298
    lack of, salary and, 280
truth, freedom in, 57

U–V

unconfessed sin, 25
unexercised faith, 25
value to employers, 112–115, 129
verbal branding, 134–142
Verbal Business Card, 134, 137–139
visioning
    Biblical role of, 34–35
    as brainstorming exercise, 59–61
visual branding, 142–147

W–Z

waiting versus stepping out in faith, 74
wardrobe in visual branding, 143, 147

Web forms. *See* e-forms
Web resumes. *See* e-portfolios
Web sites
    career sites, 246
    Christian job sites, 248–251
    company sites, 245
    employment agency information, 253
    for e-portfolios, 196
    finding target companies, 219–221
    job aggregators, 246
    for marketing blogs, 198
    newspaper ads, 254
    niche job sites, 246–248
    Pocket Prayers, 15
    posting resumes, 251
    recruiter information, 252–253
    researching career options, 65–66
    resume distribution services, 251
    for RSS news aggregators, 197–198
    salary research, 282–283
whitespace in e-resumes, 193
will of God
    in job search factors, 92–93
    surrendering to, 27
withholding from God, salary and, 280
witnessing. *See* testimony
work
    as calling, 20
    God's blessings on, 12
    God's purposes for, 4–8
worksheets
    calling, 29–31
    career assessment, 60–61
    career brand, 149
    career marketing documents, 207
    company profile, 222–223
    finalizing resume, 189
    God's purposes for work, 14–15
    interviews, 276–277
    job search plans, 110
    Master F.I.T. model, 53
    researching career options, 78–79
    resume structure, 171–172
    salary negotiations, 295–296
    SMART goals, 99–101
    SMART stories, 126–127
    success stories, 129–130
    support team, 103–104
    targeted search, 240–241
    traditional search, 257
    Verbal Business Card, 139
writing SMART stories, 123–128
written salary offers, 293